Power and Illusion: Religion and Human Need

Power and Illusion: Religion and Human Need

David W Wilbur, MD, PhD

ISBN 978-0-557-66950-9

To Connie Wilbur (1943–2010) who shared forty-two short and often happy years with me. She did not get to see the final product and would probably have disagreed with some things I've said, but she did appreciate and encouraged the old man's writing.

David W Wilbur, MD, PhD
Nov 3, 2010

Religion: A set of beliefs concerning the cause, nature, and purpose of the universe, especially when considered as the creation of a superhuman agency or agencies, usually involving devotional and ritual observances.

Abbreviated from *Webster's College Dictionary*, Random House, 1995

Religion: A way of life organized around experiences and convictions concerning ultimate power.

Adapted from Luke Timothy Johnson, Emory University[1]

Religion: A daughter of Hope and Fear, explaining to Ignorance the nature of the Unknowable.

Ambrose Bierce, *The Devil's Dictionary*[2]

Contents

1. Introductory Comments and Concerns

Man can embody truth, but he cannot know it.
—William Butler Yeats (last letter)[3]

For the believer, when myth and reality meet, myth wins—being dream and hope.

Religions are an important group of powerful human stories about the universe. They, like all human stories, are incomplete—never broad enough and deep enough to represent the reality of that complex and changing universe. They are also distorted by the human needs of those who construct them and those who retell them. Despite the risks and liabilities of such limited and distorted narratives, we do not give them up because human thriving seems to depend on what is shared. We also note that refinement in the fires of human experience may give common features to religions with very different claims about ultimate reality—for instance, the almost universal appearance among religious people of some form of prayer or appeal to the supernatural.

Someone might well ask—why another author attempting to understand religion? My current and conditional grasp of religion's place in human society has come as a result of decades of study and engagement. There are many books about religion offering a scientific or rational analysis or even a debunking—some published even since I began this manuscript. I am, however, unaware of any author following the particular road to understanding that I have attempted. Religion is often an extremely important part of existence, for believers and nonbelievers, and I thought at least some other souls on their trip through this world might find my observations interesting or enlightening or perhaps frightening.

My intended audience is anyone who suspects that religion might be about something more than future salvation. This manuscript is written for those believing or otherwise who, looking at ubiquitous religion, find discontinuities in claims and functions and wish to explore further how it shapes our world. This is an attempt to provide a fair and honest assessment of religion's many roles—a difficult task and some may think me a misguided troublemaker. Hopefully, I have at least partly answered the question of why religion often remains important even for those who have largely lost any belief in the supernatural.

This manuscript is an effort to describe how religion actually works in practice, both its intended and its unintended or unacknowledged effects. I attempt to outline the sources of its power and widespread acclaim and to describe its impact in important areas as diverse as ethics, culture, politics, science, and human health. Life being short, my effort cannot be encyclopedic, but possibly it may serve as a stimulant to some interested readers. Perhaps this text may even provide some believers with a new awareness of both the power and the limitations of religion as it's actually used in day-to-day affairs and in crises.

Religion's Importance in the Human World

For millennia religions have offered us many wonderful images. These include the solitary worshiper; the moving public ritual; outspoken concern for the sick, poor, and disadvantaged; wonderful art and music; and magnificent buildings and grand centers of learning. These great religions would seem at first glance to be above criticism, but like all powerful human tools, they also have a dark side. Religion has been used to justify persecution, cruelty, terrorism, war, the suppression of knowledge, and the power and wealth of the few from the struggles of the many. Such a wide range of uses cries out for a human explanation consistent with the rest of our growing knowledge of human nature—its limitations and strengths. Human experience, need, desire, and imagination seem to me a more believable, reasonable, and parsimonious explanation for this wonderful phenomenon than the postulate of an all-powerful, all-good, and caring Divine Will expressing itself in the world.

Thoughtful students of religion such as William James[4] have felt that some—or most—of men's greatest accomplishments have been achieved in the context or perhaps grip of a religious system. Charles Murray[5] has suggested that human creativity may be associated positively with religious belief. He has even written that Christianity has been the most effective at supporting individual accomplishment. Anyone hopeful of understanding human social interaction and civilization must study religion. Those who would sacrifice their lives for some cause or belief are almost always found to have a religious undergirding for their resolve. Those who would kill other people over differing beliefs, about this or some other world, usually cite religious convictions to justify their actions. Most wars are emotionally fueled or at least supported on both sides by some form of religious belief. The only systems of belief or knowledge about the universe that claim absolute truth are "faith-based systems" that fall in the category usually called religions or quasi-religions, such as Nazism and Marxism.

Religious systems take the defining narrative story that justifies their beliefs, their central myth, and through ritual and acculturation, give it more power than has the experience of day-to-day reality for at least a large fraction of believers. Many things contribute to this accomplishment. One factor is that most religions educate their followers to believe that their system of truth was revealed by a God or by some Divine or otherworldly force with infallible authority. The human element is downplayed, ignored, or covered up, and attempting to study this human factor is often considered a form of heresy. To question the "faith," especially the "faith in God," is in many, perhaps most, traditions treated as some sort of blasphemy that may be punished with anything from expulsion from the religious community to ritual execution. Exceptions may occur in situations of intellectual challenge—such as higher educational institutions or youthful explorations—where questions may be allowed and even encouraged, as long as the norms and rituals of the group are respected or at least resumed after adventures in the world. Within the tradition I was born into, I have seen an acceptance of higher education with its questioning, as well as a fear that such education would destroy the student's "faith"—that he would lose his soul.

Spirituality and Religion—Comments on Definitions

Spirituality is concerned with the transcendent, addressing ultimate questions about life's meaning, with the assumption that there is more to life than what we see or fully understand.

—Multidimensional Measurement of Religiousness/Spirituality for Use in Health Research[6]

This book is about religion and how its beliefs and practices affect human life. Spirituality is often thought of as one aspect of religion, and most religious people would insist that they are spiritual. In fact, many authors writing in this area do not distinguish between these terms in any significant way. The great theologian Paul Tillich defined religion as the object of man's "ultimate concern."[7] By this definition, most of us humans are religious, as we usually have some ultimate concerns. Tillich's definition of religion does bear a lot of similarity to the definition of *spirituality* given above. On the other hand, researchers studying the effects of religion on health have in recent years discovered that there is not complete overlap of the spiritual with the religious— obviously depending on how you construct the definitions and ask the questions. The report referenced above was from a study group attempting to facilitate the investigation of these two overlapping areas and their possibly separable effects on health.

Another way of thinking of these two terms is to think of *religion* as referring to organized social practices relating to ultimate power or concern that may have also private strands and to think of the *spiritual* as private religion like beliefs or concerns that exist regardless of any group practices. Private experiences of "ultimate concern" seem likely to be almost ubiquitous depending on how they are defined. Some data from a survey of pediatric oncology faculty (children's cancer doctors) illustrate the differences that may be seen.[8] Twenty-four percent reported regular attendance at religious services, 27 percent believed in God "with no doubts," and 85 percent thought of themselves as spiritual. Thus the vast majority of these highly educated people working in an emotionally stressful specialty think of themselves as spiritual, but only about one-fourth would qualify as religious by attendance at religious rituals.

Most of the people in the world are participants in some sacred tradition that would meet the usual definitions of a religion. A larger circle would be drawn by including all who have some personal spiritual experience or ultimate concern as defined above. It seems most important to distinguish these forms when one is studying the effects of belief on some behavior or outcome. Mircea Eliade, a great scholar of religion, never proposed a definition of religion, because he thought people could intuitively distinguish the sacred from the profane.[9] Most of the good and bad things done in the name of religion are inspired by one of its more public forms. Therefore this book will be minimally concerned with any private religion that is totally disconnected from some public belief system. Such "religion" would seem to be important to the holder but less subject to manipulation for public or group goals, which are important to our study. It may however affect the actions and well-being of the holder.

The French philosopher Andre Comte-Sponville has recently published *The Little Book of Atheist Spirituality,*[10] which makes a case for the importance of spiritual themes even for those who do not believe in some sort of God. He is a humanist who believes that, without God, we still need and may have ethical behavior, love, community, and an existential connection to the universe. Thus, in his view, spirituality—though it often or usually exists within a religion—may also be an important part of the life of those who neither participate in a religious tradition nor believe in a God or supernatural power.

A Naturalistic Assumption

Most of mankind's successes in understanding and controlling the natural world in the last few centuries have come using a naturalistic or materialistic assumption. This is the assumption that the world can be explained or understood in terms of natural objects and forces that are accessible more or less equally to all observers. One can argue about ontological versus methodological naturalism. Ontological naturalism is the assumption that there can be nothing but natural explanations, while procedural naturalism says simply that we carry on as though there were only natural explanations. This latter, less hubristic assumption seems more defensible. The alternative explanation that some divine power is continuously or intermittently acting has not seemed useful in understanding our world, and no such science has appeared.

Some of us would assert that this naturalistic assumption seems appropriate even for the study of religion. If we accept that humans are part of the natural world, it might reasonably follow that their creations—including their religions—are also part of that natural world. The claim that religion is magically different from other human activities and interactions with the world seems self-serving by the claimed expert, and works to deny us the possibility that we might increase our understanding by applying reason to the study of religion. The only hope we have of understanding and judging the vast array of competing religious claims, ideas, and organizations would seem to be applying our limited rational abilities to the problem.

David Hume was probably the first student of religion to look for a human, non-supernatural explanation of all religions, including Christianity.[11] At that time there was considerable danger in publicly offering such an explanation, and some of his work was published posthumously and without attribution. Some parts of the world are freer now, and books about atheism even occasionally make best-seller lists. Part of the evaluation problem is that the religionists and their apologists offer claims but do not venture into the area of providing useful, unbiased, publicly available ways for judging validity or comparing religious claims.[12] My goal is to show that human religion serves human nature and need and may be reasonably explained as a product of the interaction of human experience and human nature: the kind of beings we are and the structure and limitations of our world.

Worldly "Success" Guides Us to Metaphysical Truth?

This seems worthy of discussion here, since the almost universal belief in the supernatural and in religion would be proof of their "truth"—if such an argument were persuasive. I personally find the argument seriously flawed, but having heard it from thoughtful religious people, I would like to spend some time examining it.

Similar argumentation could be applied to studying the "truth" of particular sets of religious beliefs by judging the relative success of this particular belief system at winning, holding, and making happy its converts in the world. If this were true, one might say Christianity, having the most members, has the most truth—followed by Islam, etc. But even within these traditions, there is a great range of competing beliefs, so it is not clear how to actually apply this claim to adjudicate truth in a complex religious world. Most people, especially ones from minority ideological or religious traditions, would not want to say truth is determined by a plurality in a plebiscite. The world is a very complicated place, and many "truths" are contingent on time and place. I will attempt to illustrate some of this uncertainty.

One could tentatively or arbitrarily divide one's truths into facts about the physical world or universe (climate, seasons, rainfall, properties of materials, gravity, celestial movements, etc), the properties of human nature or human psychology, strategies for living in the world, and beliefs about the supernatural. In terms of facts about the world, such as when and where to plant crops or how to select material to build a dwelling, religions seldom compete. People, regardless of religious affiliation, usually accept the best available conventional wisdom in their culture.

Turning to human psychology, I note that there are claims about this world that, even if false, may have some real adaptive value for the person or group holding them. Such beliefs may have wide currency and durability. For instance, if one believes that there is a good God who rewards hard work with success in this world, then that belief may be self-fulfilling and self-perpetuating, regardless of whether that God exists. The only observable "truth" in such a belief would be that it had a positive or productive effect on most of those who accepted it. Most religions also address human social needs in practical ways—building some form of community. The beliefs, including supernatural claims, are invoked when doing this, but it is unclear how any test of truth is involved—except that shared beliefs are an effective way of making community. The Nazis were very good at building a powerful community—by demonizing those outside, by claiming a scientific justification of their position, and by creating or reinterpreting mythology. They failed to recognize the limitations of their strategy and eventually suffered an appropriate and terrible defeat. Despite this, their ideas still linger in a fringe movement eager for another try, a disturbing example of the power of a self-serving idea—however absurd it may seem to some of us.

Strategies for living in a complicated social world may succeed or fail depending on the situation. For instance, a belief in reproduction without restraint would, in a situation with unlimited resources, allow a group to achieve numerical and possibly practical dominance over groups with restrained reproduction. On the other hand, if resources were limited and defendable for each group, those practicing unrestrained reproduction might suffer serious loss of quality of life—even facing starvation. Beliefs may be successful in the world, though that success may have nothing to do with "truth" but instead with application of a particular strategy in a particular situation.

Supernatural claims or extravagant beliefs about some other place—heaven or hell or another galaxy—inaccessible to our examination, may have limited or even beneficial effects as part of a belief system in this world. There is no practical way of adjudicating "truth" claims beyond the reality of this world. Bizarre claims for some other place may go along with a very practical program in our reality. The principle of parsimony would suggest getting rid of the bizarre claims, but they may be the emotional power that makes the whole system work. For instance, these beliefs may function as powerful glue that holds a social group together, or they may motivate self-sacrificing behavior. We must therefore recognize that the success of a religious tradition in terms of numbers of adherents, and political and economic power, may not be related to the veracity of its claims about the structure of the universe. Time will indeed filter out teachings that don't agree with human nature and need. The "truth" that may emerge through this filter will not be some absolute truth but instead a collection of pragmatic beliefs characterized by usefulness to a group of humans in a world structured such as ours.

Some of the Limitations of This Commentary

> *There is only one religion, though there are a hundred versions of it.*
> —George Bernard Shaw, Preface, *Arms and the Man*[13]

For purposes of this text, I intend to treat religion as one generic entity—though realizing that there are many variations. I believe these variations are, in first approximation, simply different ways of satisfying the same human needs. I would agree with George Bernard Shaw, except to substitute "thousands" for his "hundred." Within each major tradition, there are usually many strands that accommodate a range of beliefs, activities, and attitudes—probably to better serve the human. Some of these strands may be more abusive and dysfunctional than others, but they are generally not the center of the tradition. Comparative religious studies are engaging but seldom address how religions work to create the human world. I will sometimes use examples from particular traditions, most often Christian, since I have always lived in a nominally Christian society.

One of my arguments for treating religions in one common category is the observation that most adherents of religious traditions maintain a single affiliation, and many cultures are largely identified with a single religious tradition, even in our modern world. Thus, it would seem that nearly all religions are capable of addressing a common set of human needs, though perhaps sometimes incompletely (see chapter 2 on usefulness). All or almost all religions make claims about the supernatural or some other reality not publicly accessible to humans living on this planet. Another related common feature of the available religions is their claim to some unique knowledge about the universe that is shared by no other human community and justifies that religion's existence.

The exclusivity demands of the Abrahamic traditions—combined with the power of acculturation—strongly discourage interfaith movement. There is however a trickle of such interfaith conversion whose benefits are not obvious enough to make it grow. There are some areas of the so-called "developing world" where unsophisticated or primitive religions have been giving way rapidly to more philosophically sophisticated modern religions, but even this has taken generations and the winner is usually a combination of Western religion and Western culture that may indeed provide a higher standard of living. This transplanted religion often comes through with particular local modifications that some would call more primitive than the proselytizing religion from which it was derived.[14] For instance a belief in exorcisms as treatment for demon possession is active in some of the new native Christianities in Africa.

I would start out recognizing that modern religions, in complicated ways, control the shape of the human world and depend on long-evolving human histories. My text will attempt to analyze some of the properties of religion itself and its uses in the human sphere—including its interactions with other important areas of human endeavor. I hope to show that religion can be plausibly explained—both in its origins and its spread and wide acceptance—by its immense power in creating and organizing our civilizations. Many groups find it helpful, or even vital, in supporting their ends.

These supernatural belief systems are adaptable, sometimes plastic, and make many "truth" claims that can never be disproved. This is one thing that has given them great currency almost everywhere. They should probably be regarded as some of the most compelling creations of the human imagination. I think of them as a product of those evolutionary cultural processes that, using human reason and creativity, built upon our previously evolved biologic nature the human world that we now experience. As we move to an interconnected global village, it might be safer for us all if more people realized that such institutions are deeply and ultimately human in their construction, modification, and application to our world. Such a realization might limit some of the darker uses of religious belief.

The goal of this text is a rational analysis and loose synthesis—to paint a picture of the many ways religion affects human life and arises from human life. One may expect to be criticized by some in the religious community for depending on "fallible human reasoning." What are the alternatives for any such complex human question? First, one might select someone else to make his decisions for him (abdication of responsibility). Second, one might try to operate at a feeling or impulse level acting on intuition (the decisions of the subconscious brain on the basis of algorithms created by an interaction of genetics and experience). Third, one might proceed with some random device such as a pair of dice (rejecting the possibility of reasoned choice). A humble appeal to our best reflective rational analysis seems the safest and maybe the only coherent option—hopefully ready to change a position in the face of new information. I wish to stimulate discussion, but know I haven't the power to change the world.

This work is an attempt to selectively examine the records of history, the searching of philosophy, the claims of religion, and the results of relevant scientific study as experienced by one mind living most of its life within a Christian religious community but trying to understand the larger world. The formative years for my mind were spent in pursuit of education in basic science and then in medicine. Professionally, my mature years have been spent in an attempt to practice cancer medicine both scientifically and humanely. A major hobby has been an attempt to understand my evolving and often ambiguous world.

My Personal Religious Journey

When I was young I believed, on the basis of my acculturation, that I knew what religious truth really was—and that my religion had that truth (Seventh-day Adventism). Critical examination of our religious truth was painted as risky and likely to lead to hell. Some doubts emerged as I pursued education—doctoral level degrees in biophysics and then in medicine—and finally at about age forty, I was able to start addressing these. Reading and discussion lead to decreasing confidence in my birth tradition. Looking at the wider world of Protestant traditions, I found a great variety claiming to be founded on the Bible. These seemed to be created by intelligent and devout men who spent their lives trying to discover the Divine Will. The very different belief systems created by these men plus my own extensive reading of the Bible lead me to conclude that such study had limited chance of solving the riddle of human existence—or religious truth.

It appeared to me unreasonable to think that a good God would have favored one geographic region or racial stock over another, so I came to believe that all religions should probably be considered more or less equal routes to knowledge of such God(s) as existed. It seemed hard to believe that if there was some good God, He or She would be less fair or kind or merciful than the best human I could imagine. This worked for a while, but my continued attempts to become familiar with a variety of religious traditions, and to become minimally educated in philosophy, history, and politics—along with my cumulating observations of current history and my interaction with hundreds of cancer patients—lead to a rising skepticism. Reading books such as William James's *Varieties of Religious Experience* taught me that human experience was very important for the religious traditions. It also seemed, however, that such experience could be explained without having to invoke the supernatural.

For over thirty years I have practiced medical oncology, working with patients who have serious, sometimes fatal, diseases. This experience is not the source of my opinions about religion, but it has informed me about the variety of ways that religion or its lack affects the lives of those who are ill. To my surprise, it has seemed that the ability to emotionally and intellectually cope with the end of life does not bear some clear relationship with religious belief. The most anxious patients I have seen have often claimed to be believers—but other believers are calm and thoughtful. Finally I have come to the opinion that how we cope with death and dying is related to how we have coped with life—and religion doesn't in some obvious way control our coping—our sense of how we are human seems possibly more important. For the religious devotee, religion will color the coping but not necessarily for better or worse—at least in my limited personal experience.

With time and study I came to the opinion that there were no truths about some supernatural reality standing behind the religious traditions. The simplest explanation (using Occam's razor or the principle of parsimony) seemed to be that we humans had evolved these magnificent, often useful, and sometimes dangerous traditions, and we needed no Gods to have done this. Finally, in my old age I have come to believe that religions are true in the sense that they interact with human nature to serve important human needs. To paraphrase Yeats, "religions embody truth, but they cannot know truth." Their metaphysical truth claims cannot be tested and are probably not true, but widespread belief in their reality provides the emotional power to drive the religious systems. This book is an attempt to provide plausible arguments for my model of religion as created by humans to serve human needs. No proof is possible, in the sense of mathematics, but there is a vast collection of information that bears on the discussion and, I believe, supports my contention.

2. Religion's Usefulness: The Human Refuge

Religion is a disease, but it is a noble disease.

—Heraclitus (~540–470 BC)

Introductory Comments

When referring to the usefulness of religion, I mean its usefulness in modifying and managing the real human world in which we live our earthly lives. No commentary will be attempted for the supernatural part of the universe—if such exists. Beliefs about the supernatural may of course affect behaviors in this world and thus may explain many features of our civilizations. Social reality may indeed be created by belief and expectation, but physical reality seems to ignore human wishes.

One could approach a discussion of the usefulness of religion from several standpoints. One approach might be from the positions of the various stakeholders, that is, the clergy or religious functionaries, the politically powerful (aristocracy or upper classes), and finally the common believers—usually consisting of the middle and lower classes. Each group seems to find particular aspects of religion that are congenial to its needs.

One might also think about the positive and negative effects of religious belief systems in relation to their powers to support exclusivity, hierarchy, and a kind of nihilism. The briefest of expositions of these concepts from a religious standpoint can be made as follows. Exclusivity refers to the ability to create a cohesive and loving in-group, usually by turning hostility outward toward those who do not share the in-group's belief system. Support of hierarchy means accepting your assigned role in society without complaint, since God created this role for you—or you for the role—and the aristocrat for his role. A kind of nihilism may come from religious enthusiasm that says the institutions and roles of this world are unimportant—all that counts is getting ready for the supernatural existence that comes after this life, for those who have prepared well.

My approach in this section will be to present areas where I think religion has important parts to play in individual lives and in many societies or civilizations. Descriptions of these functions will be attempted with an emphasis on the positive—but noting that every positive brings with it a possible dark side. "The Force" is what we humans make of it. Most of the time I will be talking about religion as an institution, but it is clear that some unaffiliated people may at times find solace in spiritual beliefs, or even solitary religious behavior. Formal religion is not necessary for all people with a spiritual approach to life (see Spirituality section chapter 1) but some sort of shared belief structures seem necessary to give religion its great power for the believing group.

Social Cohesion: That We May Love and Care for Each Other

The condition of our survival in any but the meagerest existence is our willingness to accommodate ourselves to the conflicting interests of others, to learn to live in a social world.

—Judge Learned Hand, Graduation Address, 1931[15]

If religion has given birth to all that is essential in society, it is because the idea of society is the soul of religion.

—Emile Durkheim, *The Elementary Forms of the Religious Life*[16]

In appreciating the usefulness of religion, it is essential to understand that the human animal is deeply social. For most of us, our happiest and our saddest moments come from our interactions or relationships with other people. Our tribes, our towns, our civilizations—and our wars—are built on the successes and failures of these social relationships. A major fraction of the human brain is devoted to social processing. It would seem that we must appreciate religion's social roles to understand its ubiquity. These social roles seem far more important in explaining religion's place than the posited propitiation of the supernatural.

The anthropologists suggest that our evolutionary history is intimately related to that of other primates. These primates almost all live highly social lives, usually in established groups, often with enduring or even lifelong interpersonal relationships. Thus our probable evolutionary history argues for the importance of social interactions in creating happy human lives. The earliest ancestors in the separate evolutionary line that brought humans probably had the socialization of small hunter-gatherer bands. The Neolithic revolution brought agriculture and with that the possibility of cities and larger collections of humans. Aristotle, one of antiquity's greatest observers of human life, believed that man was made to live in the polis, his highest development being a social life in a city.

In the modern world, sociologists have studied religion and confirmed its very important social roles. In fact Emile Durkheim, one of the founding fathers of the discipline of sociology, felt that the principle explanation for religion was in its social functions. He wrote "religion is something eminently social."[17] He observed that religion gave people shared morals, norms, meaning, authority figures, and means of communication. These shared interests in effect created the social group.

Shared religious belief is in fact one of the ways we define an in-group and an out-group. The religion creates shared or overlapping interests and goals. Within this in-group there may be empathy and altruism that is not displayed toward those outside the group. Early Christians were noted for their love toward one another. For instance they nursed fellow Christians during the plague.[18] One reason for the rise of Christianity may have been that this sect was more effective at creating community than its competitors. In our current world, many religious organizations support a general aid for the needy regardless of creed, but they also often have a particular emphasis on helping fellow believers, just as St. Paul collected money for the "poor saints which are at Jerusalem" (Romans 15:26).

Humans seem to have a natural tendency to simplify their world by imposing interpretation or theory on it—to make it more manageable. These theories are often used to divide humans into two groups. This is common in political and cultural practice, but religions seem to be the most powerful way to make that dichotomy as they affirm that some infallible and ultimate authority supports this judgment. To do this most successfully, religions need to be able to maintain the common denominational position—that there is only one truth: the one they espouse. This use is probably one reason that it is hard for most religions to have tolerance as a central feature.

Another great benefit of group identification is a sense of security. One shares one's ultimate belief system with a larger group, giving confidence that one has a unique and timeless "truth." This group claims a long history for their defining beliefs and a supernatural founding. Added to this is an extensive ritual system, which supports those beliefs. The believer is provided the "miracle, mystery, and authority" that Dostoevsky's Grand Inquisitor[19] claimed to be the greatest desire of the human. For most religions, the group loyalty is more important than individual development created through exercising freedom and making rational decisions. For access to the satisfaction of group membership, the individual has to give up his personal, idiosyncratic interpretations and accept those of the group. The majority of people appear to find this a worthwhile exchange. Security often seems more important than freedom in our unpredictable world.

One often admirable social use of religions is to encourage an "other"-centered life, helping us to see life in terms beyond our own needs—to get, at least sometimes, beyond our private selfishness. One way this can be promoted is through the exclusivity property of a religious system. Religious belief, as said above, is usually used to define an in-group and supports love, concern, and altruism within this group. Altruism is not confined to the in-group, yet hostility, sometimes quite subtle, is often directed toward those who reject the group's distinctive and revelatory "truths." The opportunities for strong, rewarding human-human relationships may thus be increased greatly by being a member of a religious community. Sometimes the downside of this is a form of tribalism and especially the narrowing of the "moral community." That is we may withdraw our moral and humanitarian concerns from those who stubbornly refuse to believe as we do—to share our central myth about meaning and responsibility— be it Christian, Jewish, Muslim or some other religion.

The quality or believability of a religious system doesn't seem to be important, except that systems of great fantasy appear to acquire smaller populations of believers—but these believers are perhaps more deeply enmeshed, for instance, the "Heaven's Gate" community of a few years ago, waiting for a comet, and then promptly committing mass suicide.[20] Maybe the greater the "leap of faith" to accept a religious system, the tighter that "leap of faith" will bind the believing community into some unity. A variety of other small religious groups, such as the Branch Davidians at Waco, seem to illustrate this tightly bonded community.

Another way of thinking of religion's social role is to see it as creating a modern tribe for refuge in a frightening world. Most of human evolutionary history played out in small groups that we may think of as tribes—typically 100 people or so. As recently as a few hundred years ago, a large portion of the earth's inhabitable surface was controlled by such groups of people, living by subsistence agriculture or by hunter-gatherer activities. A few such groups are still present in parts of South America, New Guinea, etc. Their primary identification is with the group, and their socialization and survival depend on that group. The modern, urban human can replace his or her lost tribe by joining some group such as a political party, a fraternal order, a labor union, or even a professional group, but a religion is probably the most universally available—and compelling—of such organizations. It tends to be largely egalitarian, to offer intense social experiences, and to provide as much involvement as the member desires, or in some cases can tolerate. It usually helps with the socialization of children and includes concern for the elderly, the disabled, the impoverished, and the sick. Religion thus finds itself filling natural and deep human social needs, often for people who have no comparable resources for filling such needs. Durkheim seemed to have such a feeling about the tribal role of religion. He wrote that "religious force is nothing other than the collective and anonymous force of the clan."[21]

Speaking from my personal experience, I will say that my parents' religious affiliation almost completely defined the social world in which I was acculturated. Besides the immediate family, this consisted of church and church schools and their many related social and religious functions. The world beyond was painted as sinful and filled with moral danger—we were encouraged not to seek serious social intercourse outside the group. An early and cataclysmic end of the world was also promised—a messianic second coming with heaven for the faithful. Education created cracks in this worldview, as did exposure to a broader range of human endeavor and achievement—both in school and in the workplace. Only with much time and study was I finally able to at least partly let go of this acculturation and accept the idea that sectarian identity was less important than our shared humanity.

Power Satisfaction: That Some Men May Be God

The charismatic religious leader, and the bureaucratic elite who lead an organized church, frequently claim to be doing "God's will" here on earth. Though they would deny it, it appears that they have in practice become gods—expecting some of the reverence and power assigned to their deity. Some are appropriately humble about their assumptions. Some may create a better world by promoting good personal and social behavior. They would, however, seem to do it by satisfying the previously mentioned Grand Inquisitor's dictum that we humans want "miracle, mystery, and authority." This power, of course, carries with it the universal risk of corruption.

A second important group consists of those with political power. The gods were in various ways used to justify kingship in the histories of ancient Sumer and Egypt.[22] In early China, dynastic rule was justified by the "mandate of heaven."[23] The United States throughout its history has often in presidential political oratory been portrayed as God's chosen nation. God's support of the political powers is offered by the apostle Paul as a justification for obeying them. In what history we know, religion has usually supported the existing political and religious hierarchy and therefore the strong against the weak. This seems a failing to those of us with egalitarian hopes or leanings. There are definite though conspicuously limited exceptions. For instance the liberation theology popular in Latin America in recent decades has tried to address this problem by rejecting the political abuses of the aristocracy. Its success has been quite limited.

Perhaps it may be that human tranquility has often been served by this religious justification of hierarchy. The stability of a society whose class structure is assumed to be blessed by a God may often increase the chance of people living a normal life span and having some satisfaction with their lives. Of course, there may be special benefits to the upper classes of society, who find it in their interests to promote a religion that supports, or at least encourages, acceptance of their favored position. This use has probably not increased equality, fraternity, or freedom. In fact, the abusive limits to access to land and education in Central and South America—usually supported by the church in the past—may have significantly hampered long-term social and economic progress in the region. One must note here, however, that I am speaking about common or frequent uses. There are exceptions to all rules like this, and it must be noted that religion is as plastic and perhaps as rigid, as the human mind, and some expression of religion will, at some point, appear on both sides of most important human issues.

From the standpoint of the typical lay believer, religion's support of hierarchy can also be very important. There is a certain nihilism that flows from a religion's suggesting that a supernatural power is in charge of the world and you, the believer, must accept this. You might improve yourself, but you can't expect to change the world. Your real hope for happiness is in the world to come. Marx's famous labeling of religion as "the opium of the people" decried this effect of religion, as he saw it supporting social injustice. Nietzsche saw it as supporting a "slave ethic" telling people that weakness and humility were good goals, but self-development—the "will to power" over one's self—and achievement were less to be admired.[24] Certainly support for the existing hierarchy does provide social stability.

Religion, as in the Abrahamic traditions, says God will reward your quiet suffering in another life somewhere and sometime to come. At times it is even conceived as validating current suffering as a form of good—to purify your soul. Dostoyevsky has his antihero make that argument at the end of *Notes from the Underground*. Such belief may lead one to accept the political powers and social arrangements that exist, since supposedly, these come from a God who could make things otherwise if He so desired. The power of a belief in supernaturally justified social arrangements is vividly illustrated in present-day India where the Hindu caste system, though outlawed, still has substantial influence on the social life of many Hindus.[25]

Finally, it seems that any man, regardless of his place in the social hierarchy, may find a remarkable power in asserting that he is doing the will of a God, not just satisfying his own desires or ambitions. Even the poorest, most uneducated believer may claim this in a religiously justified conflict with a nonbeliever and find there some satisfaction. Often for the confident believer, the knowledge of "God's will" becomes a non-negotiable truth and sometimes an overwhelming responsibility. Sadly, it also may lead to a certain arrogance in dealing with those with whom one disagrees. To know the "mind of God" is heady stuff and can be lethal to both the believer and those around him.

Existential Relief: That Men May Never Die

We find it almost impossible to contemplate a world without ourselves or to think that all we have learned and experienced will be gone after we die. We humans seem to have a natural feeling that we should be immortal. Religious traditions validate that feeling by saying, "Yes, you have some immortal component; you do have an existence beyond this time and place." Almost all religious traditions make this promise of a supernatural future, in at least some form—with rare exceptions such as the Orthodox branch of the Jewish tradition. For many people the great hope that they cherish with their religious tradition is another life beyond this one where they can find happiness, justice, equality, and all the other things that people so often struggle for but seldom achieve in this life. Perhaps such religious hope allows people to face more risky undertakings as "gods" unperturbed by the possibility of a death that they think is not real—or at least not final.

Most religions make your fate in the next existence conditional on your behavior or spiritual development in this life. This then seems to be an important bargaining chip in getting good, compliant behavior from the believers during their time here. Perhaps this is the source of the common—though misguided—belief that only religious people can be counted on to behave ethically. The hope for heaven may also be the solace that keeps some men working against almost impossible odds for some good. We all might benefit from such heroic action.

The Hindu, Jain, and Buddhist traditions believe in repeated incarnations on the "wheel of life." Their hope is to escape this wheel by spiritual development, with eventual union with some mystical goal sometimes called "nirvana." In contrast, the Abrahamic traditions usually teach that there is future life in a conditionally determined hereafter, either immediately on death or at some final judgment day. The Pythagoreans, and of course Plato, introduced a belief in immortality into Greek metaphysics. The ancient Sumerian religious traditions, such as exemplified in the Epic of Gilgamesh, did not believe immortality was possible except for their gods. Some of their stories however suggested that they believed in some shadowlike existence for the dead in an underworld. A similar picture for the dead may be found in much of the Old Testament, possibly reflecting the fact that Father Abraham's family came from Sumer. The pervasiveness of this ancient concept is seen in an underworld of less than fully human characters visited by the heroes of Homer's *Odyssey* and Virgil's *Aeneid*—in stories put in writing at least seven hundred years apart.

Some of us would think that there is a fundamental difference between accepting ourselves as mortals with a finite time on this Earth, or as immortals with other places to live, to develop, and to correct our errors. Various philosophers, particularly the existentialists, have claimed that we are never fully human until we face our own mortality. Thus religion may, from this viewpoint, allow us to deny our humanity. It is hard to deny that our bodies are part of the natural world, especially as science provides more and more details of our ancestry and our relationships with the other life forms current and past. These observations are consistent with limited types of group and of genetic immortality, but those are not the objects of most people's hopes. The claims of individual immortality must then be confined to a soul or mind that can be conceived of as separable from the body or brain. This is a tradition that is not supported by our slowly advancing understanding of the brain, but it is deeply held—and powerful—for the believer. Some religious commentators[26] are attempting to move religion away from belief in the immaterial and immortal soul. One must ask how this would affect the major religious traditions. Will they continue to ignore such concerns? Must they to maintain their place and power?

Does a belief in immortality have a significant effect on coping with serious or possibly fatal illness? My experience suggests that in daily practice both those identifying as believing in immortality and those identifying as atheistic have the same concerns with comfort, pain, weakness, progression of disease, fate of survivors, and impending death. Only a few patients report they have renewed their religious lives in some way in response to this crisis or impending crisis. A belief in a life after death has not, for most participants, removed some fear of death—as far as I can tell. Some oncology colleagues have even suggested the opposite. Yet many people, with or without a belief in life beyond, gracefully accept the finiteness of life here and the inevitability of death.

A brief story might illustrate my experience. A few years ago an eighty-year-old patient was in my office in a wheelchair, with an oxygen tank, and not looking very well. I had for many years helped him manage a low-grade leukemia that had responded nicely to therapy. Multiple other symptomatic medical problems had developed. This day he announced, "Doc, you know this is the last time you're ever going to see me." I acknowledged the possible truth of his assertion and ask if he had made his peace with his religious tradition. His response was, "Doc, you know I don't believe any of that stuff." Indeed, I had briefly forgotten a conversation from a few years prior where he had confided that he didn't believe in God. This day he seemed at peace with his belief, wanting no sympathy but instead desiring an acknowledgment of his carefully weighed conclusion.

Meaning Making: That We Might Know Our Importance in the Universe

If there is one indisputable fact about the human condition it is that no community can survive if it is persuaded—or even suspects—that its members are leading meaningless lives in a meaningless universe.

—Irving Kristol quoted page 131 in Daniel Pinker's *The Blank Slate*[27]

Religions tell believers why they were put on earth. They say that some God or force, personal or impersonal, made us and our world. This relationship is conceived of as giving importance to all people's lives and how they are lived. From this relationship flows a set of responsibilities—toward God, others, and the natural world—with assertions about the importance of fulfilling them. Since the unseen world of this God or Divine Will is more important than the visible world, the duties defined by this supernatural imperative are assumed to be man's most important obligations.

Most religions offer all humans, including the poorest and weakest, some sort of access to the powers controlling the universe, thus validating the importance of all. Religions do vary considerably in how they relate humanity to the rest of the natural world. The "wheel-of-life" religions—Hinduism, Buddhism, and Jainism—and Taoism seem to more strongly emphasize mankind as part of the natural world and not superior to it. For instance, the Isa Upanishad[28] contains the following statements (slokas 6 and 7):

If one sees all living things as if they were in his own body, i.e., feels their joys and sorrows as his own, and sees the same Universal Spirit in all things then there is no need for protecting oneself against others. ...When a man understands that all beings are, indeed, the all-pervading Spirit, then he realizes the oneness of all things and illusion and grief vanish.

The Abrahamic traditions generally define humanity as a special creation of an all-powerful God—who continues to be concerned with the lives of individual humans. A record of all their deeds is purportedly kept by the Divine administration and will be examined when assigning their fate after this life. The founding narrative story of this group of religions presents nature or the world as having been created to make a home for mankind, who seems, in this story to be more important than all the rest of creation and to be assigned control over that creation.

Some of the power of the Abrahamic traditions may flow from their claim that humans are not just another creation of nature, of evolution in a great chain of being across the natural world and over hundreds of millions of years. Instead, the believer can claim that she was created in the image of a God and has a divine mandate to control the world and to prepare herself for some utopian future arranged by this God. This mythic claim, this wonderfully satisfying dream that the human is divinely separated from the rest of the natural world by his bonds to the divine may be one reason these traditions are the most successful of all current religions.

Religion is also the source of many of the rituals that give meaning, importance, and even solace to human events both public and private. Familiar rituals are one of the ways we control anxiety about the uncontrollable or the unknown. The widespread use of ritual predates recorded history in many places, filling an archeological account that goes back for thousands of years before written records. Many of these ancient rituals appear to have been largely religious—as suggested by the relics left us. Chinese society, especially as represented by the Confucians,[29] developed an extensive ritual system in an attempt to control, and make virtuous, both public and private life. This had great currency for over two thousand years and still contributes to the structure of some Asian societies. Certainly today, participants in weddings and funerals in most of the world usually look to religious understandings of these life-changing ceremonies.

Before leaving the topic of meaning, it seems appropriate to point out that religion is not the only way we find meaning in our lives. Camus' novels (especially *The Plague*[30]) and his essay on the "*Myth of Sisyphus*"[31] present life as the only meaning we have and living it responsibly and well as the highest good. Victor Frankl in his book *Man's Search for Meaning*[32] proposes three ways in which we humans find meaning for our lives. One way is by personal achievement—such as a creative work of art or literature, winning a competitive championship, or building a successful business. A second way is by having an intense experience such as falling in love or even developing a deep personal friendship. The third of Frankl's routes to meaning is to rise above personal suffering, to turn tragedy into triumph in recreating yourself.

Thus, for the individual, there are a variety of ways of creating meanings for a life. Religion is only one possible source—but perhaps the most frequently and widely invoked. For the politician or other leader of a group, who wants to create a shared meaning, religious belief is readily available and often a powerful place to start. There are risks when a leader attempts to apply such a strategy in the presence of multiple competing religions. He may incite competition or persecution instead of the unity he intended. Where it is useful, the effectiveness of such a program may be enhanced if the leader can appeal to shared experiences and shared achievements, uniting the followers with shared meanings for their lives. Obviously, a group could also be united by the meaning of shared nonreligious experiences—for instance filling some community need such as building a school or a road.

Personal Validation: Our Parental Substitute

We grow up usually seeking validation from our parents—for our efforts in school and work, for our academic and athletic successes, and for our dreams of career and family. We derive considerable reassurance from their approval and distress if they withhold that approval. As we get older and our lives more complicated and separate from these parents, the meaning of their approval may become less clear, but the emotional need will be there for many of us until the day we die. Parental approval gives a certain satisfaction to cap our efforts in life, and even after they die we may think, "I wish I could tell them…" My mind does that.

As we grow and are introduced to our religious traditions (at least within the Abrahamic strands), we are taught that God wants us to do everything as well as we can, and is like another—but supernatural— parent who really cares for us regardless of our successes or our failures. At least in some branches of Christianity, an extensive mythology of songs and stories is used to support this—with lines like "Jesus loves me" and "His eye is on the sparrow." As time goes by, one is encouraged to seek personal validation by following the dictates of his religion—in personal devotions, in services, and in gifts. In practice this means looking for endorsement from one's personal religious advisers or from public leaders of the religious tradition, since in practice for most people God is not visible to give this support.

These religious figures, by their approval and by making that approval public, may do much to validate a believer's life and to make him feel admired by his peers and others. As we grow older and family approval is less available, or even not available, this religious substitute may become increasingly compelling for some. For instance, an eighty-year-old acquaintance of mine left a large sum of money to his church and was very pleased when a number of important clergy from that church visited him and validated his actions—and thereby his life.

Comfort in Distress: That We May Know We Are Not Alone

Most religions, at least of the Abrahamic variety, offer some claim that what happens in the world is ultimately controlled by a divine force, usually their deity. They commonly propose that this divine entity is both just and good and cares about the sufferings of the creatures that have been put here on earth. It is asserted that this deity knows what is happening to us all, and will make sure—if we only let him—that things come out for the best at least in terms of our eternal interests. At times of major uncertainty or stress religion's appeal to the supernatural seems particularly attractive to many people. A typical Christian response to illness, conflict, accident, catastrophe, and loss is to recommend praying to God and trusting that he will appropriately control the outcome. The individual is then encouraged to let go of his anxiety, and having put the problem into God's hands, accept God's management.

When the experience is urgent, frightening, and beyond the individual's control, this strategy may be particularly helpful at achieving some inner equanimity. My personal observations in the areas of illness and medical care suggest that this strategy can be reasonably effective in certain situations such as before major surgery or coping with terminal illness. Its sometimes dramatic calming effect may be used as an argument for the validity of the underlying belief system. Unfortunately, for a significant number of believers this is inadequate, and despite claims of deep religious faith, they remain fearful and anxious in the face of impending death, still seeking a miracle until the very end.

Another concern must be raised about this program of placing complete trust in God. If the individual could influence the outcome by his or her own actions or choices, but they give up that opportunity in order to place the outcome in "God's hands," they may have forgone a real opportunity to help themselves. Though this is not the common outcome, I have seen many patients over the years make this argument in rejecting a potentially beneficial medical intervention. My observations have included patients who refused potentially curative surgery for cancer and patients who declined chemotherapy or biologic therapy that might have substantially prolonged life or even had some chance of cure.

Acculturation of the Young: That Our Children May Be Good Like Us

Religion may be thought of as the most powerful ideological tool created by the human mind—perhaps a result of cultural evolution. It should therefore not be surprising to find that it is an important instrument for preparing children to play their roles in human society. In fact, we find most religious groups investing heavily in the religious education of their children. This is supported by the belief that their religious system is the only correct understanding of the world, and indeed of the universe—therefore it is in the children's best interest to learn it well. From the leadership position, it is also motivated by the need to maintain the strength of the organization by keeping up its membership. From the standpoint of the parents, the benefits of a common belief system are noted in the Christian slogan "the family that prays together stays together."

Religious instruction is a way of transmitting much of what the adults in a society have accepted as important. It tells the children what their culture expects of them in terms of beliefs and of relationships within the family, the local community, and the larger human world. It is a point of shared beliefs and feelings across generations. In some situations, such as affluent North America, even nonbelievers will sometimes arrange instruction in religious schools for their children in hopes that the values and standards of behavior taught there will have an enduring, positive effect. Equivalent nonsectarian education, including ethical and aesthetic instruction, is often difficult to find or afford. In other poorer cultures, children's religious instruction may be the only education they get beyond mundane practical matters taught at home or apprenticeship in the workplace. The madrassas schools of the Islamic world seem to be examples of this.

Identification of Cooperators: That We May Avoid Being Cheated

For economic success in the world we depend on many interactions with other people. If they cheat us, it is often very difficult to get redress—either impossible or requiring lawyers, money, and time. In a world with an increasing division of labor, we come to depend on many different specialists—to maintain our homes, our vehicles, our bodies, etc. We are always looking for a way of identifying honest, reliable, and fairly priced services. A cooperating population is thought to be more productive. We can thus think of our search for fair services as a search for cooperators who will participate in a mutually beneficial exchange.

People who share a religious belief system are probably more likely to give each other status as real people deserving respect and fair treatment. This is at least the common belief. Jared Diamond[33] noted that in primitive cultures a shared religion could make it possible for unrelated people to meet for the first time without killing each other. He felt this was one of the reasons for the development of institutionalized religion as centralized societies came to dominate the human world. It is easily observed that many religious organizations in the United States encourage their members to use each other's services. The not always stated, but at least implied reasoning is that a businessman who is a member of our congregation wouldn't cheat another member of the community. The religious group may thus serve as a first approximation to a community of cooperators.

This may work better in strict religions where in effect the price of admission is higher and people are less likely to join just to appear trustworthy. As an example it is noted that Howard Hughes, the wealthy industrialist, made extensive use of trusted Mormon associates in his old-age reclusive period. Thus even to outsiders, some religions may seem to identify "cooperators" that may be more reliable than nonreligious people. On the other hand, a failure in this area may be devastating for the naïve believer who is cheated by another member. Several of my religious acquaintances have complained bitterly of a soured employment or business arrangement with another member. Such systems are never foolproof—still human.

Prayer, Meditation, and Problem Solving

Discussing a complex problem with any interlocutor, even an imaginary one, may force us to more clearly organize our ideas. Both active presentation of a problem in the form of a petition to a deity, or thoughtful meditation about a problem while actively asking for divine guidance in solving it, may force the petitioner to think carefully and consider all the possible solutions and their implications. This would seem to be a recipe for making your best possible decision. In support of this most of us can testify that when we attempt to teach or explain something to someone else we are forced by this effort to develop a clearer and more complete understanding. Such an enhanced understanding may inform and improve our own decisions.

If we put our mind to work on a problem multiple times, it may continue this work subconsciously, sometimes bringing new and never before thought of solutions to the conscious level for evaluation. To the believer this may seem like God making a suggestion, though it is a well-known mental phenomenon; at least for those who struggle with scientific or mathematical problems. Calling it his "over-belief," William James asserted that there was some spiritual power and that this power communicated with us through the subliminal or subconscious; so there is some precedent for giving the supernatural credit for this.

Thus there are two cognitive mechanisms by which religious practice may help people to make better decisions: by repeatedly struggling with their problems and by trying to understand their options so well that they can explain them clearly to someone else.

Summary

Religion appears to be the most powerful and widely available social and ideological tool for helpful manipulation of our fellow humans. I have provided a less than exhaustive review of its useful applications—of things that make it highly valued by many human minds. One must also recognize that the majority of adherents, who claim a religious tradition, do so with the clear belief that they are honoring some divine entity here and now and possibly making their lives right for some future life. In my experience, the average believer seldom understands religion's role in making the human world work or establishing his place in that world. He looks to his religion for "God's will,"—for something more than human, and in various ways learns he has found it.

The illusion is that religion is provided by some divine power to reconcile the human and the divine realities. It appears to some that the real function of religion is to try to make human life more social and more fulfilling, as we are social animals needing physical and emotional homes, approval of others, and guidance in finding our places in the world.

One way of describing the role of religion is to say that it is a way of framing a human life. This one institution seems to provide meaning, context, acculturation, socialization, and an ethical framework for a life. People are naturally and reasonably reluctant to question the foundations of their religious belief system because so much of their lives appears to depend on it. This is partly an illusion as there are other sources for many of these things. For instance, the ethics proclaimed by religions are largely founded on our "intuitive" ethics—see chapter 6: Religion and Ethics.

3. Unique Power of Religious Belief

Let me start by noting that some of the power of religious belief flows from its immense usefulness as noted in the previous chapter. Some of that usefulness is, however, only possible because the confident believer privileges his religious beliefs as being more true than his other beliefs about the world. Here we will attempt to look at how this works in the real world.

Emotional Power and Truth

There is no evidence that enthusiasm and joy always go with the truth.
—Emile Boutroux, quoted by Ellenberger[34]

It seems that the power of an idea in the typical human mind has little to do with its ontological truth—perhaps for some well-trained and skeptical subjects there might be a relationship. The most important support for a belief seems to be how it satisfies emotional and social need, rather than how accurately it fits with a known reality. This is most clearly indicated in history when men die on both sides of a battlefield, fighting for belief systems whose truth claims are mutually exclusive. However, they often die firmly convinced that they are on God's side, dying for "truth." The objective accuracy of a belief and that belief's motivational power for the believer seem at best loosely related. The most important support for belief may be early acculturation. We are taught a set of religious and other important beliefs usually as children, and the majority of us don't stray far from these during our lives. We probably filter new religious beliefs for some rough compatibility with these starting beliefs and accept the new if we find them congruent and helpful.

Some personalities may be more readily enrolled in a demanding belief system and even easily transfer from one such system to another.[35] These people seem to need to devote their lives to some cause larger than themselves, religious, political, humanitarian, etc. Even without promises of immortality, such people may be prompted to sacrifice their lives in hopes that the movement may be successful and their contribution will be enduring and remembered. This was certainly true in the Marxist movements of the twentieth century. These compelling belief systems are usually shared by a peer group, increasing the individual's confidence in them. In some cases rejecting them may risk one's place in this world, as well as one's hope for the future. Thus people may end up enmeshed in a system dangerous to their personal survival, such as guerilla war or suicide bombing. They may be unable to extricate themselves—for both physical and psychological reasons—even if they lose their original confidence in the belief system.

The long-term success of beliefs is another matter. This success seems to depend on how these ideas interact with human nature and with the facts of the world in which humans are enmeshed. Ideas that are wrong about human nature will eventually fail. For instance, attempts to create utopian societies by means of political violence have usually eventually created some sort of hell. Think of Hitler's Germany, Stalin's Russia, or Pol Pot's Cambodia. Ideas that are wrong about the world—such as a belief that agricultural resources are indefinitely renewable and expandable—will ultimately fail—see for instance *Collapse*, Jared Diamond's major study.[36] Ideas about some other "reality" that is inaccessible to us in the here and now may survive very well, even if bizarre, as long as they are associated with successful concepts addressing human nature and physical reality. The Latter Day Saints or Mormon Church is an example of a belief system about life after death and the supernatural that seems, to many of us, rather hard to defend or to seriously entertain. This belief system is supported by an emphasis on personal industry and entrepreneurial activity, and a missionary program that also functions to confirm the youth in their belief system. The result is a rapidly growing and economically successful organization admired by many. For further discussion of this topic see the section "Worldly "Success" Guides us to Metaphysical Truth?" in chapter 1.

Presumed Sources and Reinforcements

The current sources of our major religious narratives or myths usually include documents, typically ancient and almost always with significant uncertainty about the details of their origins. There are, however, many people who believe that the ancients had great knowledge, some of which has been lost. These people find such texts very attractive in their search for that lost wisdom. This becomes one of the factors that support the power of the religious traditions. The corollary claim that God directly inspired—either as ideas or as particular words—the writing of these texts, supports the same sort of thinking. Any contradictions in the manuscripts are thought of as apparent, not real, and probably a function of our limited human understanding. Thus, for many people, a lifetime devoted to studying such texts is the supreme road to wisdom, and to knowledge of this world and the human place in the universe.

Ancient texts held in high regard by large religious groups include at least the Bible, the Qur'an and Hadith, the Vedas and Upanishads, the Pali Canon, the Analects, the Daodejing and maybe the Avesta. Expressions of this devotion include the monk who spends a lifetime reading and contemplating his sacred scriptures and the Christian layman who spends all her spare time on "the Good Book," believing there is no equally reliable source of knowledge. A further example could be Sir Isaac Newton, who spent more effort on and wrote more about Biblical prophecy than he did science or mathematics.

The other source of spiritual knowledge and validation for many religious traditions is a personal experience interpreted as an experience of God—in some way a stamp of divine approval. Within some Christian traditions this may variously include visions, trances, dreams, "speaking in tongues," and even a warm inner feeling of peace and divine approval. Common folk wisdom validates these experiences as from God, especially when the experiences are appropriately framed—for instance occurring in the setting of a religious service or private devotions. People having the experience report a powerful positive emotional event or even "high" that may be transforming for their lives. They and those around them usually take this as evidence of God's approval of their lives and validation of their religious belief.

Some religious commentators, such as Luke Timothy Johnson of Emory University, feel that such powerful personal experiences were very important in the rapid spread of early Christianity and are important in all the Abrahamic traditions.[37] Similar experiential manifestations related to religious belief were well-known in other Mediterranean religious systems at the time that Christianity was beginning. With time, the Christian church had to learn to manage these experiences to maintain control and orthodoxy. Diverse religious claims validated by mystical experience can be very disruptive to organized church life unless modulated and controlled by the church. My personal experience is that this form of affirmation is active today for at least some of my acquaintances who are believers.

Recent studies of brain function suggest that religious behavior and thought are dominated by the right side of the brain—that part of the brain that has to do with poetry, music, and art. Religion shares with poetry extensive use of metaphor. Nietzsche called this right brain, the feeling or experiential brain, the Dionysian part, the source of power for the human player. Against this must be arrayed the rational or Apollonian side in an attempt to harness the power. Artistic success would seem to come from coordinating these two to make a harmonious artistic product. Thus poetry, music, and art are often closely related to religion and readily serve to enhance its power.

One may think of theology as the Apollonian side with its attempt at rational analysis, and in contrast the Dionysian can be seen in the Pentecostal meeting with its "spirit possession," healings, and "speaking in tongues." Clearly, the latter is the more spontaneous and attracts a larger fraction of most human populations. Trimble has recently published an enlightening attempt to describe for us nonexperts current research on the cerebral basis of religion.[38] Looking at the widespread belief in typical religion and also in UFOs and alien visits, he insists that we can only appreciate this when we realize the "inadequacy of our cognitive structures and systems, which are simply not as rational as we would like to believe and which are driven far more by emotion than most commentators are willing to concede."

Complete Knowledge without Struggle: Standing in Gods Place

Once having bought into a religious tradition, the believer is encouraged not to question its validity. To the extent he is able to maintain that attitude, he can now be confident he has the answers to the great questions about human existence. He now knows why we are here, the goals of human life, and how we should behave. He knows this absolutely—as if he were standing in God's place and knowing the mind of God. This gives him a certainty in action that may allow him to destroy his own life (martyrdom) or the lives of those who do not share his views of the world.

Religions usually attempt to offer a complete interpretation of the human world—and even the natural world. This interpretation is offered as instant knowledge to the potential believer. Belief itself offers access to a complete solution to the labyrinth of human existence. To the believer, this information comes with limited struggle in comparison to that effort required for the student to understand the realms of philosophical or scientific inquiry. Sometimes rational inquiry is replaced by learning the revealed wisdom of the tradition—and acquiring varying degrees of scorn for rational enquiry. The Protestant reformer Martin Luther said, "Reason is the greatest enemy that faith has" and "The damned whore, Reason,"[39] suggesting his distrust of rational enquiry. There is even a subset of members within some traditions who believe that knowledge beyond that contained in their holy manuscripts and teachings is not needed or helpful for humans.

Playing off of these powerful beliefs, committed leaders can often get their followers to undertake major works such as a lifetime of service to the needy or suicidal terrorism against the presumed enemies of the religious tradition. The current activity of Al-Qaeda and the last-century life of Albert Schweitzer illustrate the power and plasticity of such beliefs—the promotion of a life dedicated to helping others or to destroying others both claiming to make the world better. To what actual ends a religion will be put almost certainly depends on human need, the larger culture, and the morality, imagination, and creativity of those who are in leadership roles. American "skin head" churches, Al-Qaeda, liberation theology, and the Fundamentalist Church of Jesus Christ of Latter-day Saints are all the result of creative uses of religion for someone's purposes. These may be understandable from the perspective of those who created them, but they do diverge from some mainstream in frequently frightening ways.

Lest I speak too lightly of the religious tradition and its intellectual struggles, let us recognize that there are two major areas of such struggle. One is the inward journey of the religious ascetic or mystic who seeks to become something or someone, to become enlightened, to mold himself to be like or in union with the envisioned divine. This seems to be more an attempt to change the self than to understand the self or the world. A second form of intellectual struggle in religion is the discipline of theology. Over history this seems largely to have been an attempt to rationalize the tradition and make it speak in an intelligible voice to both the believer and the nonbeliever.

Generally, this intellectual effort must start with the primary stories, myths, or beliefs of the tradition, and if these seem to disagree with other areas of intellectual development, the theologian must reinterpret or refine the tradition or rationalize it in such a way that it is no longer in disagreement with the best scientific or historical scholarship. For further discussion, see the section "The Religious Intellectual Quest" in chapter 10: Religion and Science and Reason.

Magic and Religion

In this section when I use the term *magic,* I am not referring to sleight of hand or other visual tricks used by modern magicians to entertain and surprise their audience. Instead, I refer to the so-called "black arts," including the belief that spells and incantations have power to help or harm the person(s) toward whom they were directed. Up until the European Enlightenment such beliefs were common in Europe as witnessed by the persecution of witches well into the seventeenth century. Such beliefs still persist for some primitive peoples where shamans and witch doctors control the spirit world. Even as a child growing up in the rural American South (Tennessee), I was told frightening stories suggesting a reality to these beliefs.

The practices and hopes of those who apply magic and those who use religious ritual have similarities and differences. Both offer contact with some ultimate power we usually refer to as supernatural. The practitioners of magic usually claim to be able to use that power for some desired end without regard to any moral concern. For them the power is like the "Force" in the Star Wars movies; it can be used for either good or evil. In some ways the magician or "divine engineer" is more powerful than the power he controls because that power moves at his command.

The religious person addressing his God in prayer and hoping that his prayer will change God's action in the world is apparently doing something very similar. Some differences may, however, be noted. The religious person addressing a presumed good God has been acculturated to believe that this God will not do anything immoral or bad even if requested to do so. Most practitioners of prayer, at least in the Christian tradition, have been educated to assume that their God will only answer their prayers positively if he, in his "infinite wisdom," decides that fulfilling their requests will be somehow "good" for their long-term interests. For Christians, unanswered prayers are to be interpreted as God answering no. This makes empiric evaluation of the results, purported to be produced by such prayers, a difficult if not impossible task.

Thus within some religious communities prayer is, at least theoretically, different from magic. In actual practice on the ground for the unsophisticated and needy lay member, the difference may be small. For instance, it has been claimed that there are no atheists in foxholes—all pray for divine assistance. These prayers may be seen as a form of stress relief, but they also would seem to be requests for a protection that is not clearly different from magic.

Immortality and Reward

There are widespread religious claims that humans are immortal, usually by having "souls" that never die. At apparent death here, the believer's soul goes on to heaven or some union with God or the divine, or perhaps re-enters the earthly quest for another lifetime seeking to further perfect this soul. A few religious groups offer an alternate immortality consisting of real death here followed by a resurrection—a sort of resuscitation—after which the human must face a divine tribunal where his eternal fate is decided. These claims are taken by the serious believer to suggest that the next life is more significant than this brief existence and that the present life is some sort of preparation for this looming future. Much of the current (and past) political power of the Catholic Church flows from its claims of controlling access to this promised future. For a large number of people at the level of "folk religion," the most important and powerful religious "fact" is the promise of some desirable future existence in a better place.

Thus part of the power of many religions seems to flow from their claims of control over and understanding of a human fate beyond this transitory earthly existence. There are, of course, no objective, public ways of verifying such claims. The religions themselves tell us that these claims are not testable. Their commentary includes the assertion that God can't show his power here on earth or there would be no room for us to exercise faith. There are, however, many believers who report special, personal, private experience to validate these religious beliefs. *Those who accept such claims, truly believing, must alter their thinking about life.* Not surprisingly this thinking may denigrate the current world in support of hopes for a greater, and possibly permanent, existence to come.

The other side of the offer of an eternal utopian existence for the believer is the claim that there is some alternate fate beyond this life for the sinner, or rejecter of the truths of the tradition. This alternate fate may include an eternal damnation in the fires of a Christian hell; some process of re-education, preceding a delayed admission to paradise; or endless recycling through lives on this earth attempting to get it right. These alternate fates are portrayed as very undesirable in all traditions. Some of the more famous Christian examples include Jonathan Edwards's sermon "Sinners in the Hands of an Angry God" and Dante's *Inferno*. Any organization able to make the "myth" or belief system real to its members, and making claims to hold the keys to both of these eternal fates, will thereby wield immense power over believing members.

Ritual

The strength of religious claims can be further reinforced by the emotional appeals of powerful and often beautiful religious rituals. These ceremonies are sometimes framed with attractive and compelling sacred music and usually include intense oratory encouraging some action such as personal confession, monetary donation, missionary service, etc. They may successfully elicit guilt, submission, joy, and even lifetime commitments. William James[40] describes the effects of such rituals on some people. Life transforming "conversion experiences" were common among the subjects of his study. What archeological remains we have of preliterate civilizations suggest that rituals, especially those involving death and burial, were very important in those societies. These were probably in a real sense religious rituals involving gods or ancestors. Thus it appears that religious ritual is much older than written history and has been part of the important glue holding human social groups together for many millennia.

The power of these rituals can be immense, especially for the young and inexperienced mind. James Joyce provides an example of this power in the story of his Catholic schooling and his temporary journey into a deep religiosity.[41] Most who have experienced a Protestant upbringing with sermons followed by altar calls framed by beautiful religious music have experienced some of this power. When I was young, I had direct involvement in many of these deeply guilt-producing experiences—at least that is how they felt to me. It seems that as we get older and more experienced in the world, we can at least sometimes step back in our minds and more objectively evaluate the experience. On the other hand, the ability of these traditions and rituals to generate changed lives is often used as a compelling "on the ground" argument for the truth of the underlying belief system. Many people are persuaded by this—apparently untroubled by the variety of belief systems that may be so supported.

Loyal Rue in a recent book[42] makes several comments on the central role of rituals in religious traditions. He considers them an important way of transmitting the narrative story or central myth of the religion to the next generation, a way of making the myth seem more real to those experiencing the ritual, and an apprenticeship in thinking about the myth as valid and important. These rituals are also a way of refreshing working memory so that elements of the myth come quickly to mind when we face life's decisions.

Religion and Social Psychology

Those who study social psychology have defined several ways we can, in our social world, wield substantial influence over others.[43] These depend on built-in reflex responses to particular social situations, rather than on some intellectual analysis. For most people these can be overridden but only with difficulty. Religions are often adept at using these triggers, and I will comment on the use of reciprocity, commitment, authority, and social proof. Within the religious traditions, simple explanations are about as follows: reciprocity says you owe the divine world something for all the blessings you have, commitment refers to your obligation to something after you publicly support it, authority refers to appeals to designated authorities to answer questions, and social proof refers to the attempt to establish a belief system's authenticity by an appeal to the wisdom of those who publicly support that system now or have done so in previous ages.

Within the Abrahamic traditions, it is common to say that the human has been given life and every possession by a loving God. The believer is urged to reciprocate in response to this love—by worshiping his God and giving some of what he possesses back to this God—which translates into gifts directed to the religion or church. A considerable effort is made in this regard, and it is often successful in influencing the members to give generously, sometimes beyond their means, to support causes important to the church or its leaders. Some churches are not bashful about promising eternal rewards along with relief of potential "reciprocity guilt"—or other forms of guilt.

Religious organizations have found more than one way to use a public commitment to reinforce a believer's faith. In the Protestant tradition this is often done with rituals, as described in the last section, including emotional sermons framed by beautiful religious music and culminating in an altar call for all who love the Lord to come forward and affirm or reaffirm their faith. Those who don't come forward feel guilty, and those who do come have made a public commitment that tends to block any intellectual evaluation of that to which they have committed. Another powerful form of public commitment is the work of proselytizing for the organization. The Jehovah's Witnesses strongly encourage this for all members, laud it, and actually keep a written record of it. The Mormons require two years of full-time missionary work, mostly proselytizing, from all their young men. Doubtless, this does much to cement a lifetime membership for those involved. To publicly advocate something that we don't believe subjects us to a form of cognitive dissonance and a painful perception that we might be dishonest. Thus we tend to bring our beliefs in line with our voice, suppressing questions or alternatives.

Most humans, being social creatures, tend to defer to those presented as authority figures. Churches use this regularly to control religious expression and belief. Churches almost universally have their own authorities on the interpretation of ancient texts, on what God wants from his followers, and on the religious history that justifies their particular tradition. These authority figures will dispute with the infidel, the atheist, the schismatic, and believers in other traditions, giving the concerned member confidence in his own tradition—even if he never bothers to understand the debate. At least an "expert or authority figure" is on his side and has defended his position.

Life is short and we do not have time to examine all truth claims, religious or otherwise. If something is widely believed by those around us, we tend to accept that as proof we should share this belief. This is the essence of social proof. If a belief about God is widespread in your community, you will frequently accept it without examination. In fact, you may consider the group smarter than you are and therefore fear to attempt an examination lest you come to a wrong conclusion. If your family and friends are members of a particular religious tradition, the same reasoning may apply. If the religion is large and ancient, the social proof is even more effective, as one can ask how thousands or millions of people could be wrong for centuries, or even millennia.

Rodney Stark[44] has pointed out that the founder of a new religion usually starts by converting his own family. The religion then extends to friends and neighbors. Most conversions to a spreading religion occur when a substantial part of the converter's social world has already embraced the belief system. Mass conversions are not necessary to explain most religious change. In fact Stark has calculated that Christianity only had to increase at about 3.4 percent per year for its first three hundred years to achieve its powerful fourth-century position. This conversion by social networking seems to be another example of the use of social proof in religious matters.

The Self Reinforcing Nature of Some Religious Belief Systems

Within the religions of the Bible or the Koran, people are regularly taught to believe that their successes come because of divine blessing. The Old Testament presents the whole story of the Israelites as a series of successes and failures, completely explained by worshiping and believing in the correct God, or failing to do so. Though this is almost certainly a misrepresentation of the actual history,[45] it has been accepted as received "truth" within the Abrahamic traditions. It is common for us to see this belief applied regularly in American popular culture—as our athletes, coaches, and even politicians demur to "God's blessing" in explaining success. Failure is less well explained but is presumably due to either a personal shortcoming or not providing the appropriate worship to the appropriate God.

One problem with this is that if you have any successes, you assign them to divine favor. You then come to believe that, being favored, you now owe something for that favor. You also believe that you must continue to seek that favor to maintain your success. If you maintain the approved level of humility, the more successes you have, the more you come to believe that you have been divinely favored, and the more you owe that divine power some form of allegiance—or even gifts. Since almost everyone, who tries any difficult or competitive venture, has some times of success, those who start out believing that divine favor is the route to success will receive reinforcement for their belief whether or not it is true. This will usually serve to maintain their belief system.

Some of my associates (a minority) have so enthroned religion in their worldview that they believe everything that happens must be God in action. They do not believe that they can get to the supermarket and back without divine intervention to keep them safe. Their world is dominated by the unseen supernatural whose actions they assume. This sort of belief is also self-reinforcing because lots of good or even uneventful days happen to us and may be interpreted as God helping us. This can also be thought of as "confirmation bias." We look for things confirming what we already believe and ignore things that are contrary to our beliefs.

There is a sense in which both of these approaches to the world are corrupt. They attribute failure or bad outcomes to mistakes of the human agent in selecting and worshipping the divine power. They do not make the human agent directly responsible for outcomes. Success is not represented as a function of study, foresight, the development of skills, the use of resources—overall the preparation, decisions, and actions of the agent. The important human property is thought to be worship of the divine. It is true that there is an uncontrollable randomness in the universe (call it divine or not), but it is also true that our actions have effects and are the only way we have any chance of controlling our own fate.

Summary Comments

Developed religions offer the believer the illusion of a complete solution to the mysterious labyrinth in which humans live. They offer revealed knowledge without the struggle and uncertainty of the disciplines of science and philosophy—claiming to get beyond finite human understanding. They explain how we got here, what we should do, and what possibilities the future may hold. They usually promise some form of immortality or union with the divine. These benefits are available in many cases simply upon profession of faith. Most traditions do, however, reserve special status for those who spend years in study, worship, and contemplation.

The weakness and the glory of religion is that it addresses things outside this world, things that are not empirically testable but are of deep intrinsic interest to us. One can require of religions that they be self-consistent in the sense of Wittgenstein's "word games," and one can deny them statements about this world that are demonstrably false. Clearly they are compatible with many human minds—maybe most human minds that are appropriately acculturated. Thus, for the majority of people, religion functions as a powerful core component of their mental model of reality, an important part of their framework for understanding the world, around which they organize their lives and hopes.

Religion may be thought of as faith-based beliefs created and supported by acculturation, respect for ancient texts, respect for authorities, recurring rituals, social psychology, social networking, promises of divine favor on earth, promises of immortality in some utopia, and threats of a dystopia often called hell. It seems to be a system that evolved as a response to various human needs, possibly on a somewhat ad hoc basis, but it does not appear to be the result of a plan created after any rational analysis of the world. It is, however, sometimes disturbingly more powerful than a rational analysis for the majority of people. Illusion may in fact defeat reality in many situations for those enmeshed in faith-based belief systems. Perhaps this indicates that for the human, emotional needs can frequently be more powerful than rational analysis.

4. Religion and Change

Religions do not disappear when they are discredited; it is requisite that they should be replaced.

—George Santayana, *The Life of Reason*

There is nothing permanent except change.

—Heraclitus quoted by Diogenes Laertius

When I first started to look at religions critically, I thought they should think themselves perfect at their beginnings because of their divine claims. Despite this I saw systems that evolved over decades to millennia. When I asked a more experienced observer of religion to explain such changes, the answer didn't satisfy me. It was something like "God is always revealing more truth as humans become able to accept or use it." In this section I will try to provide a more expanded commentary on how I now think about the question.

Resistance to Change

Change in religion may be at least partly understood in the light of two observations. One is that religions claim to be supernatural creations—the result of a God or supernatural force acting on the world directly or indirectly. The other is that religions are in fact human creations; constructed and maintained by fallible, flawed, human agents. The clash of divine claim and human action will allow the possibility of change but always with some resistance, and sometimes that resistance may be a major fundamentalist backlash. The divine claim is like an anchor that resists movement or change. How could the religion change in significant ways if God made it perfect at the start? If he made it, he could do nothing less. The fundamentalist strands of many religions can be seen as simply attempts to honor the tradition by returning to the beliefs of the founders who got it pure and strait from the divine. Thus we can expect to find a fundamentalist branch or wing in most durable religious traditions, especially in times of change and uncertainty.

These fundamentalist groups may become a formidable challenge to any religious authority that seeks to modify the religious tradition—even for good and altruistic reasons.

The Human Component

The possibility of change in religion flows primarily from the fact that religion is a human activity. Organized religions, like most governments and other large human associations, are virtual realities. You never see the God, the religion, or the government. You only see people who stand up and say they speak for the God, the religion, or the government. Clearly they are as human as the rest of us, and to give them special powers is inconsistent with human experience—though it may be consistent with their claims to be knowledgeable or to be in better contact with the divine than the rest of humanity. They each operate under their own set of incentives, this worldly or otherworldly, and some will have reason to push the religious tradition to be more rational, or more militant, or more socially responsible, etc. The religion will almost certainly change over time in response to the needs of its leaders, its members, and the culture in which it is embedded. An analogy to this are the "public choice" studies in economics. These have shown that public officials do not strive in response to some idealized concept of the public good. Instead, they respond to the incentive system under which they work by trying to maximize their personal rewards—usually material but maybe for some emotional.

The Problems of Language

The second strand supporting change in religion is the fact that its sacred documents are written in complex, plastic human language. The linguists tell us that languages are always changing.[46] Both semantics, the meaning of words, and grammars, the rules of sentence construction, change with the passage of time. Change is slower in written languages than in spoken-only languages, but even here, an attempt to read Shakespeare will quickly show that four hundred years have changed the English language in meaningful ways. As expected, the difficulties of interpretation increase with the time between the interpreter and the writer. However, even a document composed in current language has substantial plasticity with different interpretations by different readers. The verbosity and complexity of legal documents serve to emphasize this difficulty.

The upshot is that there can never be a "final" commentary on the Bible or most other complex documents written in human language. Current cultural artifacts such as *The Simpsons* or *Winnie the Pooh* have no final interpretation—just many meanings and uses illustrating the lack of certainty in such constructs. The postmodern strand of philosophy has emphasized this real problem. The judicial modification of the meaning of the United States constitution over the last two centuries serves as a practical though possibly extreme guide to the plasticity of interpretation. In reality, most of us can live our lives happily communicating with spoken and written language, but we will certainly find times when our "clear explanation" is turned into something completely different than we expected—by a well-meaning listener. Every religious tradition must therefore have a continual reinterpretation in its application to the real world and must establish some "authorized" way of controlling the interpretations so that they don't proliferate too wildly.

One example of how this works is the substantial range of Protestant Christian churches claiming to be founded on the Bible and clearly finding different things there. Some of the differences in just interpreting the record of Jesus' sayings can be appreciated from reading Bart Ehrman's *Misquoting Jesus*.[47] Possibly to avoid a proliferation of interpretations, the Catholic Church kept the Bible in Latin and out of the hands of the common people until the Protestant Reformation. Islam early on created one approved version of Muhammad's sayings and attempted to destroy competing versions.[48] Despite this, Islam has still experienced schism and change.

The Many Voices

The holy books or scriptures of each religious group tend to have accumulated over some period of time, and they have usually been shaped by multiple minds driven by a variety of intentions. In the case of the Old Testament, a holy book for both Christians and Jews, we have a set of documents that appear to have been written by Jews for Jews. They were written over at least hundreds of years, recording events from more than a thousand years. The writers are unknown generally but seem to have had rather different backgrounds and goals. Some small parts bear similarities to Egyptian wisdom literature and to

Canaanite hymns. Beyond broad outlines, such as existence, the details of much of the history is unverifiable, misleading, or even wrong as judged by current archeological fieldwork.[49] Within these ancient documents can be found religious ideas that range from broad concern for the weak and poor to death sentences for breaking minor ritual laws.

The New Testament, though written over a shorter time, is still a collection of works from a series of partly unknown authors, probably written over a period of fifty years or more. The included works are actually selected from a much larger group of manuscripts written at about the same time. Over several hundred years these were winnowed down to the current cannon by the practitioners of the strands of Christianity that came together to form fourth-century orthodoxy. Even within these documents we have differences of emphasis and presentation, such as the different pictures of Jesus in the various gospels.[50] He is a righteous Jew in Matthew, very interested in the Gentiles in Luke, a mystic in John, and often angry in Mark. This variety of voices in the manuscripts allows a religion to change by changing the focus of its attention within or between its documents.

The Qur'an has similar, though perhaps less obvious, difficulties in posing as a unified whole. Mohammed had his revelations over a period of about twenty-two years from 610–632 CE. He wrote nothing and commissioned no systematic written record of his revelations from the angel who reportedly brought him God's messages. During the latter part of his life, he allegedly used secretaries to record some or most of his divine missives. After his death, there were attempts to collect, from the memories of those who knew him or from those who had private written records, detailed accounts of his messages. The caliph Othman appointed a committee of four to collect and review available versions. This committee created a single authorized version—the Qur'an. There was an imperial order that all other codices were to be destroyed, and the claim is that this authorized version comes to us today unchanged from its form about twenty years after Mohammad's death.[51] The reality is that other versions persisted for at least several hundred years, and the Muslim world arrived at a canonical version of the Qur'an in the early tenth century CE.[52] The other major textual source of the Muslim tradition is the Hadith, and this also did not achieve its present form for at least two to three hundred years after Mohammed's death.[53]

Even within the Qur'an there is evidence that Mohamed's testimony changed over time as his political and social situation evolved first in Mecca where he was politically weak and then in Medina where he obtained political power. Wright in *The Evolution of God*[54] provides an extended commentary on the varying emphasis on violence versus peace and diversity in different parts of the Qur'an; its selective quotation by both Muslims and non-Muslims; and certain often ignored historical anomalies that may bear on what we now have in the official document.

Similar stories can probably be told for Buddhism and Hinduism, though I am less familiar with their documentary history. Ultimately we hear, within the documents of an established and ancient tradition, the voices of many people with many visions of God or the supernatural and of the world. Change in selective emphasis is one way that these many visions can be utilized to evolve or change a particular religion.

The Essential Plasticity of the Central Myth

Loyal Rue in his theory of religion[55] has commented on the central narrative myth that he considers to be the heart of any religious tradition. He believes it must have enough ambiguity or plasticity to be reinterpreted in the face of new religious or intellectual challenges. As examples he gives St. Augustine's neo-platonic reinterpretation of Christianity in the fourth century and St. Thomas Aquinas's thirteenth-century creation of an Aristotelian understanding of the Christian story. In essence, each generation needs to re-examine its mythic tradition to find what it has to say about human life as they are experiencing it. This is probably more important in the modern, high-tech, instant-media world, where life is really different for every generation.

The substantial dependence of interpretation on the interpreter is readily seen if one looks at the religions of the world. All or almost all religions of significant antiquity and a large following have evolved, creating many strands. Christianity may have been the most prolific at producing offspring—especially in the last five hundred years with the great number of Protestant sects. Many of these groups have claimed to found their divergent beliefs on the Bible and the Bible alone, clearly indicating the complexity of voices and views contained there and the uncertainty of interpretation of this ancient, widely translated, and greatly revered document.

Limitations on Religious Self-Analysis

Much of the power of religious traditions depends on maintaining the illusion that religions were created and are directed through divine interventions in our world. Therefore they cannot be seen as created by humans to meet human needs and as often reflecting the wisdom and wiles of the founding fathers or mothers and of the continuing human leadership. To look at the human motivations and forces involved might vitiate the supernatural claims. This would weaken the emotional power of the religious tradition for those who truly trust it. Leaders who would risk supporting a psychological, sociological, or anthropologic analysis of their religious tradition or comparison with other traditions are likely to bring their leadership into question and stir up distrust among the laity. Some of the more sophisticated members have probably already figured this out and only maintain their involvement for its social utility—but they are not the heart of the tradition. My life experiences suggest that the vast majority of members buy into this model of their tradition—"God did it"—even if it means painting white over black.

Summary

The illusion is that a religion being founded by a divine power would be perfect at its initiation and change could only be degradation or deterioration. The reality is that we find frail humans working with plastic language can readily, reasonably, and maybe unavoidably develop or change a religion over time. The anchor that limits such changes is the ancient documents and traditions that are claimed to underlie or found the religion and which are also claimed to have supernatural connections. The constant tension between the supernatural past and the changing present gives a perpetual opportunity for a fundamentalist reaction to the current changes, as people try to get back to the "faith of our fathers"—fathers to whom God talked or directly revealed his will.

These fundamentalist movements seem to have a remarkable tendency to be intolerant, to inspire hatred, and to develop political goals that may lead to violence. Ready examples include Messianic Zionism, Al-Qaeda, Wahabi Islam, and in the United States the Christian Right. The latter would like to outlaw abortion and substitute religious mythology for science in the classroom to force wider conformity to their beliefs. These fundamentalist groups do not seem to bear good will toward the rest of humanity. Often they elect themselves a chosen elite with a "divinely" appointed mission to force their vision on a reluctant and sinful world.

Religions seem unable to admit their human origins, the plasticity of the interpretation of their texts and their central myths, and the actual evolution of their beliefs over time. Proponents of religions therefore seem unusually incapable of engaging in a critical analysis of religions' roles and places in our world.

5. Religion's Corruption and Abuse

Men never do evil so completely and cheerfully as when they do it from religious conviction.

—Pascal (1623–1662)

Among all the causes which degrade and demoralize men, power is the most constant and the most active.

—Lord Acton (1834–1902)

Anyone who has the power to make you believe absurdities has the power to make you commit injustices

—Voltaire (1694–1778)

In the seeming eternal struggle of good and evil that occupies so much of great literature and art, religion always tries to position itself on the side of good—sometimes by defining good. Certainly the founders of the great religious traditions viewed themselves as making the world better. Unfortunately, we all know of the abuse of religious authority for personal gain, sexual desire, and political power. Martin Luther wrote a scathing attack on the Jews after they refused to convert to his version of Christianity. His pamphlet or book (65,000 words)[56] was violently anti-Semitic. The Nazis considered it justification for the attitudes that lead to the Holocaust and it was introduced as supporting evidence for the defense in the post–World War II Nuremburg trials of Nazi leaders for crimes against humanity.

By corruption of a religion, I do not mean it's changing from some original version to some following version, which would then be interpreted by the founding generation as a corruption of their tradition. Instead, I use the term *corruption of a religion* to mean its use to support private or public actions, rules, laws, or institutions that arbitrarily decrease the quality of human life here on this earth—for particular individuals or groups. Examples might include the isolation and degradation of subpopulations such as the "untouchables" in India and the Jews in Medieval Europe and the killing of people solely because of their religious beliefs—for instance the Inquisition, the wars of religion after the Protestant Reformation, and even the killing of non-Jews by Jewish Hasmonean rulers during first and second centuries BCE.

Essentially, all human institutions, including political, religious, fraternal, business, etc., are at risk of corruption as a function of the power they hold and the money they control. The greater this power or money, the more attractive they are to potential corrupters. The corrupters would use the organization for some private advantage while maintaining the appearance of continuing its public mission. The risks of religions in this regard have to do with their claims of dealing with ultimate power and having to do that through the agency of the largely private experiences of all too fallible humans. Thus those who would take over a religious movement always present their goals as those of the deity and claim long-term benefits for all true believers, at least in the next life, if not here. Disagreements about such claims can never be adjudicated objectively since these people are making claims about the supernatural—and about their contact with it. The air would be much clearer if the metaphysical claims were thrown out—but that isn't an option for religion. Ultimately, one appeals to religious "authorities." This is illustrated in the Islamic tradition by appeals to a terrorist tradition and supporting texts that go back for hundreds of years.[57]

Charles Kimball has written a book about the bad or evil uses of religion.[58] On the back cover of his book, he gives five warning signs for corruption in religion. In the order in which he presented them these are claims of absolute truth, demands for blind obedience, claims of access to God's chosen time, ends justify means, and Holy War is demanded by God. I will attempt to amplify these concerns.

Absolute truth claims must be present to give people confidence in their tradition. Religions and some ideologies are, of course, the only human belief systems that make claims of such perfect truth. The second item, blind obedience, follows readily in the train of absolute truth. Questioning religious leadership is usually viewed as the road to heresy and perdition. If this view is adequately driven into the followers, they will not question the evil tasks that they are assigned to carry forward. Kimball's third item, establishing the "ideal" time, applies to particular events such as the coming of a messiah, gives urgency to action, and justifies the leader's call for specific acts by the followers. One well-documented early example of this was the Jewish Zealots' uprising against Rome in Palestine in 66 CE. It was portrayed as getting ready for the messiah, the hoped-for savior of the Jewish world who would come when they had shown themselves ready.

The fourth sign is the use of the widespread misrepresentation that the "end justifies the means"—a phrase uttered repeatedly by those employing violence and deceit. Its most egregious abusers in the twentieth century were probably the Marxist and the Fascists who have left a frightening history that should be a lesson for all future ages. In fact, all ideologies that depend on blind faith and authority have the same risks of corruption as do religions. Marxism did not meet some people's criteria for being a religion, but it occupied the same ideological place in the lives of the majority of its devoted followers— its God was the "forces of history," its prophet Karl Marx, and its cannon his writings. The anarchist Emma Goldman's response to this claim was to assert that the ends and the means are inseparably part of one whole.[59] If one is evil, it corrupts the other, and the whole becomes corrupt. In this regard it should be noted that those who created the French Revolution and those who brought the Bolsheviks and the Nazis to power were in a large part destroyed by the systems they helped create—in the Reign of Terror, in Stalin's purges, and in Hitler's "Night of the Long Knives."[60]

The final sign, declaring Holy War, is almost a contradiction as war is never the route to someplace good or holy. What is clear is that all wars lead to death, destruction, cruelty, and long-cherished hatreds—the downsides of such holiness. In a very real way war demeans the humanity of all who participate, both winners and losers. A defensive war may satisfy St. Augustine's criteria for being a "just war" but is perhaps acceptable only as an alternative to something worse, such as violent destruction or enslavement.

Violence in the Traditions

The killing of masses of human beings,
  we bewail with sorrow and grief
Victory in battle,
  we commemorate with a mourning ritual.
                                    —Tao Te Ching[61]

The flames of thy mouths devour all the worlds. Thy glory fills the whole universe. But how terrible thy splendors burn.
                                    —Arjuna to Krishna in The Bhagavad Ghita

The God portrayed in the Biblical Old Testament, the Qur'an and even in parts of the New Testament is a violent actor. The Biblical stories have this violence very early in them—Cain kills Abel after God accepts Abel's offering and rejects that of Cain. To the reader, it seems almost arbitrary that God accepts one and not the other. This is followed by a long list of violent stories, including Noah's flood, Abraham, Isaac and his sons, and finally the Israelites, the "Chosen People," who often—per God's command—kill every living human being when they capture a city. The God of the Qur'an is no less violent since many of these Biblical stories are repeated in Qur'anic versions and Mohammed assumes the same God is the center of both traditions.

This Abrahamic God does not restrain himself from genocide and usually prescribes a violent end for those who have not obeyed him compulsively. In the Hindu tradition as portrayed in the Bagavad Gita,[62] there are also wonderful images of a violent God, so violent they were reputedly quoted by Robert Oppenheimer at the first nuclear explosion in New Mexico. Though God is also often portrayed as loving and merciful in these sacred texts, such passages are often less memorable than the violent parts. Jesus, who is usually thought of as teaching love, had his violent moments, such as throwing the merchants out of their usual place in the temple and saying in Matthew 10:34, "I did not come to bring peace, but a sword." Certainly the New Testament book of Revelation is filled with violence and bloodshed.

Jack Nelson-Pallmeyer has made a thoughtful attempt[63] to expose the traditions of violence that are embedded in most of our religions. A brief quote from his introduction will illustrate his contention. "My fundamental claim is that *religiously justified violence is first and foremost a problem of "sacred" texts and not a problem of misinterpretation* of the texts.... The problem is actual violence at the heart of these texts that can be reasonably cited by people to justify their own recourse to violence."

The Support of Hierarchy

A [passionately proletarian] religious prophet may be...founder of an organization of fools, conducted by knaves, for the benefit of wolves. That fate befell Buddha and Jesus, it befell Ignatius Loyola and Francis of Assisi, John Fox, and John Calvin, and John Wesley.

—Upton Sinclair, *The Profits of Religion*[64]

The involvement of the elite in society with "the gods" probably precedes recorded history. The Egyptian pharaohs claimed to be gods themselves, who would be elevated to the pantheon after death. Similarly, the Roman emperors eventually claimed to be gods, as part of the state religion that they believed to be necessary to preserve order and civic virtue. The idea that some human born of a human mother and dying in battle or of disease should somehow be a god is so preposterous that only the power of religious belief and ritual would seem able to sustain it, and then only for the less thoughtful and well educated. As Santayana said, "The fact of being born is a bad augury for immortality."[65]

The lesser idea that the gods have special communion with and support for the ruling elite is also common in many cultures. In medieval Europe this was expressed as the "Great Chain of Being," which put everyone in his place or as the "Divine Right of Kings," which asserted the king's rule is ordained by God. In the Christian tradition, St. Paul is cited supporting this in Romans 13 where he says, "Everyone must submit himself to the governing authorities, for there is no authority except that which God has established." In antiquity, the Chinese spoke of the "Mandate of Heaven" that justified the ruler's place.

Though it is possible for religion to be subversive of civil power, most of the time throughout human history it has sought the favor of those in power. The early Christians, who were persecuted by the Romans, were probably not subversive to the state, but they were subversive to the belief system that the leaders felt must be maintained to guarantee the order of the state. The Peasant's Rebellion in the time of Luther and liberation theology in the late twentieth century were attempts with very limited success to use religion to relieve oppression.

The support of the powerful by the religious establishment seems to have been more clear and strong than any calls by that same religious establishment for restraint and justice in the exercise of power—at least most of the time. Hitler found ready support from the Catholic Church and signed a treaty with it, as did Mussolini. Many Protestant denominations also officially supported these Fascist governments. The lower classes seem to be expected to make do with hope for a better next life while the ruling classes are given solid political support by church organizations. The churches do this, of course, to maintain their own wealth, power, and official access to and control over their believers. The leaders clearly have interests, and these are served, but it is less clear if either God or the common man is served by such official ties.

The Suppression of Inquiry and Reason

From Socrates to Galileo to stem cell research, certain religious groups have sought to force their views on the world and to deny people the opportunity to consider alternatives for themselves. This is presented as being demanded by the divine or as being necessary to propitiate it. It is never presented as the suppression of inquiry, but instead as supporting some form of "truth" against those who would use their weak and impaired human reason to question revealed wisdom from God. To carry this off usually requires absolute confidence that one knows the mind of God—a malady sometimes experienced by those of strong faith. Those who make such claims often demonstrate a very limited understanding of both science and of alternative interpretations of the world. Their hubris seems remarkably unjustified. In his book *Conjectures and Refutations* Carl Popper wrote that "truth is hard, and often painful, to come by" and "once found it may be easily lost again."[66]

When religions have political power, they often feel obliged to force others to conform to their views as though this were something they did for God, at his behest. Authoritarian belief systems have difficulty with reasoned compromise to solve differences. They can only appeal to their authority and can only exercise it by violence—if they have that option. With the passage of time it is often seen that the religious tradition can be adjusted to new scientific or social concepts without damage to its most core ideas. Thus we have Galileo being forgiven by the Catholic Church but only after a few centuries. Currently Darwinian evolution is a major center of controversy in part of the Christian world. The Catholic Church has already accepted this approach to natural history, and I suspect that if you came back in a century or two most of Christianity will be in the fold on that issue.

One of the reasons that religions get used in this way is that they are ultimately human institutions and their leaders may be mostly concerned with their own political power or prestige. Confusing their personal needs with the needs of the religion seems to come easily for some who claim to represent a divine power.

Religion and Terrorism

The worst atrocities have their source in the zealous pursuit of a sublime ideal that is believed to be so majestic, so magnificent, and so grand, that it is worthy of every sacrifice, every hardship, and every abomination.

—Shadia B. Drury in the preface to *Terror and Civilization*[67]

Christianity, from its very beginnings, has held several beliefs that have immense implications for how the church will deal with the world if it has political power. These apply in varying degrees to different versions of Christianity and also substantially to Islam. Such beliefs include:

Original sin—the demonization of nature, guilty at birth and deserving any punishment.
Unbelief is sin—right belief is more important than right action.
Hell and damnation—an angry God's justice requires terrifying punishment.
There is only one truth—you are either on our God's side or justifiably damned.

The Abrahamic traditions have usually not accepted a pluralism of the good or multiple ways to God or salvation. Shadia Drury in the reference above finds such concepts in the words of Jesus and traces them through Augustine, Luther, and Calvin of the Reformation, the Puritans of England and New England, and today's Christian fundamentalists. When political power comes to such an organization, it can hardly restrain itself from trying to force belief or eradicate unbelief. The control of belief is more difficult than the control of action. In fact, it often seems to require some form of terrorism. The Christian attempt to control belief started early after the Church got political power, even with the Council of Nicaea in 325 CE, and climaxed in the violence of the Inquisition and the religious wars of the Reformation. The loss of political power and the fragmentation of Christianity have in the last two centuries largely protected Western civilization from violent attempts to control Christian belief, though ideological orthodoxies still drove millions to their graves. Those seeking a revival of religion in politics need to remember this along with their other remembering. The Islamic world has largely mirrored the Christian world at seeking right belief and demonizing those who don't have it. The recurring battles of the Sunnis and Shi'ah are examples that have weakened Islam for over a thousand years.

Assuming there is only one "truth," religion can readily be used to dichotomize the world into good and evil, ignoring all the fine nuances of human belief and action. This makes it useful for demonizing a competing group who can be portrayed as sinful enemies of "God" and therefore not worthy to be treated as fully human. By this means theft, cruelty, dishonesty, and murder are portrayed as doing "God's" holy work. Hatred is created where there is no other reason for it by invoking a God who demands hatred toward the "other," who has rejected this God's truth—that is those who hold wrong belief. Political power may then accrue to the people who manage and guide this manipulation. Of course, if there are other cultural or economic issues, religious groups may pretend such issues are unimportant relative to the religious issues, which are used as emotional fuel for the contest. The last thirty years have seen religious terrorism involving at least Islamic, Jewish, Christian, and Sikh sub-strands.[68]

Another important claim of religion that makes it useful in the world of terrorism is its promise of personal immortality for the believer—particularly if death comes while acting to support a "righteous" cause. This is uniquely applicable to the support of terrorism and war. Suicide missions become more reasonable for any cause, if you are told that somewhere after death you will be rewarded very well for your dedication to the God, the Committee, the Force or whoever or whatever runs the ultimate good place. This belief can be a powerful ally for good causes that are also risky, but it can readily be turned toward the "dark side" of death and destruction. For instance, note the widely publicized promises of heaven and seventy-two virgins for male Al-Qaeda terrorists suffering death in action. What female terrorists should expect is less clear—at least heaven?

The Exploitation of Believers for Private Gain

One can hardly pass a discussion of the corrupt use of religion without mentioning the many religious organizations, or as they are often called "ministries," which have been established with no clear justification—except possibly to provide a luxurious lifestyle for the founders or leaders. Most often this is done under the large tent of "Christianity," but similar games have been played by Indian gurus. The leaders offer healing, blessings of wealth from God, happiness in this life, and happiness in the life to come, all as inducements for the followers to contribute. In the United States, such contributions are nontaxable income to the religious organization and can be used without any accountability for the support of the leaders. James Randi's book *The Faith Healers*[69] documents the deceptions, dishonesty, and greed that permeate much of this segment of public religion.

Several properties of religion seem to make it useful for those who would exploit their fellow humans. Properties this observer thinks important include religion's usual support of hierarchy (reviewed earlier this chapter), its common use to define a group of trusted economic cooperators, (see the section on this in the chapter 2: Religion's Usefulness), and its demand of unskeptical faith toward the tradition by the member. The attitude that God controls history and puts in place the leaders he approves, prepares membership to be trusting—not to ask questions. The belief that someone else shares your inspired religious ideas makes you think these people must be as reliable and honest as you are yourself. Thus they can be expected to behave honorably with your money, property, etc.

In practice most religions are not schemes for examining the world—or for finding truth. They generally function as "belief" systems, claiming they have the answers to the great human questions such as the meaning of life and the meaning of death. The religious devotee is encouraged to accept by "faith" the religion's positions; to strengthen this faith by reading the religious literature, verbally and publicly asserting his belief, and participating in religious rituals. Some would say he is to "walk by faith not by sight." Skepticism is considered close to heresy. Thus the average believer is poorly prepared to bring a questioning mind to institutions with clerical leadership or even clerical approval.

These attitudes toward other members, but especially toward clerical leadership, leave the membership relatively open to exploitation. This exploitation may be of the straightforward "con-man" type—privately or the use of public ministries as mentioned in the first paragraph of this section. The exploitation may also be more complex and sophisticated such as the manipulation of institutional boards for private gain.[70]

Summary

Religions are powerful systems for manipulation of our human world. They maintain the illusion that everything they sanction is approved by God and is for the ultimate good of humanity. Violence is part of the religious tradition—often built into the original documents. The leaders of religious organizations may have substantial control of this power, wealth, and even violence. These people are humans living with particular incentive systems. Being human, some of them will lead the organizations in corrupt ways for personal reasons that they will camouflage behind the mask of doing God's will. Others may truly serve "an angry God" who makes rigid demands that they must obey on pain of eternal damnation. This also may lead to a charge of corruption in the eyes of those of us who have a more humane hope for religion.

The reality of some religious groups is that in day-to-day function they have become more devoted to power than to anything good and admirable in their tradition. The fundamentalist strands of most religions, with their lack of self-criticism, tend to fall into this category. In fact Salman Rushdie, a famous target of fundamentalism, has noted that fundamentalism isn't about religion, it's about power.[71]

6. Religion and Ethics

In all of my years, one thing does not change…
The perpetual struggle of Good and Evil.

—From *The Rock* by T. S. Eliot

The Common Belief

To the believer in religion—both casual and devoted—it seems that morality flows from the religion. Many think that moral behavior is defined by God's command. This provides an anchor especially for nonreflective adherents who wish to understand their moral obligations in the world. The majority of believers would judge that the moral standards of their religion are exemplary and should be extended to all humans if possible. When I take my own personal survey, I find that most people who believe in a religion assert that without that belief they would have no reason to behave morally. They often claim that they would have no restraint from murder, theft, adultery, etc. Most formal religions support this position by claiming that only believers can be trusted. The claim that God will reward good and punish bad behavior in some other time and place are apparently the chief justifications for this attitude. The limited success of the criminal justice system certainly weakens the claim that future rewards will create moral behavior.

John Stuart Mill reported[72] that in his day, the British court system would only accept testimony from a person who affirmed a belief in God. He then comments that in his own experience, his atheist acquaintances had been at least as honest and reliable as his believing friends. There are good reasons to think that most of us share an intuitive morality that is then built on by acculturation, education, and religion. Perhaps the most powerful component of our morality is our ability to identify with others as fragile humans like ourselves. This chapter will try to explore some of the things underlying morality and how religion relates to this essential component of civilized life.

It is probably worth noting that the ancient polytheisms usually did not assign an ethical role to religion. Certainly this was true of the

Greek and Roman versions of polytheism.[73] Some think that one of the important developments of the Axial age was ethical religion.[74] Zoraster seems to have given us one of the first visions of a conditional ultimate fate dependent on the morality of the life of the individual human. His traditional dates were during the Axial age (800-200 BCE) though more recent scholarship suggests he lived at least 1000 years BCE. His religion did become the dominant belief system of the Persian Empire for over 1000 years. Some of his innovations such as an ethically determined existence beyond this life and an apocalyptic end of the age may have reached Jewish minds during the "Babylonian captivity" and thereby also affected both Christian and Islamic world views.

The Observed Difficulties

Religion has been widely used to promote, or at least to support, war. Augustine tried to deal with this by giving rules for a "just war," but these rules have frequently been ignored or the situation has been interpreted to fit his rules with some bending to the current "special problems." The post-Reformation Thirty Years War and the Hundred Years War were justified by religious claims, though there were certainly other interests involved. Crimes such as murder are, unfortunately but not infrequently, committed by people claiming religious justification.[75] Terrorism, with its atrocities against the uninvolved bystander is exonerated with claims that God's will is being done. In acts of war or terror the violent believer is often promised absolution for any crimes and a wonderful heavenly reward. Salvation seems to come from creating destruction in the service of an angry God.

Some authors such as Jared Diamond and Upton Sinclair have skeptically noted that religion's chief day-to-day use is to enable the powerful to exploit the weak. Karl Marx had similar feelings about religion when he wrote that "the social principles of Christianity" were used "to defend the oppression of the proletariat, although they make a pitiful face over it...it (religion) is the opiate of the people...the criticism of religion is therefore in embryo the criticism of the vale of woe, the halo of which is religion."[76] See our previous discussion in chapter 5 on the corruptibility of religion.

Incarceration in the U.S. federal prisons doesn't seem to be correlated with atheism as the U.S. population supposedly is 8 to 16 percent atheist, while the prison population is only 0.2 percent.[77] Murder and divorce are not less common among societies with high levels of religiosity. Overall we seem to find that professedly religious people are not more moral than those who do not profess a religious belief.[78, 79] Thus religion's stringent ethical demands seem unable in actual practice to create a higher moral standard for the average believer than the standard that the nonbeliever sets for himself on other grounds.

Religion is readily bent to support violence and to justify oppressive hierarchy. Those who profess to follow a religious belief system seem to have about the same morality as those not so professing. Such observations suggest that there may be some alternate source of morality that is important for both theist and non-theist. One suspects that in actual practice religion really isn't the source of moral judgments for most people, most of the time. *In fact, religion's particular ethical innovation may be to excuse the believer from normal human morality so that he can in good conscience do evil for the sake of his religion or his religious leaders.* Otherwise religions generally advocate a high standard of interpersonal ethics, similar to the standards of the majority of nonbelievers.

Exclusivity Problems

Any religion that proselytizes must go into the world claiming that its beliefs, ideas, and way of life are better than those of its competitors. The tendency over time is then for adherents of a particular religion to disrespect those who persist in following an alternate belief system. This seems especially true in the Abrahamic traditions—of which I have some personal experience. Eventually, the unbeliever is seen as rejecting God's truth and therefore less honest, less good, and less human than the believer. When this position is taken it is a short step to say that the ethical behavior demanded of believers toward other believers no longer applies to these evil people. This is readily illustrated in the Biblical Old Testament with Israel's dealing with the inhabitants of Canaan. It was the approach sometimes taken as the Europeans destroyed the native peoples of North America—the settlers thinking of themselves as the Children of Israel destroying the Canaanites. It is also illustrated with the internecine battles in the Muslim world, especially the violence of the Sunnis versus the Shiites. In our shrinking world, this source or justification for violence appears to be an increasing problem. The fundamentalist wings of the Muslim, Jewish, and Christian traditions are especially prone to this interpretation of the world. In the last few decades Islamic terrorism, antiabortion terrorism, Northern Irish Catholic–Protestant killing, fundamentalist Jewish killing of both Palestinians and their own prime minister (Yitzhak Rabin) and the Balkan wars of the 1990s have illustrated religion's potentially devastating effects on civil life.

Thus in practice, religions, with their frequent claims that there is only one "true" set of beliefs, become frightening tools for those who would control human society. They can and often are used to support a dichotomized world where the believers are good and everyone else is consigned to some sort of hell they are thought to deserve. In such cases, any atrocity toward the nonbeliever may be justified (see section on religion and terrorism in the prior chapter). In trying to understand this we might note that the sociobiologist E. O. Wilson has suggested that human brains are programmed to partition other people into friends or non-friends, to fear the non-friends and regard them as less than fully human, and to solve conflict by aggression.[80] Religion may thus build on already existing mental tendencies. At its best, religion goes beyond this tribalism to be a universalizing and civilizing influence, but its leaders are often successfully tempted to use it for something more narrow and limited. Such tendencies to serve a limited tribe may have been successful in a hunter-gatherer world, but in the present "global village" they may lead to a great deal of human pain and suffering. Wilson hopes that by building a "confusion of cross-binding loyalties" we might defuse our natural turn toward partitioning the world.

The Euthyphro (Authority) Problem

In his dialogue *The Euthyphro* Plato explores the foundations of morality.[81] This may also be called the "authority problem." Plato has Socrates ask Euthyphro (paraphrased): are actions good because God commands them, or does God command them because they are good? Plato, Aquinas, and Kant believed the latter. Assuming the former makes God the source of right and wrong—a sort of "Divine command morality." If you think you know where God's words can be found, then studying them becomes the road to morality. In this case there is no reason to attempt to understand morality as a human problem—

since some divine entity has already addressed it, and with appropriate effort we can apply his recommendations. Often religions seem to operationally subscribe to this "divine command" theory.

Most religions do have a set of very good moral injunctions that they can put on display. The difficulties come with interpretation—particularly with the possibility of exceptions—especially for divine commands reported by the leaders to the members. Many people believe that they or their religious leaders communicate directly with God. The leaders assure them of this. If in this situation a God given command is received and can be seen to be in conflict with some prior moral injunction recognized in the religious tradition, that conflict will usually be ignored. The fact that the new command came from the God who is the source of all morality will justify the presumption that this God gave the new command after taking into account the moral concerns. Since he is the source of morality, the believer is not to question such commands; questioning may be heretical.

If your God's words define "truth," you are then often at the mercy of his interpreters since you do not speak directly with him. You are as the Israelites, killing every man, woman, and child in cities they conquer, and a terrorist killing thousands of people, all on your personal road to salvation. Some religious people would define away this problem by saying that God is identical with the good so there is no difference between the above options. In the practical world of human life and decision making the problem is, however, very real.

By claiming that your God is the only valid source of ethics or truth about the world you place your tradition above all other interpreters of morality or reality. You say that only your tradition can rightly understand the ethical responsibilities of humans. The sad result of this is not that God is in charge, but instead that humans have assumed God's mantle and would for all practical purposes act for him in the world—they have become "gods." They act on the basis of their personal set of motives and drives created from years of public and private experience. Like other humans, their behaviors and decisions reflect the incentive structures with which they must deal—as they perceive them. Though we may try to create the internal goal hierarchies of a God, we will forever be finite, limited, partially blind, and never too impartial humans.

If there was some God who came to speak truth to us about our moral obligations, this source of morality might make some sense. All the evidence available suggests that, if there is some God, she does not talk with humans—especially not with those in political power. My best judgment is that the humans who claim to talk with God are actually talking to some part of themselves, even if in trance or vision. It would appear that the belief that God is the source of morality opens the possibility for delusion and evil since one's morality is now in effect dependent on the humans who claim to speak for this God. The "divine command" theory of morality is the great risk in using religion as a source of morality. It allows the believers to be manipulated into doing things contrary to usual human moral emotions—emotions that are based on intuition, fairness, empathy, respect for life, and for others.

Nonreligious Sources for Understanding Morality

The oldest strand of moral guidance not seeking its sanction in the rules of a religion or the claimed dictates of a god is that known as natural law. This starts as we know it with classical Greece and is still alive. Starting with the Enlightenment period, some intellectuals attempted to understand the human drives that lead to moral behavior—without invoking a divine actor. Kant, Hume, Bentham, and John Stuart Mill are some who were influential in this area. Most recently the field of intuitive morality has developed, as students of psychology and evolution have sought to explain how altruism may have evolved. They have discovered that most humans come with a form of morality already built in, probably at birth—with reinforcement by early life experiences. The following sections will attempt a brief review of these sources for understanding morality.

Natural Law

The natural law tradition goes back at least to the classical Greek period especially to Aristotle. Some would carry it back to Antigone's protest against Creon that she was right, by a higher law than Creon's law, in burying her brother. This tradition sought from studying a variety of human cultures to find obligations or rules that were respected in all the traditions and infer these as universal obligations or laws.[82] The stoics especially developed the tradition, and the great Roman moralist Cicero was much indebted to it. It is also appealed to in the introduction to the famous sixth century compilation of Roman law called the Code of Justinian. One of the definitions there (citing Paulus): "The word *ius* (law) is used in a number of different senses:

in the first place, in that in which the name is applied to that which is under all circumstances fair and right, as in the case of natural law (*ius naturale*)."[82]

The most notable recent application of natural law was probably the Nuremberg Trials of Nazi leaders after World War II. They had acted within the existing laws of Germany and could not reasonably be tried under the laws of some other jurisdiction. Thus a natural law argument for crimes against humanity was used by the winners of the war to justify punishment of the losers. The losers seemed to richly deserve their fate. The winners, by winning, were protected from a similar court of inquiry. This only shows that regardless of how good or bad a law may be, it is usually applied within some power relationship by people who must live with a particular set of incentives. *Alternatively one may say that no law is better than the people who manage its enforcement.*

Philosophical Attempts at Moral Reasoning

Other attempts to understand morality originated in the Enlightenment period and these efforts have continued to the present. These include the recognition of sentiment or identification with others as a vehicle to help us achieve a good ethics in our behavior toward them. The Scottish Enlightenment, including David Hume, Adam Smith, and others, developed this understanding in the eighteenth century, and it still has appeal today. Some would say this was a rediscovery of the work of the Confucian philosopher Mencius who had lived two thousand years earlier. He taught that *Ren* (humanity) involved sympathy or "fellow feeling" and was the origin of all the Confucian virtues. Both Hume and Mencius believed that proper moral education was necessary to make this work in human society.[83]

Emanuel Kant, also in the eighteenth century, developed his Categorical Imperative, which suggests that we should act in such a way that we would want our behavior to be generalized to everyone or alternatively that we should never use people as objects. This seems to be an argument supporting our intuitive feelings about "fairness." Please don't behave in "such and such" a way unless you would like other people to also behave that way. In some situations it becomes very much like the golden rule with a different derivation.

Later, Jeremy Bentham and John Stuart Mill developed utilitarian theory, which says that the right decision is the one that brings the most happiness to the largest number. Applying this requires a great deal of interpretation of both happiness and pain, but it has been thought useful especially in public policy decisions. It ignores the principle of justice or fairness, which may be especially important in the decisions concerning individuals—at least most of us would think justice highly relevant in our individual fates.

Various philosophers have proposed a contractarian approach to achieving social justice. These have included Thomas Hobbes, John Locke, Jean-Jacques Rousseau, and maybe most recently John Rawls. Rawls, in his twentieth-century book *A Theory of Justice,* addressed some of the moral concerns in running or arranging a political system. His justice was the justice of a political system chosen or created by an agent blinded to how these choices might affect his own life. This construct may have limited applicability to individual private ethical decisions, but it could be helpful in addressing our societal problems such as poverty and health care and how they may relate to our politics.

These attempts to ground morality outside of or beyond sectarian religion have given us many options for thinking about our moral decisions, but no single system has come to have a pre-eminent position in the modern world. Religion is still able to claim to be the source of morality for the average believer—and the believer agrees. At its best, religion can be a wonderful force for good ethics, but sadly its tribalism or exclusivity can sometimes drive it into serious conflict with important ethical concerns.

Intuitive Morality

Two things fill my mind with ever-increasing wonder and awe: The starry heavens above me and the moral law within me.

—Immanuel Kant in *Critique of Pure Reason*

It is also worth reiterating the point, better clarified now, that religion does not support morality. Instead, the moral intuitions and emotions that humans, as a species of cooperators, already possess support religion.

—Todd Tremlin in *Minds and Gods*[84]

There are reasons to think that we come with some form of intuitive ethics or morality—shared by most humans. This seems to be independent of any religious profession and probably to be in place before any religious education. Cognitive studies and the development of evolutionary psychology have in the last few decades greatly expanded our understanding in this area. It appears most likely that this morality is the morality that was necessary for a small-scale hunter-gatherer existence. It would be as variable in its expression as are other human traits that are at least partly genetically determined. This genetic determinism is always modified by the experience of the environment—ultimately making the bulk of individuals ethically similar but also providing a small minority of serious outliers.

There are evolutionary or survival reasons for expecting altruistic behavior within a kinship line. If someone shares many genes with you then their survival is your survival in terms of genes. You would expect that evolution would have favored genes that supported this form of altruism—and perhaps still does. Family dynamics, parental devotion, and kin versus the world interaction and conflict may be better understood in the light of this observation.

Altruism between unrelated individuals is often referred to as "reciprocal altruism." It may be explained as what happens when organisms trade favors. Cooperators tend to do better—and therefore better transmit their genes—than hermits or misanthropes. Some think that reciprocal altruism is the explanation for the development of the social and moral emotions. Sympathy, trust, guilt, shame, anger, and contempt all may be involved in encouraging cooperation and suppressing cheating. Reputation in a community and memory of past behavior are further components in this system. Steven Pinker has given a lucid and engaging discussion of these topics in his chapter "The Many Roots of Our Suffering" in *The Blank Slate*.[85]

Studies of altruistic or empathetic animal behavior suggest that what we call morality is very old and very common in social species. Frans de Waal has written "the possibility that empathy resides in parts of the brain so ancient that we share them with rats should give pause to anyone comparing politicians with those poor, underestimated creatures."[86] Dr. de Waal is a noted primatologist who is especially interested in the types of morality seen in the nonhuman animal world.[87, 88] He has collected a large number of both experimental and anecdotal reports of animals helping other animals, conspecific or not, sometimes at significant inconvenience or even serious risk. One of the most interesting is a report of monkeys housed in adjacent cages with one monkey's taking food possibly triggering an electric shock for his neighbor. Two thirds of the monkeys decreased their food taking to avoid shocking their neighbor, and a few of them starved themselves for days—five and twelve days in two cases reported.

Loyal Ruc[89] has argued that the core of a religious tradition is a narrative myth that relates the cosmos with morality—what is with what ought to be. He thinks that religion came into being initially to support an ad hoc morality that became necessary as human societies expanded beyond the original hunter-gatherer groups that occupied most of human evolutionary history. The changing and more complicated social system needed new or expanded rules to make it work. Rue imagines that the religious myths may have developed or evolved to support these changes to supplement the intuitive ethics already in place.

Cognitive studies have shown that human decision making can be characterized as occurring at two levels.[90] One is a subconscious decision making that occurs rapidly (usually in seconds) and without effort and comes to consciousness with associated emotional overlay. It apparently operates by algorithms that are at least partly genetically programmed and only changed with difficulty. These rules seem to be adequate for an intuitive cosmology, physics, psychology, and morality that are applied to problems immediately and without conscious exertion. The other decision process is a slower deliberative, conscious, reasoning process. It comes without emotions and can be used to override the rapid intuitive process, but it may be uncomfortable for the individual to make such an override. It appears that when we say we know something intuitively, we are saying we know it because these unconscious mental algorithms have made this decision and sent it to our consciousness.

The following is from a 2004 lecture by Dave Frohnmayer, president of the University of Oregon:

> We have a well-developed ability to process information slowly, deliberately, and fully within conscious awareness. But recent research in social psychology suggests that responses to moral dilemmas mostly emerge from the intuitive system— quick gut feelings that happen within a second or two when a particular situation is presented. People then search for supporting arguments and justifications using their reasoning

system, which is the rational tail that got wagged by the emotional dog.[91]

Religion and the Development of Written Law

Though religions have no unique claim to founding morality, they have sponsored the development of systems of law allowing groups of people to live together under specific guidelines for settling disagreements. Perhaps the oldest of these sets of laws are in the Jewish Torah—Genesis, Exodus, Leviticus, Numbers, and Deuteronomy—also part of the Christian Old Testament. These documents contain complicated mixtures of religious and civil rules for living and worshipping. Parts have to do with religious rituals including sacrifices that are no longer used and dietary and behavioral restrictions that are variously interpreted. Parts have to do with punishment of criminal behavior when there is no reliable civil authority who will undertake this responsibility. Other parts include somewhat egalitarian redistribution of wealth and forgiveness of debts at recurring intervals.

It is unclear if there ever was a society that was run using these rules; possibly the rules were modified or markedly embellished when put into final written form hundreds of years after their supposed promulgation. Regardless of this, many Jewish and Christian commentators have felt that at least some parts of these rules should apply to humans living in our current world and the Ten Commandments have been a centerpiece of that discussion. Some would like them posted in public buildings, but most of us would agree that the last six rules, which govern human-human interaction, are worth serious consideration. The admonitions to avoid murder, theft, adultery, and false witness are enshrined in most human legal systems and probably older than Hebrew law. The admonitions to honor one's parents and to avoid covetousness seem good rules of life, though they are less easily incorporated in a formal legal system.

In contrast, the first four of these rules define obligations toward the deity and illustrate the problem with all attempts to universalize codes of conduct developed by religious groups. Such groups assume that their codes will apply to members of their own religion—which ought to be all—so mix rules for ethical living with rules that have to do with the particular supernatural beliefs that the group shares. The group, being confident that it has the only real "truth" about the universe is sometimes willing to make nonbelievers toe that mark. This may cause difficulty in a religiously pluralistic society as a combination of secular power and religious conviction is and has been a common road to violent abuse of those who dissent.

Both the Canon Law of the Catholic Church and the Sharia Law of the Muslim world have made significant contributions to the legal systems of modern societies. Whether the world would have done as well without these is anyone's guess—history only runs by once—but they have left major marks on our world. There were also times in the past when they were probably the best legal systems available, and even today many devote Muslims would prefer to live under Sharia Law. There are multiple strands of this legal tradition that draws on the Qur'an and the Hadith, supplemented in varying ways by reason, consensus, and prior jurisprudence.[92] Many applications of this system are possible in the modern world with the Taliban being at one extreme and at another pole some political administrations offering it as an alternate, elective, dispute resolution process.

Though Buddhists have advocated for compassionate resolution of disputes, and there is intent in some Buddhist countries to make law consistent with Buddhist values, there is no particular Buddhist legal system.[93] In the Hindu world we find dharma or personal law (marriage, adoption, inheritance …) applied to Hindus' living in India. Such law goes back to ancient Sanskrit texts (Vedas, Dharmasastra, …) and was written into the new Indian constitution at independence but does not seem to have been exported.[94]

Religious groups have clearly contributed to development of human legal systems. They have done it in ways that are related to their fundamental beliefs about human responsibilities to both fellow humans and to some concept of the divine. Much of this corresponds to our common concepts of fairness or justice (intuitive morality?) and where it does not because of sectarian preferences it may not always be an improvement. In our imperfect world large groups do seem to need written rules so as to know what to expect of each other and that need seems to have driven some religions to make useful contributions to the development of human law—which still evolves. These contributions were usually made at times when religious and civil authority were combined or deeply enmeshed.

Final Comments

It seems likely that for thousands of years most humans have believed in some form of religious tradition and at least in recent centuries have thought of this as the main source of their ethical responsibilities. The problems of exclusivity and of authority plague this source of ethics, though they also give it a unique power. It seems likely that in our shrinking and pluralistic world, the continued dependence on these traditions will only lead to more and escalating violence—both between traditions and within traditions between those who offer different interpretations. The world might be a better and more peaceful place if people would reach beyond their religion for some human and therefore possibly universal ethics. This may be only a dream as the power of religious traditions over the believer is often complete, and to death. It is true that most religions have tolerant strands promoting peace but at the same time other strands invoking violence in the name of God. A small group of the violent may dominate a large group of the peaceful. Many examples can be cited, but Jewish resistance to Roman rule in the first and second centuries CE is one sad example.

The illusion is that religion is man's only good source of ethical guidance and that all other sources are inferior, incomplete, and not to be trusted. The functional consequence of such a belief is that the believer may be open to manipulation by those who lead the tradition as they, in practice stand in God's place, becoming gods themselves, and claiming divine authority for sometimes evil commands and actions. The often ignored fact is that humans have an intuitive morality built in from early childhood. It may naturally be limited to some "in group" and religion may enlarge that group but in our global village we need to develop it as a more universal source of moral behavior—though we can never completely escape human limitations.

7. Religion and Culture

Culture: The sum total of ways of living built up by a group of human beings and transmitted from one generation to another.

—Webster's College Dictionary, 1995

Both religion and culture are ways of defining or identifying groups of humans who have shared interests, moralities, and approaches to living. They are not identical as may be seen by the fact that people of Hispanic origin living in the United States may share an American culture, a Hispanic subculture, and also be involved in a variety of religious traditions, for example Roman Catholicism or Jehovah's Witnesses. Clearly religion and culture interact, overlap, and conflict in important ways as religion may sometimes limit the part of the larger culture in which a believer may actively participate and culture may limit the expression of religion.

Our understanding of the human world is very largely conditioned by the cultural models to which we have been exposed. Our expectations for the behavior of others, our gender and family relations, and our responsibilities toward and expectations of the larger society are all educated by the cultural models we have incorporated. It might also be noted that Thomas Sowell has written a book[95] defending the thesis that interracial conflict is better understood as conflict between different cultures. Thus, when we see ethnic conflict, we should recognize that differing cultural models—including differing religions—may be one important source for that conflict, perhaps more important than race.

Ideology and Religion as Cultural Tools

My limited experience of the world suggests that religions can be easily and usefully understood as ideologies. Ideologies are readily seen to function as cultural tools, and religions fill such roles quite powerfully. One great example is the effect on the Arab world of almost universal acceptance of Muslim teaching. Their prior intertribal warfare stopped, and their violence was directed outward. Within 100 years of Mohammed's death, their empire stretched from Spain to India. The following will attempt to provide some argumentation supporting my claim.

First some definitions. Culture has been described as "the sum total of ways of living built up by a group of human beings and transmitted from one generation to another." Ideology can be approximately defined as "the body of doctrine, myth, belief, etc., that guides an individual, social movement … or group," including sometimes the plans for putting these beliefs into practice (Both of these are adapted from Webster's College dictionary 1995). It should be clear that there is a major overlap of the definitions of ideology and culture. It should also be clear that religions fall broadly in the category of ideologies.

Some religious people insist that religion is not comprehended in the category of ideology. They would separate the two by accepting the supernatural claims of religion contrasted with the presumed human origins for other ideologies and also by claiming a better ethics for religion. Other writers use ideology for a system that most prominently has political goals versus religion's claimed supernatural goals. The overlap is, however, large, and I find the distinction arbitrary as did some other writers I located using a Google search for "ideology and religion." Overtly Christian sites usually disdained the application of the term *ideology* to religion.

One way of changing human culture is to bring in a new ideology that makes novel stipulations about our ways of living. New ideologies often demand changes in values, ethics, hierarchy, hopes for the future, respect for the past and for the natural world, etc. Those who accept a new ideology are often forced to make changes in their manner of living and thinking—in effect change their culture. Religions are definitely in this business as are systems like Fascism and Egalitarian Communism or Bolshevism.

Those who promulgate a new or variant ideology usually do this because they desire to alter our culture—behaviors and beliefs—thinking or hoping that the new will be better. In effect an ideology—including a religion—can be looked on as a way of getting people to make the desired changes. Those who offer new ideologies usually have high hopes for the desired changes. These ideologies may in effect function as tools for creating social groups, acculturating the young, organizing the family, focusing ambition, directing charity, etc. Religion's force in this area relates partly to its use of a supernatural mask.

As decades or hundreds or thousands of years pass a vast array of people come to leadership in the evolving ideology or religion, perhaps controlled by different goals and different fears. Within the original complex sources for the ideology—Bible, Qur'an, *Das Kapital*, Book of Mormon, etc.—are many ideas and by changing the emphasis these leaders can alter the behavior of committed believers. The religion or ideology then has become a tool for the leader allowing him to create and control both "good and evil," charity and violence, while always claiming to be serving the ideology and its great mission—fulfilling the dreams of the founder(s). Some would make a kinder world; others seek power at any price.

A current example of an attempt to use religion as a cultural tool was described in the journal of *The Institute on Religion and Public Life* in 2009. The Chinese Communist Party, having abandoned Maoist thought in their drive to modernize China, seems to have created a spiritual or ideological vacuum. They have now recognized this and are attempting to find remedies—looking at both Buddhist and Christian sources. One official has written that the party "needs to learn how to use religion to enhance social stability and to avert rebellions and revolutions."[96]

The Mix

The idea of a secular culture separate from religion may have started with the Enlightenment and its encouragement of tolerance and religious pluralism especially in Europe and North America. In this environment, religion can be seen as a powerful ideological tool for molding, educating, and controlling people. This is not always bad—sometimes it may be the best way to educate and improve. We would also note that elements of culture currently thought of as secular may have been thought of as religious at some time in the past. By serving human needs, a piece of culture may persist despite changes in the religious tradition of the group and thereby come to be thought of as secular. Alternatively, it can of course be added onto a new religious tradition and continue to have a religious flavor and explanation.

In the pre-Christian era in the Northern Hemisphere, there was in some societies a winter festival of the sun celebrating the start of the sun's return north eventually bringing spring and new life. The Christian festival now known as Christmas replaced this celebration of the winter solstice and has now evolved, at least in North America, into a festival with both secular and Christian strands. The secular part is illustrated by Santa Claus with music, art, and stories, and the Christian part maintains the theme of the birth of Jesus.

In the modern world cultures are often seen as some mixture of elements—viewed as sacred or controlled by religious concerns, and as secular and outside of usual religious considerations. This mixture tends to be fluid being different for different subgroups, etc. For instance, a monk may live a monastic life almost completely controlled by the religiously determined rules of his order. The lay followers of the same religious organization have much more freedom in how they live their lives. The Amish enclaves in the Eastern United States are examples of groups whose culture seems dominated by their religion. The alternative is post–World War II Western Europe where the majority of people have largely given up on religion as an important part of life. Religion remains a strong influence for the citizens of the United States today; in fact, so strong that religious posturing is considered advantageous for the politician. It has been claimed that no American politician dare admit he is an agnostic or atheist as he would be considered unelectable. The Religious Right has taken a strong stand that some of their beliefs should be made into law and forced on those who disagree with them. Examples include abortion and drug control legislation. They think the God they pray to demands this.

The intertwining of religion and culture is demonstrated by the work of religious missionaries and the course of the institutions they have founded. These missionaries exported religion and culture together. With varying degrees of success, they have spread religion combined with Western dress, nutrition, medicine, agriculture, and family relations. Often these Western ways offered a higher standard of living to those who accepted them, and this gave more power to the religion and allowed it to impact local culture in ways beyond just the religious. The local cultures also pushed back in ways that have and are changing the religious institutions founded by these missionaries. Philip Jenkins has written[97] about what is happening to Christianity in the lands where the missionaries took it. He finds the move in non-Western Christianity to be toward a more primitive and supernatural form of worship. There is more emphasis on the direct intervention of the divine in human life and on the action of evil spirits—including a role for exorcisms, etc. This emphasis may reflect the prior religious practices, such as animism, that dominated these cultures before Christianity came.

Over the centuries, religions given political power have shown a significant tendency to become totalitarian. The Medieval Catholic Church with its Inquisition, and the Puritans under Oliver Cromwell, give ready examples—the latter with only a few years in power. Religious leaders, already considering themselves authorities on God's will, that is ultimate "truth," find it easy to apply that knowledge to every detail of human life. Some, given opportunity, would control the culture to make the details match the perceived will of the God they serve. Proselytizing and evangelizing institutions cannot lightly give up such an opportunity.

Religion and Family/Gender Relations

The dominant religion in a culture is usually interpreted to support the family and gender relationships found in that society. The move to liberate women and empower them equally with their male counterparts did not originate in the Christian church, though some of the actors may have been Christian. Certainly in my day, feminism has carried more of a secular connotation, and resistance to it has often been found among Christian groups, who interpret their documents as privileging men with power over women. In the 1970s, one of my patients, a good Mormon lady, testified against the feminist-sponsored Equal Rights Amendment to the U.S. Constitution. One commentator[98] has suggested that in early Christianity, women were more or less the equals of men, but when Christianity became the official religion of the Roman Empire, it was also molded to Roman patriarchal culture.

The Abrahamic traditions support the typical nuclear family life with heterosexual marriage and children. This is not usually a belief or practice required for membership, but I have observed that in some conservative Christian venues long-term singles are looked on with suspicion. There is a current North American movement called "family values" that does insist that this family life is a God-mandated arrangement and seeks to increase its exclusive legal protection. This has gotten a lot of attention because same-sex marriage and gay and lesbian clergy have often been the focus of political agitation within North American Christianity in recent years. The same-sex marriage question has even created opportunities for political posturing by national figures calling for a constitutional amendment protecting heterosexual marriage, as though same-sex union might somehow be a threat to heterosexual marriage.

Religion and Educational Factors

There is some correlation between social or educational status and religious preference, at least within the Christian world. The Jehovah's Witnesses and most Pentecostal organizations (whose members speak in tongues, are possessed by the "Spirit," practice exorcism...) tend to prosper best among the economically less advantaged groups. This is to some degree self-perpetuating, as they often encourage their members not to seek higher education, especially secular, for fear that education will lead them away from their belief system—a fear that is perhaps well-founded. I have personally heard these fears expressed within the Jehovah's Witness tradition and when I was young among Seventh-day Adventists. Adventism seems to be changing on this point, with its growing higher education system—but the Witnesses at least recently still maintained a recommendation to avoid education beyond high school.

The pursuit of intellectually demanding professions and the education required for this appears to have an impact on the attractiveness of religious belief. Surveys have shown that the more successful scientists are less likely to believe in God or immortality. In 1914, the psychologist James Leuba surveyed American scientists and found that 42 percent believed in God. Separately tabulated results from 40 percent of his surveyed scientists, those labeled "greater scientists" in the AAAS directory, found only 30 percent believed in God. Using the same questions, this survey was repeated in 1996 for all scientists and later just for members of the National Academy of Science.[99] The results were that 39 percent of all scientists believed in God but only 7 percent of the elite scientists shared this God belief. For comparison, a Fox News Survey in October 2005 reported that 91 percent of Americans (registered voters) believed in God.[100] A Harris Interactive poll in 2006 done online and probably representing a more technologically sophisticated group reported 73 percent of Americans believed in any form of God or supreme being.[101] A 2007 survey of 1011 Americans at least age fifty, by AARP[102] found that higher income and education both had a modest negative effect on belief in heaven. Heaven was real to only 78 percent of the higher income versus 90 percent of the poor and to only 77 percent of the college-educated versus 89 percent with less education.

Attempts at Culture without Religion

History records only a few attempts to organize human society without an important religious component. As one might expect, we find attempts to substitute some alternative rational system for religion as religion's role is too important to be ignored. The French Revolution proposed to do away with religion and God but substituted the Goddess of Reason. Their whole program included many changes, even attempts to alter the weekly seven-day cycle. French society was indeed turned upside down but the result was not a stable and happy system. Instead they produced the Reign of Terror, and finally from the rubble Napoleon Bonaparte rose to control France, and briefly, much of Europe. Religion came back but not the Inquisition. A few good things were introduced then that are still with us, such as the units of length and mass that are universal in science—but the religious reforms were a failure. One might note, however, that a recent Harris Poll found God or "supreme being" belief in only 27 percent of French people—the lowest believing fraction of five large European countries surveyed.[101]

Communism as practiced by the Bolsheviks introduced the Communist Party as a substitute for a religious organization. In his book *Socialism*[103] first published in the early 1920s, Ludwig von Mises pointed out the similarities between the Communist Movement and a religion. The god of the Communist Party was the invincible and irresistible forces of history as described by its prophet Karl Marx. His writings were the scriptural canon of the party and contained its eschatology. The party's role was to help those forces bring into being a new and just world. They destroyed any who resisted or were thought likely to resist these changes. They misunderstood human nature as do most utopians (see comments of Steven Pinker in *The Blank Slate*), thinking that with the right education, they could create perfect people to inhabit a world where each contributed according to his ability and received according to his need. They organized extensive systems for education and control, especially of the young but were never able to move beyond central authority and the use of violent power against any dissent. Their outposts in the world such as China, Cambodia, Vietnam, and Cuba, had the same problems of violence and an inability to create their dream of justice. The center has broken down, and the pieces are evolving in ways the founders would never have imagined. Customary or typical religion, both

Christian and Muslim, has returned to most of these societies, especially Russia. The average working person was not a party member, and such people were probably caught in the Communist system without being intellectually committed to it. For more discussion, see the section "Atheism and the Marxist World" in chapter 13: Atheism and Religion.

Limited Secularism

Shortly before the French Revolution, the British colonies of North America undertook a revolution. This revolution has had remarkable success in that its political institutions endure today and have been much admired—sometimes copied. The main goal of its founders seems to have been the creation of a coalition of colonies to resist outside interference. It appears that they had neither the desire nor the opportunity to destroy and remake their society. They did have to deal with about fifty different religious groups—some with strong political opinions. For instance, they had to deal with Rhode Island and Massachusetts knowing that the founders of the former had fled there to escape the religious persecution of the latter. To satisfy the needs for peaceful pluralism, they resolved to separate state and church and limit the power of the state as regards the affairs of the church. The secular state then came into being, agreeing that its powers came from the consent of the governed, not from some divine right.

This government continues to the present though always in an evolving form. The confident fundamentalists among the religious still try to get control of the government to impose their God's presumed will on others, not realizing that success in such a project would be terribly harmful in the long run, to both politics and religion. For the sake of appearance and public morality, political leaders, both conservative and otherwise, in the United States have often claimed that they were leading God's Chosen People. Despite this, the relatively open and pluralistic society that has been created in the United States has become, for those who can choose, one of the most desirable places for living a life. In this society some men live religious lives and others purely secular lives, and most of the time they do this cheerfully, side by side, without anger toward the opposite approach.

The ideals of this state and its public educational system have been the creation of a society of free people whose freedom is restrained by law to avoid damaging other people's equal opportunity for freedom.

This has required the development of a form of shared secular culture that has allowed people to follow their own uncoerced religious convictions in public or in private as long as they don't force others. The shared secular culture and its political institutions have sometimes been referred to as an "American civil religion."[104] Over the last two centuries millions of people have immigrated to the United States, and the majority have willingly learned this secular culture—to the apparent benefit of all of us, for we have been a nation of immigrants.

The Religious Marketplace

When a religion has the political support that gives it a monopoly position in a culture it tends to become more interested in its political power than in the welfare of its individual believers. Competition may enter the religious marketplace if the state allows more than one religion to coexist, and if the rules of eligibility are not too restrictive, a genuine market for religion may develop with religions competing in trying to make their followers happy here—and possibly in some future existence. This may make for a very vigorous religious sector that wins support from a large part of the population by serving many needs in its competitive fervor. Adam Smith was the first one to make these observations, which were included in a less well-known section of *The Wealth of Nations*.[105] Rodney Stark has an excellent review of Smith's contribution with a discussion of its application to the ancient Roman religious world that at least sometimes looked like a marketplace.[106]

Compared to Western Europe the United States has a larger fraction of professedly religious people or believers in God. For instance, the previously reported *Financial Times*/Harris Poll in 2006 found 73 percent of Americans believing in God but only 27 percent of the French people. Perhaps this is at least partly because over a long period the United States has maintained a more free and diverse religious marketplace. This has forced both new and old religions to compete for adherents and their financial and personal support—most likely making the religions more attractive, more flexible, and more sensitive to the needs of the average human.

Happiness and Religion

Some religious people, both fundamentalist and otherwise, have claimed that people, without God or religion, are selfish and immoral and have neither freedom nor dignity. In response, the sociologist Phil Zuckerman has written about the virtues of godlessness, rejecting the idea that religion is necessary for happiness or social justice in a particular society.[107] Among other sources, he cites a Dutch expert, Veenhoven, who has been a longtime student of human happiness and finds that the citizens of Denmark lead the world in overall happiness and those of Sweden are not far behind. These same countries rank very low in their religiosity but are tied for number one in a German-sponsored worldwide ranking for social justice.

Two thoughtful letters followed Zuckerman's commentary.[108] A psychologist, David Myers, agreed that "traditional religious values are most practiced in the most irreligious countries" and extended this observation to a comparison between the individual states of the United States. In contrast he noted that within a country religious people were more likely to be happy, to have donated to charity, to have done volunteer work, and to have avoided arrest and divorce. He offers no reconciliation of these observations.

Alexander Zubatov, an information specialist, thinks that "it is societal unhappiness that is an important cause for high levels of societal religiosity, not vice versa." He believes that religiosity is driven by alienation related to low standards of living and high levels of inequality. Thus the Scandinavians have little need of the "compensations offered by the supernatural" since they are happy in the here and now. By his analysis, the United States has a lot of racial and economic disparity and this may contribute to our relatively high religiosity—compared to other first world democracies.

It is not easy to reconcile these observations, but I would speculate that within any society the most socially responsible people may also be more likely to participate in religious life. Perhaps both social responsibility and religious participation are significantly related to some basic personality trait(s). The overall happiness and social justice of a society may be related to its productivity, its cultural homogeneity, and possibly to its ideas of what it means to be human. Religion, though it seems to offer positive help in these areas, may in actual practice, if too powerful, be more a sign of failure as excess religiosity may be evidence of a search for supernatural solutions for a hard life and social justice may seem unimportant in the common religious portrayal of good religious people versus the "rejecters of truth."

It is unclear if religion is a major source of good in a society or a person or simply an expression of the kind of society or the kind of individual that has been created by some complicated confluence of factors and forces. The two world wars of the twentieth century were largely contested on European soil and they with their associated atrocities may also have contributed to Europe's loss of religiosity.

Cultural Achievements Associated with Religion

Here we will attempt to address some areas where religions have often been admired for the artistic or scholarly creations and utilitarian accomplishments they have sponsored. For some people these areas of accomplishment are arguments for the importance and even "truth" of religion. Such people feel that the religion directly and divinely inspires these items while others of us would say that it is in the religion's best interest to arrange or provide the output of skilled specialists in these areas, as their work may direct admiration and adherents to the religion. Sometimes the limitation of offering this work to the larger society is the sectarian nature of the product, but good artistic work can usually be appreciated by a cultured audience regardless of its own religious orientation. The most important value of these efforts may be that they give the religious myth a vivid kind of reality that keeps it living and active in the believer's mind, especially his working memory.

Literature

A Google search on "religion and literature" August 2009 got 163,000,000 hits suggesting the large amount of interest in this topic. There is even a journal with the title *Literature and Theology* published by the International Society for Religion, Literature and Culture. Certainly religion has been extensively involved with literature throughout historic time. Our oldest available epics are deeply infused with the gods and the religion of their days; for instance the *Epic of Gilgamesh, The Iliad, The Odyssey,* and the *Tanach,* whose stories have lived on to influence the Western literary canon.

The Christian Bible and the Muslim Qur'an have made major impacts on the development of the languages and cultures where they have been used. Many Muslims regard the literary beauty of the Qur'an as proof of its divine origin. Translation of the Arabic text is, however, officially discouraged, and it has had limited literary influence where Arabic is not spoken. On the other hand, the Bible has been translated into many languages over the last two thousand years and often had a major impact on the evolution of the new language. Luther's German translation set an enduring standard for use of the German language. The seventeenth-century King James version of the Bible is still read by many English speakers, at least partly because of the beauty of the language; though there are a host of more recent and more accurate translations.

A great number of the most respected writers of my lifetime have addressed religious themes in their writing; for instance, in no particular order, T. S. Eliot, Salman Rushdie, J.D. Salinger, Albert Camus, James Joyce, and Samuel Beckett. In my small world, other notable writers who used religious themes in their art include, naming only a few, Alfred Tennyson, Fyodor Dostoyevsky, Leo Tolstoy, Herman Melville, and Franz Kafka. Some of them questioned the received truths of religion, but they did not question its large role in their world.

Art, Music, and Architecture

Religions often make use of the best art, music, and architecture available in a culture. Attendees of Christian religious services have frequently remarked to me on how they enjoy the beauty and glory of the rituals and the music that usually adorns them. These services intend to make the religious myth more real to the believers; and they seem to do it best when they achieve great artistic beauty, giving a sense of the sublime that the worshipers cherish in memory and delight in relating to their tradition.

People often can be persuaded to devote a large amount of their disposable wealth to support their church, thus religions may have more discretionary funds than anyone else in a culture, and they find it beneficial to direct significant amounts to high quality art, music, and architecture. This is reportedly done to "glorify" their God, but it especially seems that they make their religion more attractive to potential members and reinforce the reality of the central myth that justifies their religious belief system. There are always limited exceptions as the English Puritans, and the Muslims have rejected artistic depiction of the divine.

In our current culture, examples of this abound, including fine vocal and instrumental music for Christian church services both on weekends and for great festivals like Christmas and Easter; "Gospel music" on American TV and radio; wonderful devotional art such as the Sistine Chapel and countless beautiful stained-glass windows; the architecture and decoration of great Christian Cathedrals, especially in Europe, of mosques such as the Great Mosque in Damascus, and of Hindu Temples in Benares.

Good architecture seems to be appreciated by the religious regardless of its origin as the Great Mosque in Cordoba, Spain, was consecrated as a Christian church after the Christian reconquest of Cordoba in 1271, and after the Ottomans conquered Constantinople in 1453 they turned the huge Christian church there into a mosque, the Hagia Sophia; made a museum in the twentieth century.

Higher Education

The first medieval universities in Europe probably evolved from schools in churches. Besides teaching religion, they added law and medicine. Over centuries, they evolved to become research institutions, many publishing their own journals by the eighteenth century. Thus schools started with a main goal of providing a religious education, especially for clerics, became great secular research institutions with religion only a small part of their offerings. The European research university has become a model, used worldwide, for advance educational institutions.[109]

In North America, Protestantism has usually encouraged education, and many of our most well-known universities were founded by Protestant groups or churches to provide a good education, both secular and religious, for the children of members. The Catholics have not been far behind, founding such great schools as Boston University and Notre Dame. Many of these, originally religious schools, for instance Harvard, Yale, Dartmouth, Duke, Baylor, Vanderbilt, and the University of Southern California, are now known primarily as secular research universities, though they often have associated seminaries still devoted to the founding vision. It seems that the broad interests of a great research university don't mesh well with a religious view of the world so that control has largely passed to university administrations that have tried to move beyond the sectarian.

Despite the changes at the most eminent universities, the Christian religion in the United States remains very involved in education at primary and secondary levels and in smaller colleges, many set up specifically to promulgate the sectarian religious views of the sponsoring organizations. The Muslim world also has an extensive network of madrassas schools whose main job seems to be providing religious instruction. In less affluent areas this may be the only education available to most children and young people.

Medical Care

In antiquity, medicine and religion were often intertwined as the most common form of medical care was an appeal to the supernatural for healing. This was practiced at Egyptian temples and at Greek shrines dedicated to the god Asclepius, a physician added to the Pantheon after his death. In the third century BCE, Ashoka the Buddhist king of India, reportedly founded hospitals for both people and animals. The Romans continued the worship of Asclepius and eventually developed limited institutions for care of at least sick slaves, gladiators, and soldiers. When Christianity came to political power, it expanded the care of the sick; in fact the Council of Nicaea in 325 CE ordered the construction of a hospital in every cathedral town.[110] From then through the sixteenth or seventeenth century, medical care in the Christian world was usually associated with religion and was often mixed with care for the traveler and the indigent.

The Muslim world also developed medical care, including hospitals. They built on an older Persian tradition of medical knowledge that had been augmented by Nestorian Christians fleeing persecution by the Orthodox and also Greek academics going east after Justinian closed the Academy in Athens. These Muslim hospitals spread across the Mideast and North Africa and continued through the time of the Ottoman Empire. At least some of them had endowments for support and offered free medical care along with mental health care and medical education.[111]

Some scholars would date increasing medical knowledge and the secular hospital to the eighteenth century with huge advances in the nineteenth century and thereafter. This development of secular knowledge has not kept religion from having a large continuing role in medical care. Medical missionary work has been an important activity for perhaps the majority of Christian churches in both North America and Europe. Even smaller organizations such as Seventh-day Adventists have a substantial and almost worldwide medical presence including hospitals. The medical work of many Christian groups includes proselytizing and health education. My limited exposure suggests the education is partly sectarian but still may fill a significant empty place in some cultures. Besides their foreign commitments, many religious organizations have been involved in founding and operating hospitals in the continental United States, including at minimum Catholics, Methodists, Baptists, Presbyterians, Jews, Lutherans, and Seventh-day Adventists.

There are at least two explanations for this tendency of religions to support the provision of medical care. Most current major religions have somewhere in their foundational documents or traditions a goal of caring for the sick and needy, and this goal is served by providing medical assistance that ranges from modern surgery to hospice care for the dying. Many members identify with these goals and are willing to donate significant parts of their lives to such projects. The other important goal is a form of advertising. If the medical work is done well, the religious group may point to it as something done according to the ideals and principles of their faith. Grateful recipients of care may be encouraged to study the religion further and possibly convert or at least make financial contributions. A supplemental benefit is that the medical work may sometimes serve to get political recognition or favors for the religious group.

Conclusions

Where religion exists, which is essentially everywhere, it is part of culture—sometimes almost all of it, at least in the eyes of those involved. There have been no known successful attempts at establishing a human society without religion. There have been at least two large-scale public attempts to move in this direction, and they have been terrible failures: the eighteenth-century French Revolution and the twentieth-century Marxist states. One cause of these failures may have been the arrogance and violence of those who tried to create the new societies—driven by their own "faith"-based belief systems. Less arrogant and violent men would probably also have failed but with much less blood spilt. Another cause of failure may have been an inadequate appreciation of religion's powerful roles so that these were not all or adequately cared for in the new arrangements—if such is even possible. The daunting task of figuring out what is possible and how to defuse the violence associated with confident ideologies must be confronted if we are ever to have a somewhat peaceful world.

Societies that allow individual men to live their lives without religion have, however, done well. Whether a particular individual is better off with a religious belief system is another question. Sociologists may report that members of religious communities are better off in terms of satisfaction with life, social support, or longevity—but this can never answer the question of whether a religious belief system is better for a particular person. Individuals vary widely in their appreciation for different aspects of human life and accomplishment, and it may be that religion is essential for many people's fulfillment, and yet is detrimental to the happiness and fulfillment of some minority. It appears that there are creative and rational minds who find the available religious traditions limiting and frustrating, though they have great respect for their fellow humans and for the beauty and complexity of the universe. That is my impression of some scientists I have read such as Albert Einstein and also my feeling when I listened to an interview with Salman Rushdie.

Many religionists would promote the illusion that a culture must be dominated and controlled by their particular religion for it to be most desirable and happy—a closed society. My own impression is that the best and most admirable human cultures are open and come from a fertile mixture, allowing many forms of religious expression, including unbelief, without official built-in bias or violence for or against any religious position. The very uncertainty and pluralism this produces may be a stimulant of creative thought and activity—even as it is frightening to the adherents of the fundamentalist strands of religion who believe they know the mind of God where resides final truth for all time. One hopes that the visible contrasts between peace and violence may somehow weaken the power of the violent.

8. Religion and Politics

All that man seeks on earth, that is: someone to bow down to, someone to take over his conscience, and a means for uniting everyone at last into a common, concordant, and incontestable anthill—for the need for universal union is the third and last torment of men..

—Fyodor Dostoevsky, *The Brothers Karamazov*

The garb of religion is the best cloak of power.

-William Hazlitt, *"On the Clerical Character" in Political Essays (1819)*

The art of politics consists in hiding the face of power behind the mask of doing good.

Historical Commentary

Religion, culture, and politics are certainly related, and maybe I should have merged these comments into the prior section, but politics seems too important for that. Throughout most of human history, religion has been enmeshed with politics. State religions have provided support for the state and that state has demanded that the citizen give the religion both assent and money. Socrates was executed for impiety—but maybe more for asking questions. Some sort of religion was important in all the ancient civilizations of historical time, and if you too overtly rejected or questioned the religion, you might put your life at risk. Early Christians were not persecuted so much for what they believed about Christianity as for their absolute refusal to render any homage to the state religion of emperor worship. In the Greek and Roman religious traditions the worshiper was usually not required to render complete and solitary devotion to one particular deity but could seek approval from several. The exclusive devotion required by the Christian God was a significant though not unheard of innovation that probably should be attributed to the Jewish roots of Christianity.

Starting with Constantine, the Christian church became officially enmeshed with the civil powers and sometimes in competition with those civil powers for ultimate control. This power grew gradually, especially after Roman emperors were no longer elected. However, even early after getting official recognition the church was active in persecuting Paganism and in forcing orthodoxy. At the height of papal power, Pope Gregory VII (1073–1085 CE) used the perceived power of church sacraments to humble Henry IV, king of Germany.

Beginning with the European Enlightenment of the eighteenth century, religious freedom has now come to much of the world, and at the same time much of the world has abandoned having a coercive state religion. The Islamic faith, however, includes many groups and individuals who believe religion and politics are inseparable. In fact historically, starting with Mohammed himself, Islam has usually chosen to have civil and religious authority combined in one political entity. They have intended to make religious law the civil law for all citizens. Iran, Saudi Arabia, and Afghanistan under the Taliban are or have been examples of attempts to apply Islamic law to all citizens regardless of their personal religious orientation. Of course, in the past, Christianity has attempted the same program. Examples include the Inquisition, Calvin's Geneva, and the Puritans in England and early Massachusetts. Today's Christian Reconstructionists have ideas of the desirability and validity of Deuteronomic law (Old Testament) for the modern world that are similar to the Muslim idea of applying Sharia law universally.[112]

Some Rudiments of "Politics"

People sleep peaceably in their beds at night only because rough men stand ready to do violence on their behalf.

—George Orwell

The goals of politics are ostensibly to create or realize some vision of justice and security for the inhabitants or citizens of the political entity. In actual practice, one may think of three broad strands of politics. One strand envisions its goal as the creation of freedom where individuals may pursue their personal hopes and dreams, as long as they don't interfere with others doing the same. At best it tries for some rough equality of opportunity. A second strand seeks to create a utopian dream, where all subjects may lead happy lives, usually with some sort of equality of outcome—often referred to as social justice. This happiness will come from living in just the way that the utopian planners see as most necessary for human fulfillment.

Usually, only a single vision can be implemented, and it has to be binding on all. The third strand of politics seeks to advantage one group at the expense of the larger society. This may be the most common use of politics, but it is usually hidden behind some mask. The Marxian Communist regimens were essentially utopian in their organization and hopes. The United States of America started out as primarily a system to achieve individual freedom for its citizens. For most of its existence it has been increasing freedom by expanding its definition of a citizen but at the same time has gradually added more and more utopian elements—with their unavoidable price. The increasing power necessary to provide the utopian pieces—so called socialism—has also brought greater opportunities for corruption, and the third strand to enter political life.

Progress toward realizing any of these political goals is attempted by creating a set of laws or rules to limit and protect the actions of the citizens. The way in which these rules are created is of course a matter of intense interest to those affected. The rules may be created by democratic assemblies, political tyrannies, religious elite claiming theocracy, and various combinations such as a democratic tyranny of a minority in a state with severely limited citizenship. A less happy situation applies when the law is simply some person's word (the chief or king or a representative thereof). This then becomes a rule of men instead of a rule of law. However, even a laudable set of written laws may be systematically interpreted to get a result you would never have expected—having read and reread those laws. The brutal purges of Stalin were carried out under a Russian constitution that sounded good, humane, and a reasonable basis for a happy society. Ultimately, no law is better than those who have the power to interpret it.

One must remember that democracy of itself is no guarantee of justice or wisdom. In his *History of the Peloponnesian War,* Thucydides described significant failures of the Athenian democracy.[113] At times it had become irrational "mob rule." Without the restraint of a respected and enforced constitution, democracy may easily become a form of tyranny of the majority. The founders of the United States were afraid of such a tyranny, so they attempted to create a republic with restraints on the will of the majority. So far, democracy in the United States has been somewhat restrained by a strong judiciary since the legislative and executive branches have often shown significant willingness to ignore constitutional concerns.

Despite the good goals and the crafted laws, politics is always about power—access and application. Real political power flows from violence or the credible threat of violence. If the power is limited, the contest to control it can be played under rules of fair play with goodwill at the end and hopes for another future contest. If the power being contested is unlimited or totalitarian—the contest will have no rules. The most clever and ruthless will almost always win. The stories of the rise to power of the Marxist dictators of the twentieth century, such as Lenin, Stalin, Mao, Pol Pot, and even Castro, are recent examples of the contest for unlimited power. Hitler and Mussolini rose to unlimited power by the route of first winning significant popular support then changing the character of the office they had acquired.

Every political entity needs some source of validation for its authority. Much of ancient history suggests that the first important validation for leadership of a political unit was a claim of support by the gods or even of being one of the gods. The idea that political authority should be built on a foundation of the consent of the governed seems to start with Greek democracy and Roman republican forms. It appears to have largely disappeared by the late Roman Empire. Switzerland did revive the idea in Medieval Europe, and it gained a new lease on life with the eighteenth-century Enlightenment, which spawned the Constitution of the United States, among other democratic documents.

The power of a particular political entity flows from the fact that that entity demands to be the sole legal user of violence within its domain. Chairman Mao reputedly asserted that "political power flows from the barrel of a gun," and anyone who carefully examines the political world—at any level—finds that when laws or rules are made, then men with guns are engaged to enforce those rules. *Thus in a crude but very real sense, politics is the discussion of the legal use of violence in society; to what ends.* This is the part that politicians in discussing their utopian goals, whether great or trivial, almost invariably ignore. It sadly may haunt the polity and is often the seed of everything from libertarian dissent to violent revenge. The Waco Massacre and the blowing up of the Murrah Federal Building in Oklahoma City are extreme but clear American examples. No one benefited by either, but violent political power created one and those who resented that power created the other.

Power, Utopia, and Religion

Religions have many reasons to seek political connections or political power. Frequently, the very existence of a group with a particular religious orientation depends on tolerance by the political system. Churches therefore seek at minimum recognition by the political authorities for their organization and its legitimacy. (There are some fundamentalist Christian groups who would avoid this as a pact with the devil, but they are a tiny minority.) As church members may become more common in a political unit there is a tendency to seek greater accommodations from the political authorities so that the church may operate more easily and widely. In turn the political leaders start to see benefit from having the approval of the church. Eventually, it may be a win-win situation for both leaderships to support each other. This seems to have been the case when Constantine recognized the Christian church in 313 CE with the Edict of Toleration. An astute politician used this move to get a major increase in support for his emperorship—originally won in battle.

A further perceived benefit of political power is that a religious organization may be able to start to universalize its recommendations for how people live by putting them into the civil law. Because religions claim to deal in matters of ultimate power and immortality, they find it easy to convince themselves that their recommendations would be followed if men only rightly understood the human condition. It seems then only a small step to force the protection of a man's soul even over his objections, even at the cost of his freedom or life. By the end of the fourth century, Rome had banned support of the pagan temples, and in fact there was only one official religion, Christianity. That religion was already persecuting pagans. Plato's Academy in Athens was also closed early in the sixth century, and its teachers eventually sought refuge in Persia where their students contributed to the Islamic preservation of Greek science.

The cycle of a minority achieving political power and then persecuting those who disagree with them has been seen many times in history. John Calvin found political power in Geneva and ended up burning those who disagreed with his theology. The Puritans fled England to escape persecution but once established in New England started to persecute those who disagreed with them. It seems that Dostoevsky's Grand Inquisitor was right when he said: "For the care of these pitiful creatures is not just to find something before which I or some other man can bow down, but to find something that everyone else will also believe in and bow down to, for it must needs be *all together*."[114]

This utopian or universalizing strand that runs through most religious belief systems or organizations finds more than one outlet. Its safest expression is in a belief in some idealized heaven as the goal of earthly existence. This is only inhabited by good people (those who believe) in some other time and/or place. There have, however, been many attempts at some sort of implementation here on this contingent and fragile earth. Examples include Calvin's Geneva, the Puritans of the seventeenth-century English Revolution, the Spanish Inquisition, the Taliban in Afghanistan, and even Charlemagne the Great's hopes of establishing St. Augustine's *City of God* in his domain. These have all proved transitory and fraught with the risk of bad outcomes for those who disagree. The closest thing to an enduring possibly happy implementation of a religious utopia in North America would seem to be small civilly constituted groups such as the communities of the Hutterites and the Mennonites.

Corruption, Diversity, and Religion

Power, especially political power, brings an often irresistible opportunity for corruption. The greater the power, the greater the possible corruption, and what is possible will happen at least sometimes, and maybe often. Religious people think they may by their good belief systems and ethics be protected from this corruption, but that is often an illusion. They are real people who are usually constrained to act by the incentive systems under which they live. Paul Johnson[115] relates the early corruption of Christianity after it achieved official status in the Roman Empire. This consisted in people seeking church office to avoid taxes. Political power may bring greater monetary income, larger buildings, and grander rituals, but there is little evidence it leads to greater concern for God or one's fellow citizens.

Political recognition is usually given to a specific church organization. This recognition encourages the development of an orthodoxy to which all are expected to adhere. The expression of diversity is to a significant degree discouraged by this need to present a single face to the political powers. For example, Constantine provided Christianity with recognition and political power and encouraged the development of a single orthodoxy and the suppression of alternate interpretations of the Christian tradition. In fact, the Council of Nicaea in 325 CE was called by Constantine and was used to suppress Arianism or the belief that Jesus Christ was less than fully God. The decision was made by the selected elite and forced on all. As an "authorized version" of the Christian church grew stronger in its first few centuries, other strands of Christianity also disappeared, including the Ebionites, the Gnostics, the Marcionites, etc.

Religion and Political Freedom

Ideas of human political freedom are at least as old as Greek civilization and were central to the Roman Republic. Lord Action has presented a brief history of such ideas both in antiquity and more recently.[116] Throughout history, freedom has probably not been a primary goal of most political systems or peoples. In the last few centuries, it has most likely had its greatest development in the English-speaking world—perhaps with an exception for Switzerland. According to the political commentator George Will,[117] it is an acquired taste, requiring effort to maintain. In my opinion, religions have not generally supported freedom except for the "freedom" to follow their own particular religious tradition. They are generally found advocating respect for authority and the group instead of respect for reason and the individual's considered evaluation. The rise of Protestantism and the splintering of Christianity into many strands created new possibilities in the Western World. To some degree this empowered individuals and gave them many options instead of a single conformity—but still religious choice seems largely limited by acculturation.

Dostoevsky's Grand Inquisitor gave us a remarkable commentary on what people really want, telling Christ that they didn't want freedom but preferred "miracle, mystery, and authority." Of this story Sigmund Freud wrote *"The Brothers Karamazov* is the most magnificent novel ever written, and the story of the Grand Inquisitor is one of the peaks in the literature of the world. It can hardly be over praised."[118] In practice for many, religion seems to fill these needs. Claims of miracles are widespread in religious traditions along with the frequent assertion that at least some of the beliefs of the religion are mysteries that can never be understood by reason. Of course, authority is almost always present in the religious tradition: in documents, clerical leadership, or respected elders; so the three identified needs are usually met within such a tradition.

As previously mentioned, religion when held by a small or weak minority demands or requests freedom, but with political power, it tends to demand conformity of others to its rules and beliefs. This seems a common rule with few exceptions. Human freedom appears almost irrelevant to a typical religious group unless the humans hold the correct belief system—and they are eager to help you achieve this orthodoxy. Certainly in the visible Islamic world, conformity to belief seems far more important that any idea of human freedom. The most noble goals some Muslims seem capable of are not the creation of some great good—literature, art, music or even sporting success—but instead the destruction of someone unknown to them but viewed as an enemy of the faith by their leaders. The moderates among them probably have a different view, but that voice often seems muted compared to the voice and actions of the violent.

Buddhism might possibly be an exception to the violence found in much of the religious world. During my life I have known of Buddhists who sacrificed themselves as martyrs for a political cause, but I have not heard of Buddhist terrorists killing others for some political or religious goal. Sadly, however, even Buddhism has occasionally been put to seemingly disgraceful ends. In an article titled *Buddhism: Blood and Enlightenment,* Joseph Grasso[119] reports that Buddhist leaders supported Japanese imperialism in the fifty years leading up to World War II, resisted modernizing an oppressive feudal system in Tibet, and more recently tried to sabotage efforts at making peace between the Tamil Tigers and the government in Sri Lanka. This only seems to say that all major religions are powerful ideologies that can be applied to many goals, often good but some appearing quite tarnished.

The diversity of religions in the United States of America is probably the main reason it still has great religious freedom. Some people would insist that America is a Christian nation. Through most of history, being a Christian nation has not meant being a free nation. In fact, there is little in history to suggest that in practice Christianity values human freedom. Most Christian nations in the last 1,700 years have found themselves suppressing alternative religious views, at least subtly, and often violently. Those who would make America a Christian nation seem to be tending in the direction of political enforcement of their beliefs, a return to the attempt to create a utopia through political violence.

Political Revival and Religion

Religion has been often used in human history to attempt to revive the political fortunes, unity, and vigor of a national, ethnic, or cultural group. The Biblical Old Testament is filled with stories of the Israelites forgetting their religious heritage, falling into political bad times, and being called back to their God by a reformer who then leads them to political or military victory. These stories are especially found in the books of Judges, Samuel, Kings, and Chronicles. For many of the stories, there are no alternate sources of information, but for some parts of the time covered by these documents, there are now revealing glimpses of the past provided by archeology.[120] These sources suggest that the "sacred record" of God's recurring action in Palestinian political life may be systematically distorted for national religious reasons. This record has, however, had a large and enduring effect on Jewish and Christian history. Those who deeply believed that record, created the wars of the Maccabees and the disastrous Palestinian and Alexandrian rebellions against Rome, and are still active in a fundamentalist wing of Judaism. Christian fundamentalists of the present day look at this record and long to make the United States a "Christian Nation" by forcing everyone to worship their God or at least not do things that might make him frown.

Similarly, Augustus, after becoming established as emperor, sponsored a revival of the worship of the classic Roman Gods.[121] It was publicly urged that the civil wars had happened because people had failed in their piety toward these gods. Augustus also attempted to legislate an improvement in Roman morality. The emperor's own daughter was exiled for adultery, and the great poet Ovid was sent to the Black Sea for the rest of his life. Several more episodes of official revival of the old Roman pantheon occurred over the next three hundred years—usually at times of political stress for the empire. These were typically associated with persecution of the Christians since they would not participate in the revivals.

In the modern era, Joseph Stalin, facing a German invasion in 1941, relented in his persecution of Christianity. He called for a revival of the Russian Orthodox Church and provided some loosening of his repressive regime.[122] This was part of an attempt to create a strong emotional response of the Russian people to this overwhelming event. The Bolsheviks had been both repressive to religion and an internationalist party, but for this war they needed the inspirational power of religion and patriotism. After the war, the repression returned. Even more recently, after his defeat in the first "Gulf War," Saddam Hussein sponsored a revival of Islamic religion in Iraq, portraying himself as deeply religious, adding "God Is Great" to the flag, outlawing drinking and gambling, and building many new mosques.

One great problem with this form of revival is that those who dissent from the majority religious beliefs have to be demonized or even destroyed because they undermine the goal of obtaining political and social unity and renewal; and divine favor for the political entity. The Jews of the Old Testament supposedly did this by destroying those who strayed too far from Yahweh worship; the Maccabees did it by exiling or killing those who would have reformed Judaism trying to make it more universally appealing.[123] The Romans did it by persecuting the Christians. Today part of the Muslim world looks for renewal by reviving the "faith," and we have seen the Taliban try to build a new Muslim community in Afghanistan based on the Wahabi interpretation of the tradition with violent suppression of those Muslims who disagree with this interpretation.[124]

Religion and Place

Religions have a remarkable power to set aside some things as special or holy and deserving of different treatment than other similar things. This has been used to designate pieces of this earth as uniquely holy because of an experience of the divine claimed for that place. This is an ancient and Old Testament sort of notion that seems to assert that the divine is limited and cannot move on to express itself equally well elsewhere. The power of this claim is then illustrated by the demand that this "sacred dirt" must be controlled by true believers at all costs even if that cost is the misery of war. Thus we have the Crusades that changed medieval history—and got thousands of both Christians and Muslims killed. These are still remembered angrily in the Islamic world. Though the historians of culture and commerce can point to some benefits, it would seem that similar benefits might have been available by peaceful means at almost no cost in human life.

Similar claims are still at work especially in Palestine—particularly Jerusalem—and in places like Mecca and Medina. Unbelievers seem to be banned from at least parts of Mecca on pain of death. The greater difficulties, however, are associated with Jerusalem where the three major Abrahamic faiths intersect. The most vigorous of the claims is that of the fundamentalist Jews who think they serve a God who demands that He have a temple there. They also seem to think their God has given them an enduring right to control this unremarkable pile of dirt and rocks, regardless of who they have to kill to get it. The geographic claim is treated as more important than any other ideas—even ethical demands. This has created an insoluble problem—a war or pending war without foreseeable end or resolution.

This scene has also given the world a picture of a small god not much to be admired; a god who seems more invested in geography than in ideas, ethics, or knowledge.

Fallibility, Freedom, and Religion

Human freedom requires the toleration of diversity. To cheerfully tolerate diversity one needs to accept the possibility that there is more than one way to lead a rewarding and useful life. One must also have enough goodwill to think that others are intelligent and seeking to live their lives well—in the best way possible, considering their options. If one understands the world in this way one can easily come to desire a government of laws that do not restrict individual freedom beyond that necessary to protect this freedom for all. This seems to have been the broad picture aimed at by many of the framers of the United States Constitution. The details are always subject to discussion with the understanding that we are all fallible.

The philosopher Carl Popper wrote about the idea of such a society in his book *The Open Society and Its Enemies*. His student and admirer George Soros has extended this commentary[125] to point out the radical nature of our fallibility and to urge the importance of openness in our civilizations. Soros has also spent a large personal fortune and much of his own energy trying to foster open societies, especially in post-Communist Europe. His political activities at home and abroad have earned him demonization by the political right, especially the Christian Right.

Those who know truth with absolute certainty—our "truth," the only "truth"—often feel a responsibility to spread that truth and to force others to agree with it or at least to suppress any who would dissent publicly. Faith-based systems can achieve the certainty about truth necessary to support tyranny—locally or in a wider world. They reject uncertainty and tell their followers that skepticism is evil, of the devil, or a deep flaw in character. Preferably this indoctrination is started when the subject is a small child. God or the "forces of history" are on the side of this "truth." It doesn't work for all believers, but these confident beliefs have propelled violent minorities to power using Christian, Islamic, and Marxists belief systems. Unfortunately, our world is structured so that a violent minority can often control a quiet, peace-loving majority (for some related comments see the section on Religion and Terrorism in chapter 5).

Truth, Politics, and Religion

Both political and religious systems can be addressed as ideologies that place a structural template on the world and expect the facts of the universe not to conflict with that model, to which they are very deeply committed. Both are therefore tempted to reject accounts of reality that disagree with their template. Despite this similarity, religion and politics are very different in their day-to-day dealings with "truth."

Telling lies for political advantage is at least as old as recorded history. The leaders of the United States have told many a public falsehood and justified it as protecting American interests at home or abroad. The twentieth century saw new heights in the use of political propaganda. After the greatest conflagration of the twentieth century, George Orwell wrote,[126] "Political language—and with variations this is true of all political parties, from Conservatives to Anarchists—is designed to make lies sound truthful and murder respectable, and to give an appearance of solidity to pure wind." Thus most of the time for the educated person there is no expected relationship between political speech and some absolute or perhaps even relative truth. *Political speech seeks political advantage.*

Religion asserts a different relationship to truth. At its very heart, in its central story (or myth), it claims to know and represent absolute truth. It has a variety of ancillary strategies, and these can be seen as efforts to reinforce the reality or "truth" of this central story. Most people think their religion is an example of "truth." We also expect our priests to give us true words about the world and our responsibilities. We do not allow them convenient lies, and most of the time most of them seem to expect truth telling of themselves.

The obvious next step is that the politician would desire to get religious authorities on his side of a political debate. A significant religious presence on one side of a political debate adds plausibility to that position at least for those who share the involved religion. People who regularly claim to be dispensing the truth of God will be expected to maintain a higher standard of truth in the political arena than the usual politician. Thus many political leaders are eager for religious support. There are some negatives that may limit this. In a society of religious pluralism, political support from one religious group may alienate other religious groups. Also the religious leader who actively enters the political world will usually be tarnished with the reputations of the professional politicians with whom he competes. Thus Jerry Falwell, now deceased, and Pat Robertson, politically active conservative religious leaders, have come in recent years to be considered more as politicians than religious people. They have played the buffoon in many a political cartoon. Despite this, their side has had a significant impact in recent elections, and this is likely to continue.

Political Benefits of Religion

It would seem that religion may be beneficial in the political world when it is wielded by men who have an inclusive vision of freedom, who want, not to control people, but to open up their options—to relieve oppression. Martin Luther King and his work for civil rights is one great example. His religion seemed to be a great source of comfort and strength for him, and it resonated with the people whose lives he was trying to improve. Mahatmas Gandhi's drive to free India from the British was also built on a respect for Indian religious traditions. He, however, went far beyond the usual Hinduism, rejecting the caste system and respecting the Islamic tradition. He was in fact assassinated by a member of a radical Hindu group that couldn't tolerate his pluralism.

The Quaker tradition has usually stood in opposition to political violence and for equality and dignity for all men. The American Colony of Pennsylvania was founded by one of their leaders as a refuge for those who had dissenting religious belief systems. Their religious descendants are still actively working for peace and against violence. Though most of the mainline German churches supported the Nazis in the 1930s, Karl Barth, Dietrich Bonhoffer, and others formed a "Confessional Church" that took a public stand against the Nazi machine. They left us a positive memory, but their work seemed to have little effect on the course of events.

Thus we see that religion can have good and admirable uses in the world of politics. It can be used to support respect for our fellow humans, even if they don't share our particular religious tradition. Unfortunately, because it is so powerful and because it is based on faith, not public evidence, on emotion, not reason, it can be readily bent by charismatic leaders to support many different goals—some wonderful, broad, and humane, and some narrow, tribal, and ultimately evil in their overall impact on the quality of human life.

Summary

We have seen that religious and political systems are powerful human constructs for organizing civilized life. They almost invariably interact and sometimes quite strongly. Throughout most of human history religion and politics have been formally connected—supporting each other. The Roman government did allow some degree of religious freedom—as long as the state religion was supported. The modern ideas of religious pluralism and tolerance seem to date to the European Enlightenment but have spread widely in the world. They appeal to those who recognize honest diversity and seek peace. Of course, there are those who disagree, including a fundamentalist Christian movement that would make the United States a "Christian Nation" and Islamic movements that would force a fundamentalist Islam on all within their political reach.

Political power will drive a religion toward having a single orthodoxy. Religions are not usually interested in human freedom beyond that freedom necessary to implement their specific belief system. Religious leaders easily come to think that they have a direct line from God about all aspects of how a human life should be lived. Given political power, they often feel a responsibility to force the wider society to conform to some or many of their views. This along with politicians' frequent tendency to propose some form of utopian goals may lead to a politics that is dangerous to dissenters and ultimately a real failure in terms of creating a desirable place to live.

The illusion is that religion will elevate and ennoble politics. Sometimes it does this, but there is the ever-present possibility, often realized, that it may become a tool for manipulating and controlling people and achieving, maintaining, and justifying political power that couldn't be created otherwise.

9. Religion and Health

The relationship between religion and health has become a popular topic for research, commentary, and speculation, especially in North America in the last few decades. June 2010, a search on the phrase "Religion and Health" in the National Library of Medicine database using the search engine at www.pubmed.gov found 15,262 references from about fifty years. Over half of these were published in the last ten years. There is now a journal devoted to this topic published by Springer and titled the *Journal of Religion and Health*. I cannot completely review this body of work but will try to report some of the difficulties of studying the topic well and some of the interesting correlations that have been described. We will include studies of prayer and healing since in this area there might be more possibility for "rigorous" study of the effects of interventions.

Difficulties of Studying the Health-Related Effects of Religion

Since one cannot administer religion like a medicine, it is difficult to study the health effects of joining, leaving, or changing a religion. Though these things happen, you cannot split a population into two halves and have one group on demand acquire a new religious position whose effects you wish to study. Thus randomized trials are unavailable as to most possible effects of religion on health. A researcher can look at the health status or health outcomes for people professing various religious or spiritual beliefs or following particular practices. Observed differences in health as a function of religious belief or practice may be related to these measured parameters or to some hidden or unstudied parameter. Religious belief systems usually come in extensive and enduring packages that affect many parts of a person's life—dietary, behavioral, emotional, etc—over a long period of time. Separate evaluation of the effects of the supernatural beliefs seems impossible.

We are not currently able to say that Mr. Y would be better off if he took up religion xxx. We can say that the followers of religion xxx have longer life, greater affluence, or happier lives by some criteria of measured associations. If the associations are strong and the effects highly desirable, we might come to believe there was a clear relationship, but scientific proof is a difficult and high standard. Many mistakes of this type have been made in medicine in the last few decades. Two widely believed fallacies based on epidemiologic data were the benefits of estrogen for postmenopausal women and the anticancer effects of beta carotene. Both had good plausibility arguments and less well-known counterarguments. They were finally and unexpectedly disproven by randomized trials. For most people, a religion or lack thereof is nearly a life history, and there is no way to provide this as a random intervention.

If I am told people who believe xxx are happier and healthier, that doesn't mean that I can choose to believe xxx or that I will be happier if I try personally to acquire such a belief system. On the other hand, there are some religious items that may be used as interventions in a random or unbiased way to study their effects. These include visits to the sick (such as chaplains' visits) and various forms of intercessory prayer. Attendance or participation in various religious rituals has been used as an objective measure of religious participation or commitment, but I am unaware of its use as a random intervention. Except in the case of remote intercessory prayer, it is very difficult to isolate supernaturally provided benefits, if they exist, from the effects of social interaction and support. Quantitative measurements, especially of religiosity or spirituality, remain imprecise—frequency of attendance at religious rituals is one that has been studied. Sincerity of attitude or participation can usually only be gotten from a self-report.

The difficulty of studying the effects of religious belief on health does not in any way suggest that there is no effect of religion on health. Powerful belief systems that affect the believer so strongly as to create major self-sacrifice (even martyrdom) are bound to affect mental and probably physical health. Many observational studies support this, but as mentioned above, they must be interpreted with some restraint as there may be hidden or unrecognized variables, such as personality type or aspects of childhood acculturation, that explain all or part of the observed correlations. One would also like to know the mechanisms through which religions affect health and whether secular substitutes such as social support, education, and encouragement to healthy behavior may have similar benefits.

Well-Being and Believing

Since religion does so many seemingly good things for people (see our section on its usefulness), one would expect to find that belief and/or participation in religion would be associated with better mental health. Indeed, recent reviews have shown that religious participation is associated on average with a greater sense of well-being and with less depression. People with positive religious coping (accepting) and an intrinsic form of religion (internalized) have better control of anxiety and stress while those with extrinsic (utilitarian or escape) religion may have more anxiety, stress, and depression than non believers.[127] Overall, there seems to be a positive correlation between religious participation and mental health, for the vast majority of believers. The differences are sometimes small and may require a large study to be statistically significant. There is thus substantial overlap between believers and nonbelievers.

Along the same line an April 2008 Harris Poll[128] reported 45 percent of people who labeled themselves as very religious were also in the poll's highest happiness category. In contrast, those who classified themselves as nonreligious only reached the highest happiness level 28 percent of the time. Either religion helps make you happy or people who are intrinsically happier are attracted to religion.

The various supportive features of religion such as socialization and encouragement of good health habits may be able to explain the benefits, but some investigators would disagree. These students believe, on the basis of some supporting data, that people who consider relationships sacred—for instance marriage—treat these relationships with greater care and thereby have on average more successful relationships.[129] Thus belief in the supernatural, whether that supernatural exists or not, may give some people a positive increment in their quality of life.

Mortality and Morbidity

Correlations between religious behaviors and health-related parameters have been investigated in many areas. One of the most consistent findings has been a reduction in overall mortality (adjusted for confounders still about a 25 percent reduction) for those who regularly attend public religious services regardless of denomination.[130] It has been much more difficult to show an effect of religiosity on progression of cancer or recovery from acute illness.

One can't tell if religion leads to a health improvement or if the same personality traits that lead to greater religious participation also lead to better health habits. Religions usually provide social support and encourage respect for authority, which may lead to a lower likelihood of being involved in crime and substance abuse. Religions often recommend good health habits such as avoiding tobacco and not using alcohol in excess, and many religions place a high value on human life, encouraging good medical care, etc. On the other hand, maybe people who already share these attitudes are also more apt to maintain participation in religious rituals.

Membership alone in some religious organizations is associated with better survival. Mormons and Seventh-day Adventists strongly recommend (even require this) against the use of tobacco and alcohol, and in general try to encourage healthy lifestyles. Compared with American norms, life expectancy is prolonged in both groups, and both have lower incidences of cancers, especially tobacco-related cancer.[131] In contrast, mortality was increased in the graduates of a mid-Western, Christian Science college as compared to a secular college.[132] This latter comparison was undertaken presumably to see if Christian Science's good health habits made up for their rejection of usual medical care. The lack of good medical care apparently overwhelmed their good health habits and religious rituals.

Habit Modification/Addiction Control

Alcoholics Anonymous is the model for many programs for the treatment of addiction. In its twelve-step program it appeals to a higher power for help in breaking the addiction. AA also brings into play other factors, including external supervision, a substitute dependency, and a set of caring relationships. Its wide usage suggests benefit, but I could find no reports of randomized therapeutic trials comparing it with other approaches to addiction control. There is a Secular Organizations for Sobriety (SOS) that is oriented toward nonbelievers or people who don't want to mix their religion and their addiction problems. A randomized trial comparing these would be interesting, but even here, comparative studies might be difficult, because the twelve-step/higher power approach may work better for those coming to treatment with a belief in God and the SOS program might work better for those who don't believe. A very informative discussion of religious and secular approaches to addiction management—with some references—is available on the web.[133]

A major survey of the literature on religion and addiction has been developed.[134] The authors found over 1,350 relevant papers from a sixty-three-year period. They reported that common findings included decreasing substance abuse/use with increasing religiosity and with meditation. Involvement in twelve-step programs seemed also to be protective for persons in "recovery."

Healing

Requests for healing were a part of ancient religions—probably as far back as there are records and beyond. Certainly ancient Egyptian religion included gods who heard the entreaties of their worshipers.[135] The Old Testament records requests for healing, addressed to both the Jewish God and some of his competitors. Asclepius, a Greek god of healing, had shrines in the Mediterranean world before and into the early Christian era. He had been a physician in life then elevated to the Pantheon after death and was thought able to give healing to supplicants. His shrines had many testimonials to the success of this belief.[136] The stories of Jesus in the New Testament include many reports of miraculous healings given in a narrative style that was common to reports of supernatural healing in that era. These are considered by many as convincing proof of his divine mission.

Healing continues to be an important feature of many religions. For instance, both public and private prayers for healing are widespread in the Protestant Christian community. Public healing services are also widely available in the Pentecostal subset of Protestantism and may often be found on religious television programming. The Catholic Christian community has healing shrines and relics. The healing Shrine at Lourdes in France is perhaps the best known of these—visited annually by thousands seeking health.

The history and ubiquity of religious stories of healing are likely based on universal human frailty and illness and our desire for release from that burden. Our need is so great that claims of miracles (mostly healing) have been considered one important proof of the existence of divine power. Only a few days ago, in an attempt to convince me of God's existence, an eighty-five-year-old patient (prior Christian missionary) brought me written stories of two "miraculous healings." These unreferenced stories seemed to be from devotional literature of a few decades ago. Such literature is usually hard to evaluate as often its stories can't be verified, sometimes seem highly exaggerated, and sometimes appear to reflect the natural process of healing.

Several factors about human disease explain much of the public success of such healing traditions—without requiring any actual interventions by the gods. First, many human illnesses are self-limiting and given time, there will be recovery. For instance, many infectious diseases that can be fatal are self-limiting in some patients, and recovery starts in days to weeks. Some infections that are not cured (at least without modern interventions) will have quiescent periods where the disease is inactive and the patient seems well. This may happen in malaria and in tuberculosis. Other diseases may have unpredictable courses. For instance, the central nervous system disorder multiple sclerosis may have periods of remission where the patient almost completely recovers from prior neurological loss, usually for months to years, followed by further episodes of relapse. Thus the natural history of disease is remarkably variable, and unless that history is understood, one may mistake a normal improvement for a miraculous healing.

Second, some human illness is psychosomatic and can be relieved if the victim can be gotten to change their thinking— sometimes subconscious thinking. For instance, a patient may become paralyzed or even blind as a result of some psychic trauma. This is sometimes called a hysterical conversion reaction. A skilled psychotherapist may be able to relieve the problem. In fact, this is one of the illnesses that Freud dealt with in his early work. There is no reason why a supportive and forgiving religious service or ritual might not also relieve these symptoms resulting in an almost magical recovery of function.

Third, and to some degree related, is the observation that expectations have a powerful effect on perceptions, symptoms, and even the course of an illness. This is the explanation of the so-called placebo effect. A sugar pill given with expectation of benefit will find symptomatic relief in substantial numbers of people with pain, itching, depression, etc. An intramuscular injection of placebo may be even more effective than an oral medication. Thus if people enter a healing service expecting to be healed, a substantial number of them will have improvement of symptoms and will report that they have been healed.

Into this mix we must also introduce our human bias to remember success and forget failure. This is emphasized further by the religious leaders in charge of the shrines or services taking care to publicize success and ignore failure. The faithful quickly spread rumors of healing but seldom word of failure. In this setting failure is frequently interpreted as "lack of faith," which of course means that the supplicants enduring failure are not likely to publicize that failure. They may consider the failure to reflect their own lack of confident belief. Few if any people die of chronic illness without prayers for healing being offered by friends or relatives. Some would say this tells us something about the effectiveness of such rituals.

James Randi, a magician by avocation, spent considerable time studying healing in the modern public religious world of North America and reported his findings in a book, *The Faith Healers*. My own take after reading his book is that the successful healers use a combination of misrepresentation, dishonesty, and the placebo effect to get their results. People to be healed often have their disabilities upgraded to a more serious level before healing. Most importantly, however, the healer's achievements seem to depend to a very significant degree on having a credulous audience who truly believe in divine healing. Both the placebo effect and need to publicly demonstrate your faith by your personal healing seem to come into play. We would also note that with the crutches, often piled up by the healed, there are no artificial limbs—this kind of healing doesn't work for everything.

A miracle is often understood as an event that seems to be contrary to the normal operation of nature. This is assumed to be the action of some divine actor and seems to be the point of requests for healing by the gods. David Hume wrote[137] that when something is reported that was truly remarkable and contrary to nature, the report should be examined to see which was more likely: the truth of the report, an error in observation, an error in interpretation, or an error in reporting. He thought that usually reports of miracles consisted of errors in these latter areas. The Committee for the Scientific Investigation of Claims of the Paranormal (CSICOP) has been actively investigating such claims for decades and so far has been able to provide natural explanations for those called to its attention—at least they have not found anything that seemed to demand divine intervention as an explanation. See their journal the *Skeptical Inquirer*.

Intercessory Prayer

The prayer of a righteous man is powerful and effective. —James 4:16 (New International Version)

If prayer is included in a survey of complementary and alternative medicine (CAM) it is found to be the most common form of such therapy. In a Harvard Medical School Study, 35 percent of respondents reported prayer for health concerns and 70 percent of these thought that their prayers were helpful.[138] Prayer may relieve stress and engender positive mood. It may also have a placebo effect as mentioned above. However, most people who use it now or have used it throughout history, within any of a large variety of religions, have expected that prayer would bring the supernatural interventions that they needed. This is about as close to magic as religion gets, but it escapes the label by saying "if it is God's will" even as the sometimes desperate supplicant is sure it must be the will of a good god.

A prayer to God by one party asking for a benefit for a third party is often referred to as intercessory prayer. If the third party is unaware of the request, its success can be studied as a blinded experiment. Francis Galton, one of the father's of statistical analysis, first reported an attempt[139] to study such prayer. He looked for effects of prayer on the longevity of English royalty (regular beneficiaries of public prayer) and clergy (assumed to pray for themselves), on infant mortality (assuming believing parents pray for their children), and success of business enterprises, especially shipping by sea. He found no effects on longevity or infant mortality and reported that the insurance companies believed the chance of shipwreck for missionary ventures was the same as for slave traders.

Early modern attempts to study this phenomenon included two randomized blinded studies of intercessory prayer for patients in cardiac care units, which were both reported as positive by the investigators. These have been reviewed and criticized by Tessman and Tessman[140] who found serious procedural problems with each study. The first study had problems with the blinding, and the second study would not have been judged positive if appropriate adjustments had been made for the multiple statistical comparisons that were used. Thus though publicized as positive, these studies at best left the question unanswered.

In 2007, two meta-analyses appeared, attempting to evaluate the effects of remote prayer on health. Roberts et al.[141] reported that they found ten published trials of the effect of prayer on health involving over seven thousand subjects. They felt the overall results were interesting but inconclusive. One of the smallest trials was reported as showing a higher success rate in "prayed for" *in vitro* fertilization.[142]

The authors of this particular trial report, however, called it "preliminary" in 2001, and I have been unable to find a definitive follow-up report. One of the largest studies showed an increased risk of post-operative complications in patients who knew they were being prayed for but otherwise found no effect of prayer. The second meta-analysis in 2007 reported that "no discernable effects (of intercessory prayer) can be found."[143] The Cochrane Database authors returned to this topic in 2009[144] again with a report of equivocal findings and now with a recommendation that further resources not be invested in the area. They found some positive studies, but the majority were negative, and nothing was positive in meta-analysis. They looked at death, general health, and the risk of readmission to the hospital or the coronary care unit.

Despite the failure to confirm an effect of prayer, the believer can point to our inability to measure either the quality of the prayers offered or the quality of the relationship with the divine nurtured by those praying. The question of whether the correct divine entity was being addressed can also be raised. Additionally, one can ask if the proper rituals were used with the entreaty, the ones required by the addressed divinity. Thus it will never be possible to assert that the prayers of some righteous men are not powerful and answered. Further study will probably shed no additional light on the concern, since there are too many uncertainties. Regardless, the use of prayer is unlikely to be affected by any such studies. We humans are sometimes desperate and have few alternatives that offer hope.

My own personal experience with prayer for healing has been an unsystematic but long series of negative observations. I have not had the good fortune of seeing a patient clearly healed as a result of his own or someone else's prayer. I suspect that most of my seriously ill patients are the objects of prayer, at least by concerned friends, though they usually don't offer to talk about it. A few have told me of specific healing services or events and ask for tests to be done to confirm their healing. One said he had seen Jesus enter the room and touch him—he was especially disappointed. On the other hand, I recently had an elderly patient who rejected therapy for his metastatic cancer. He had a spontaneous regression that gave him almost an extra year of life. I asked him if prayer might explain the tumor improvement, and he denied that possibility.

Summary

People who are religious seem on the average to have better health both mentally and physically. This supports the belief that God's blessings are actively improving the health of his faithful followers. This may be an illusion as it is quite possible that these effects are the results of the religious participants having better social support, better health habits (less tobacco, alcohol, street drugs), better compliance with medical care, less conflict with authority, and more positive expectations for life. At this time we cannot be sure if the details of the beliefs about God, the divine will, or the supernatural have any impact on health—at least in this world. Religions are, however, unique aggregations of beliefs and behaviors, and it is almost impossible to isolate with confidence the effects of one part of the system. It is also possible that respectful belief in the sacred may elevate some parts of human life in ways that are not readily reproduced outside of religious belief.

It has been impossible to demonstrate an effect of prayer for an unaware third party, but this can never prove that prayer doesn't benefit some beneficiaries sometimes. Despite the thousands of papers written, it remains unclear whether an educated person with a healthy lifestyle and good socialization would have any measurable health or longevity benefit from adding a religious belief system to his repertoire. The religious establishment, and many individual believers, some wealthy, are eager to prove that belief in the supernatural is not only important but also "true," so much more research may be forthcoming.

10. Religion and Science and Reason

"There are forces, Lucius, infinitely more powerful than reason and science."
"What are they?" asked Cotta.
"Ignorance and folly."

—From *Thais* by Anatole France

Throughout most of human history, religion and science have not been in conflict. In the ancient Greek and Roman worlds the gods did not usually make ethical or exclusive demands. In late classical times, the Epicureans did not believe that the gods had anything to do with men, and the Stoics believed that there was a great power or spirit but no personal god. In their early centuries, Christianity, Islam, and the "wheel-of-life" religions (Hindu, Buddhist, and Jain) had little reason to conflict with any science. Though there clearly was some development of science in the classical Greek and Roman world, it seemed to have little if any impact on the life of the common man. A local Roman governor, Pliny the Younger, wrote to Emperor Trajan that he had examined some Christians[145] and found only "squalid superstition," so perhaps highly educated people even then had difficulties with some religious claims. Certainly his naturalist uncle, Pliny the Elder, whom he admired, had written against a belief in any gods.[146] Science as we know it today seems to have started with Galileo and Newton in the seventeenth century. Galileo was a religious man who had some conflict with religious authority. Newton spent huge amounts of his energy in studying Biblical prophecy and thought of his science as revealing how God worked. Religions have founded great universities where science is encouraged in both Europe and North America. The natural world has also been characterized in Christian societies as God's "second book," and studying it has been and is thought an important way of learning about God.

Yet we have a common current perception that religion and science are often in some form of conflict. The greatest such conflict of the last century, at least in North America, was related to evolutionary biology and the origins of man. Perhaps the second most divisive conflict of this time period was about the status of the embryo—a conflict at least partly related to definitions and meanings—soul versus mind. Is the mind an expression of a functioning always developing brain or is it some essence provided by a divine act intervening in biology?

As I have looked at religion and science, it has seemed to me that religion must at some critical point depend on an appeal to the emotions—perhaps to multiple emotional needs of the human. Science appears to be dependent on a rational analysis of the world, on the predictive success of that rational analysis, and on the beauty and simplicity of its explanations.

The Criteria of Belief

Some have characterized all religious beliefs as essentially irrational.[147] Though possibly correct in some limited way, this seems too easy a dismissal of a widespread human phenomena, one that appeals to at least a majority of human minds. If you ask a religious believer if he is rational or irrational, you would surely hear that he is rational. In fact, it might be said that all humans are, at least on some level, involved in a struggle to be rational. The difference between the believer and the unbeliever, and between believers in different religious traditions, does not seem to revolve around who is behaving rationally and who is not. It seems to revolve most centrally around the selection of the criteria for belief. Science has spent the last few centuries refining its criteria of belief. It still gets wrong answers, at least temporarily, still has questions it can't answer and still offers rationally argued speculations that are constantly evolving—such as those about the history of the universe. As far as I can tell, religion has not been in the business of refining its criteria of belief. Here I will attempt to examine the differences in criteria for belief in these two systems.

Science seeks to understand the world by examining it. A scientist gathers observational facts and then analyzes them rationally to the best of her ability. She operates with the assumption that there are some consistent discoverable rules about how the world works. She hopes to create some understanding that can eventually be shared with others and that may allow one to cure a disease or send a rocket to Mars or simply satisfy a personal curiosity about some aspect of nature. In the modern world, scientific research has been a universalizing force in that there is one science based on publicly verifiable observations and almost unaffected by religion or culture. The best scientific work is published in respected journals, usually European or North American, and reviewed critically by a worldwide audience. In a typical week, I may review articles about the management of a disease written by medical scientists in any of a long list of countries, including but not limited to Sweden, England, Russia, China, France, Japan, Belgium, or America. Science remains a very human activity—subject to errors, delusions, and misinterpretations—as has been noted in the criticisms of science given by the post-modernists and some feminists.[148] It is, however, largely self-correcting over time, as it continues to explore that reality available to human investigation.

The criteria for religious belief appear to be much different. Simple observation of how the world works suggests that acculturation is the most powerful factor in determining religious preference. If your parents and your grandparents hold a belief system and teach it to you as a child, in a setting in which your peers also share these beliefs, it seems very likely you will always follow that system and die there. Looking at the world, this seems true for 99 percent or more of us. Camus wrote, "We were Catholic like we were French, we never thought of it."[149] Of course, within some parts of Islam the barbaric mandate to kill anyone who leaves the faith tries to guarantee this lifetime faith.

When a religion must compete with other religions it usually seeks to draw on supplemental resources to support the acculturation. One source of validation for religious belief is documents (often ancient) whose origins are shrouded in some mystery. The Bible, the Qur'an, the Vedas and Upanishads, and even the Book of Mormon are some examples. When one tries to systematically treat these as divine messages, one must cope with uncertainty in source, plasticity of human language, conflict in visions—often within the documents if they are long and complex—and finally the evolution of human language since the original composition. The result is far more uncertainty than the faithful can accept. The proliferation of Bible-based Protestant sects within Christianity is an example of the uncertainty of interpretation—and of the insistence on certainty.

Another source of religious validation or belief confirmation is mystical experience (see chapter 11 on the sources of religion). These are private experiences outside our normal rational conscious state and may include dreams, visions, trances, talking in "tongues," etc. These have from antiquity been interpreted as ways that the supernatural interacts with the human. Luke Timothy Johnson has provided a brief survey of such experiences[1] for the Greco-Roman world in which Christianity developed. Ann Taves has written about this in the Protestant tradition during the eighteenth and nineteenth centuries in England and North America.[150] A human explanation of this type of experience and of the unconscious has been provided by Ellenberger[151] in his discussion of the development of psychotherapy. A completely human explanation seems quite believable, but these experiences are very powerful and may be life altering for those having them.[152] The Pentecostal tradition within Protestantism is one example of the current vibrant life of this approach to belief and its validation.

A less dramatic but similarly private validation of religious belief is also found in more traditional Christianity. It seems to consist of a deep sense of happiness and satisfaction framed by events that relate it to the religion such as church services. For example, I have a traditional Seventh-day Adventist friend who says that she knows that God exists because he has spoken to her in her heart, and this is an experience that gives her confidence. Many members take this feeling as proof that God accepts their life and beliefs. They experience it as a validation of God's existence and of their being "right with him."

Thus confident religious belief depends on a variety of sources, none of which would seem to stand up under the type of public scrutiny that is applied to the world of science—or even investigative journalism. Some have insisted and continue to insist that faith and reason are both valid ways of obtaining truth or knowledge.[153] Though faith is widely used as a justification for belief, I find no evidence that it can be a reliable source for truth or knowledge about our world. Both religions and ideologies such as Fascism have demanded it of their followers.[154] This itself might be little problem if the beliefs were confined to a private world, but when they are pushed into the public arena, held confidently, and there is then an attempt to universalize them, trouble seems inevitable.

The Reasons that Religious Beliefs Cannot Be Examined Critically

In activities such as business, farming, or investing, or even just going about our daily lives, we find that if we are told something that seems very improbable—as judged on the basis of our prior experiences—it is more likely to be an error of observation, interpretation or reporting than it is to be a truly rare and anomalous event. For instance, if we are told by e-mail or word of mouth, that investing our money in a certain "penny stock" will get a 100-fold return in six months, we usually ignore the helpful advice—or we would become quite poor. Thus when we come to religion, it seems surprising that we do not have the same demands for evidence. In fact, in the Christian tradition, someone who demands evidence is often referred to as a "Doubting Thomas." Religions seem to systematically stigmatize those who require proof. As an example note how some versions of Christianity exalt those such as Abraham who make Kierkegaard's "leap of faith." Since requiring evidence and being skeptical are ways that successful people usually cope with the world, one asks how religion can escape this burden.

Several factors may have contributed to the development of what is, for most religions, a taboo against both skepticism and humor concerning the "truths" of the tradition. If religion substitutes for the lost tribe that our ancestors evolved in for thousands, even millions of years—then religion occupies a very special place. If so, it can demand that its teachings are protected by unique strictures and taboos. To question the teachings is an act of disloyalty to the group. Such disloyalty can be dealt with harshly, and questions about truth are actually, in practice, irrelevant.

Another related point is that religious truths are neither obvious nor testable, and in fact to a skeptical questioner, they seem quite vulnerable. The weakness of the religious position may be best defended by a refusal to even debate with anyone who is not already sympathetic with the underlying claims. In my experience, this position has been supported by asserting the weakness of human reason and the likelihood of men being easily deceived by those—men or devils—questioning religious "truth." The only safe solution is portrayed as using your "faith" in what you already "know" to be true, and in rejecting the questioning. A vast majority of believers, inculcated in childhood with this system for defending their faith, remain loyal. Time has proven it successful for most traditions. It is also probably true that a form of social proof is often in play as the individual is encouraged in his religious beliefs by the fact that his ancestors, family, and friends all share the beliefs.

It is also of note that books of religious humor are in rather short supply. God jokes may be told on the golf course or on late night TV, but you don't usually hear them in church services, especially about the central religious myth. In my own limited experience, I have found deeply religious and believing Christians to have almost no tolerance for comic material that may involve God or the Bible. The recent Supreme Court decision supporting suspension of a student for holding a sign (off school property) saying "BONG HITS 4 JESUS" is perhaps further demonstration of limited humor in this area. Judged by the reaction to cartoons of Mohammed in a Danish newspaper in 2005, the Muslim world is also deeply hostile to humor about its religious icons. The reasons for this may be related to the observation that using humor about a subject tends to make it more life-size and human. It detracts from the awe and fear that are probably necessary for the religious traditions to function most forcefully in organizing, controlling, and giving significance to human life.

The Religious Intellectual Quest

That which science refuses to grant to religion is not its right to exist, but its right to dogmatize upon the nature of things and the special competence which it claims for itself for knowing man and the world. As a matter of fact, it does not know itself. It does not even know what it is made of nor to what need it answers.

> —Emile Durkheim in *The Elementary Forms of the Religious Life*

Religion also involves an intellectual quest for some individuals. It appears to me that there are at least two strands of this religious quest. One is exemplified by monks, nuns, and holy men who spend their lives on the inward journey, trying to change the self to be like God or to be "enlightened" or some equivalent. The goal is not to change the world but to become more like Jesus, Buddha, or some other figure deserving emulation. The monastic tradition of Christianity and of Buddhism and the Hindu and Jain holy men give examples of this struggle that may completely occupy a life. The lay believer is also adjured to spend at least some of his time on the same journey. The journey is apparently quite satisfying for the individual. Sometimes its effects are only private, but practitioners such as Mohandas Gandhi and Mother Theresa have certainly done things to try to make the world better for other humans.

The other religious quest is that of the theologian who spends his life reorganizing and rationalizing the tradition and working on its interface with the rest of human knowledge. Someone critical might call it a word game (as in Wittgenstein), but it does seem very important in the tradition of an institutional church. For instance, it is important in helping the religion maintain credibility with an educated class of constituents who provide its leadership and have much to do with its place in the world of human affairs. Some theologians may be quite creative in trying to reconcile the teachings of their tradition with the changing worldviews of a modern, science-based society. They are limited by the claimed core beliefs of the tradition and by the fact that if they are thought to have strayed too far from these, their work is likely to be ignored or denigrated.

Most religions do not spend much time examining their fundamental beliefs about the supernatural (God, Immortality ...). These are givens and are not offered in ways that can be readily subjected to testing. Within the fundamentalist strands of most religions (at least Christian, Islamic, and Jewish), there seems especially little interest in such inquiry. For a member of such a group to question or wish to debate the beliefs may be considered an act of heresy rather than an open mind seeking truth. To question is to raise uncertainty about the reality of the central myth that gives the religion its power in the world. If you question its myth, you question the very role of any religion in controlling the world. These untestable beliefs are what separates one religion from another and are one reason we can have many religions and only one science.

How one understands one's fundamental beliefs and relates them to the world may however have some plasticity and certainly theologians from St. Augustine to Paul Tillich have done much to change Christianity's understanding of itself and its key doctrines—at least for some of its sub-brands. In our current world, for example, theologians and church members must deal with strands of Christian belief that hold that the Biblical creation and flood stories are literal and reliable stories of historical events, or in other venues an understanding that these stories are remnants of ancient narratives, probably mythic, told by our ancestors to explain their world. The latter interpretation would suggest no need for conflict with any earth or biologic sciences. The role of authority and education or specialization also comes into play in these interpretation controversies.

Another observation is that religions generally spend very little time actually trying to understand how they function in controlling the human world. Many thinkers have tried to investigate the role of religious systems such as sociologists (Durkheim, Weber, and Stark come to mind, followed by many others) and political scientists/philosophers such as Hume and Marx. Religions themselves have been notably absent from sponsoring such studies, maybe because they look on such work as "breaking the spell" (to quote Daniel Dennett[155]) they have over their believers. Some religions (at least some Christian and Muslim groups) are also unable to conceive of themselves as part of a community of organizations carrying on the same or very similar work in the human world. They seem only to think of themselves as unique entities vying to convince the world of their absolute and saving "truth." In this situation, each one has little reason to study anything beyond itself. Other religions, especially in the Protestant Christian world have sought to be part of a wider community—for example in founding and supporting the World Council of Churches.

Paradox in Religion and Science

It is certain because it is impossible

—Tertullian, *De Carne Christi*

Science has some paradoxes, such as the particle-wave duality of matter of very small particle size, but careful evaluation suggests that this paradox is related to our attempts to model the situation. The particles are unaware of our problems and behave in predictable ways in specific situations. Generally scientists survive and thrive by resolving inconsistencies and paradoxes. When these are unresolved, it is thought that a problem needs more effort and maybe new ideas. Much remains to be understood in science, but it glories in resolving its paradoxes and opening up new understandings.

Religion, since it requires at some point a step beyond clear public evidence, seems to be more open to leaving paradoxes unresolved. For instance, Christianity has trifurcated its god while still claiming to be a monotheism. The Jews and the Muslims have stayed with claims of one god. At times the Christians have thought that failure to share their Trinitarian belief justified a charge of heresy. All these Abrahamic traditions add other supernatural figures, including angels and an evil or satanic figure. They have also proposed that God made us, loves us, and wants the best for us, so we should love and obey him with gratitude. Then they turn around and offer us a selfish reason for loving and obeying God—it will get us a chance to eternally share some heaven or utopia. Otherwise, we will be going to a hell for the damned. Buddhism claims there is no self, then offers the eight-fold way to help this no self escape the sorrows of rebirth on the wheel-of- life. Authority is the source of such beliefs, and they are passed on—not to be questioned. One is supposed to try to understand, but to recognize one's limited finite human capacity and believe— even if it doesn't make sense. It is a test of being a "true believer" that you believe things that don't make sense to you initially. You overcome this by repetitive work on your belief until you achieve the "peace that passeth understanding," an experience confirming your belief.

The anthropologists have made extensive studies of cultural practices, some of which may apply here. The aspect that I find particularly interesting has been summarized as a rule of thumb by Steven Pinker[156] and I will borrow. When a society (advanced or primitive) has a cultural practice that seems bizarre to us (outsiders), the practice may serve to manipulate "intuitive biology to enhance feelings of communality." This at least supports the observation that some of the social power of religions may come from the sharing of highly improbable beliefs.

Attempts to Resolve the Conflicts of Religion and Science

There are several ways that one might think of resolving the disputes or disagreements of religion and science. The possibilities include giving science precedence when it has data and theory (not just light speculation) that bear on a religious claim, giving religion precedence when it disagrees even with well-tested science, and finally making a division and saying that they deal with separate human concerns.

Separate Magisteria

Stephen J Gould in his book *Rocks of Ages*[157] has taken the latter course. He proposed that there are separate realms of authority for religion and science and that there doesn't need to be any conflict between them if they confine themselves to the appropriate roles. He thinks religion is concerned with what ought to be (for instance with ethics) while science is concerned with what is—with the facts of the world. This would appear to be a hopeful political commentary with limited chance for either side to be satisfied. Religion and science may be in conflict about human nature, the interpretation of human experience, and the understanding of the geologic, archeological, and historical record. As mentioned above, the question of origins has been important and a source of conflict because of overlapping claims: biological evolution versus special supernatural creation. Time and the development of molecular biology have increasingly made evolution the fundamental explanatory paradigm for creating a rationally organized and understandable biological world. This has been rejected by the fundamentalist or right-wing Christian groups who offer alternatives based largely on the Biblical book of Genesis, without equivalent explanatory power for the current natural world or for the buried records of the past.

Another public conflict that might be interpreted as between science and religion has been fueled by the availability of legal abortion in the United States. Many religious groups claim that God puts a soul in place at conception, which makes this embryo immediately a full person. This claim ignores all the biological and psychological development and the great risks and uncertainty that stand between the potential of an embryo and its realization in a developed human being. This religious belief, which seems to conflict with science and reason, nevertheless fuels tremendous anger and violence as people seek to control those who don't share their beliefs by denying them the possibility of having or providing an abortion—of damaging an embryo. Thus the claims of "separate Magisteria" have not been satisfying, or helpful, for some problems and some religious groups. Conflict persists in one case because of an insistence on interpreting ancient mythology as literal history and in another case because of the belief in a nonmaterial soul that represents the essence of a human personality and is actively supplied by a deity for each person.

If religious claims were confined to metaphysics, to what might happen in some other place, or at some other time, where science has no reach—then science could go on without commentary on the religious enterprise and the idea of "separate magisteria" might seem a reasonable solution. Even for such religions, however, reason might rear its unwelcome head by providing a commentary on the criteria of belief.[158] This commentary may be unwelcome because the faithful have elevated the belief system and its documents to be the very words of an infinite god, holy and immutable. Thus science and reason will frequently have a commentary on religious belief that is unwelcome for some religious leaders and their followers.

Religion Trumps Science

For some fundamentalist Christian groups this has become an accepted solution. They believe that where science suggests their religious traditions are wrong, science itself is mistaken. They dedicate money to "creation research," publish books about alternate interpretations of the geologic record, and build museums in honor of their interpretation. The creation and flood stories of Biblical Genesis are given absolute authority versus scores of other creation and flood myths in the traditions of the world. Their rejection of science has so far gotten little traction outside the fundamentalist Christian world, but the related "Intelligent Design" movement has gotten substantial attention in the public media. It is my understanding that so far no unique scientific contribution has come from the "Intelligent Design" perspective.[159]

These groups often insist on Biblical inerrancy thus making the Genesis record history instead of the almost certain mixture of myth and history usually found in such ancient documents. They have made a short earth history, with a special divine creation, an important part of their central religious myth and are trapped by their interpretation, even as science recreates, probably irrevocably, our understanding of the past. Most of them accept science in other areas and possibly their attitudes towards geology and paleontology may change someday—but most likely only over generations.

Science Trumps Religion

This school of resolution would say that when science and religion seem irrevocably in conflict, religion must revisit its central myths and find at least some plasticity there. This can lead to new interpretations that may remove the conflict and the possible embarrassment to religious belief. In fact this has been done—at least in the Christian world—in coming to terms with the structure of our solar system. Also many Christian groups have revised their interpretation of Genesis, thus resolving their conflicts with science over evolutionary and geologic history. By evolving its belief systems, religion can defuse its disagreements with science, but sometimes it takes several generations to get the newer systems to be widely accepted. Galileo's "errors," his conflict with authority, took centuries to be forgiven. Sixteen hundred years ago St. Augustine advised Christianity not to be in conflict with science—I think still good advice.[160]

E. O. Wilson, the sociobiologist, sees an eventual resolution favoring science because scientific materialism will be able "to explain traditional religion, its chief competitor, as a wholly material phenomenon."[161] Wilson wisely notes, however, that though science may explain religion, the explanation will not destroy religion. The emotional power of religion is such that its intellectual defeat will not emasculate it in the minds of many or even most of its believers, for those beliefs were neither formed nor sustained by an appeal to rational understanding.

Conclusions

The illusion here is that good science and "true" religion are never really in conflict. The study of nature presumably reveals nature's god—that god being the same one whose existence and authority are taught by the Abrahamic traditions. Therefore, there can be no conflict between these two sources of knowledge about God—if only they are correctly studied and understood. The reality is that science is about the facts of the world. Religions are ideological tools honed over thousands of years to fill a variety of real and urgent human needs. When created, the religions were not in any obvious conflict with the known facts of the world, except for the unprovable but powerful postulate of the supernatural. Our changing understanding of the facts of the world has put varying degrees of pressure on the religious traditions, and their coping is evolving. Science finds order in the universe, but it doesn't address the possibility of an all-powerful, all-knowing, and loving being at the center directing traffic. A flood of books in recent years have offered rational arguments against such a God, and I won't directly enter that battle.

In my mind, both religion and science are powerful human tools, and both have been used for terrible evil and also for great good. They are however rather different activities—perhaps unavoidably in conflict at times. Success in science can usually be judged objectively, publicly, and by most interested observers, while success on the inward religious quest is largely private and personal, and success on the theological quest is judged by other practitioners of the tradition and by institutional leadership. This is not in any way meant to denigrate religion, which is central to all human civilization but to emphasize how different it is from science—as an intellectual quest.

It takes considerable effort to learn something like the scientific criteria for belief. It doesn't require indoctrination at the preschool level, but seems to require intense educational efforts, especially at the college and graduate level. Having mastered these and become employed in some way in the scientific enterprise seems to make one less likely to be a religious believer. As mentioned previously (see the section on religion and educational factors in the chapter Religion and Culture), scientists are less likely to be believers than are nonscientists at least among US citizens. The most elite scientists are even less likely to be believers in a personal god. This suggests that applying the rules of evidence used in science tends to make some people question the claims of religion. On the other hand, I have been acquainted with scientists employed in religious institutions who claimed that they had separate ways of thinking about their religious beliefs and about their scientific work. For them, this seemed to be a compartmentalization that allowed some degree of comfort in both areas—a solution that does not satisfy all of us.

Science is the most successful endeavor our species has ever undertaken. Starting with the seventeenth century, science as we now know it—with its practical expression engineering—has become increasingly more important in human life. In fact, the drastic changes in the circumstances of our lives in the last two centuries, as a result of evolving science, are more dramatic in speed and degree than anything prior. Probably the greatest previous change in human life had been the Neolithic revolution, which brought agriculture and urban civilization. This required a few thousand years and occurred at different times in different places. The changes brought by modern science already affect to some degree most inhabitants of the earth and a more complete spread is rapidly ongoing. Though the pessimists downplay science—the optimists see a future with almost unlimited positive changes in both the quality and duration of human life as a direct result of scientific development. It would seem that, in the long run, a successful religion must accommodate science, its methods, and its discoveries. It is at least a hope but will likely take a long time, maybe centuries. One wishes that it happen without some overwhelming human catastrophe. Religious fanaticism in a nuclear age will always be a risk.

11. Possible Sources and Shaping Factors for Religion

O my brothers, God exists. There is a soul at the center of nature and over the will of every man, so that none of us can wrong the universe.

—Ralph Waldo Emerson, *Essays: First Series*

An honest God is the noblest work of man.

—Robert Ingersoll, *The Gods*

We do not know when our human ancestors first told stories about the supernatural. Human artifacts from the preliterate past suggest that such systems were widespread, thousands of years before our first written records. This is strongly suggested, both by burial artifacts and tomb construction. Grave goods started to appear, along with unequivocal attempts at careful burial as long as 45,000 years ago, and maybe earlier.[162] Tomb complexes became important burial sites, at least for the elite members of some communities. Some of these religious belief systems seem to have held sway for long periods of time. For instance, the Megalithic tradition in Western Europe goes back to the fifth millennium BCE and continued well into the third and at least at one site into the second millennium BCE—for more than two thousand years.[163] Avebury (Stonehenge is part of this complex) in England and Carnac in Brittany are two of the important sites for this tradition. These seem to be part of a religious ritual system without written texts but leaving extensive tomb complexes and arrays of erect stone monuments in circles or rows.

With the appearance of writing, we find records of the gods included in our earliest documents. The Epic of Gilgamesh has the gods on display, as do ancient Egyptian records. The *Iliad* and the *Odyssey* of Homer are filled with the activities of supernatural beings—who seem almost human in their ambitions. The most ancient Indian Sanskrit records are the *Vedas*—a collection of religious documents. If there is anything one might learn from this, it would seem to be that civilization needs religion, or something a great deal like it, to thrive. Some details must be there to fill universal human needs and therefore present in some form in most traditions while other features are highly variable possibly because they address secondary needs or particular cultural concerns or histories.

Since religion of some form seems to be very ancient in human history, it is likely that all current religions found fertile soil when they first started, as they built on pre-existing beliefs in the supernatural. Daniel Dennett, in his study of the evolutionary origins of religion[164] outlines how divination may have originated and takes this as the first step down the road to religion as we know it. My own belief is that religion arises in the dissociative experiences of mysticism—especially the belief that one is hearing the voice of God or an angel and even seeing the supernatural. Once there is belief in a power above and unconstrained by nature (God), then his or her duties, powers, and especially ways of being influenced would tend to proliferate. In historic time, new religions have frequently come as refinements of older traditions or at least borrowed major pieces of older traditions. For example, Christianity was built on the Jewish tradition, and Buddhism was built on an older Hindu tradition. Mohammed appears to have borrowed substantial pieces from both the Jewish and the Christian traditions in creating the Qur'an and the Muslim tradition.

We do have written records from the followers of Gautama (Buddha), Jesus, and Mohammed, and these may give us some insight into the possible factors and processes in the development of a successful, powerful, contemporary religious movement. These include the canonization, after the death of the prophetic figure, of a body of literature giving this figure divine or magical powers or direct contact with those powers. This canon also includes a variously rational body of teachings about the duties of men toward the divine power, toward themselves, and toward other men, especially believers. This body of literature was almost always created by those with a deep interest in the widespread acceptance of the particular religious tradition. Though the followers received this literature as divine instructions delivered through special servants or prophets, there are good reasons to think that many human factors were in play. These may explain what happened, without necessarily suggesting dishonesty on the part of any of the human agents.

Some Reasons to Consider Natural Origins for Religion

Observations of both the universality and diversity of religious belief have some possible implications for understanding the sources of such beliefs. Looking, on a worldwide basis and over a long span of time, the claim that there is one true religion and that all the others are false seems to require a great deal of hubris—and perhaps aggressive acculturation. This has, of course, not restrained the claim. At this time, Christianity seems somewhat more successful, but at times in the past both Islamic and Confucian societies seemed more favored. An extraterrestrial observer not acculturated to any of the world's religious systems would probably consider it somewhat humorous to claim one system is divine and the rest are false rivals or degraded copies.

Those reared within a religious tradition, which is most people in the world, are often acculturated to believe that their family or group has the only "true" religion—that all other religious systems are false and morally inferior. *Only as we get older and have more experience of the world do we realize the tremendous asymmetry that such ethnocentricity requires. It is, in essence, the assumption that the other people in the world who do not share our beliefs are naively, stupidly, or maliciously resistant to "our truth," the "only real truth." The well -intentioned and honest people of the world are thought largely or exclusively confined to "our group."* Outsiders must be converted or demonized. Without this belief the system loses much of its power to unite and demarcate an "in group" loyal to its fellow believers and fearful of becoming enmeshed in the larger, evil, and frightening world of sinful outsiders. Some of the exclusivity problems that come with this belief structuring were addressed in the section on ethics.

In a further attempt to understand the diversity of human religion, one might look at three possible explanatory schemes. First, there may be one god—who delights in diversity—and has founded many religions without particularly favoring one. Second, one might think that there are many different gods, and each has founded a religious system according to his needs and wishes. Third, it might be that religions are products of the human mind applying its powerful imagination and rational faculties to the complex world in which it is embedded. Religious thought and behavior might have given an evolutionary survival advantage that supported the development of a biological propensity for religious belief—of course this is a speculation but a not unreasonable one. Regardless of any biological predisposition we have over millennia, in a process that might be called "cultural evolution," created the modern religious world. Religions have survived and thrived because they filled many human needs both social and individual. This latter, naturalistic hypothesis seems more plausible to some observers of the human situation, and it in no way detracts from the power, importance, and usefulness of religion. It does make obvious the often embarrassing possibilities for the corruption and abuse of religion. It also raises the hope that by understanding the needs that religions serve and their limitations, the future may be innovative and not just a return to a fractious fundamentalist dream of the past.

The details of an evolutionary origin for religion may not be important to many people, but accepting the general possibility of a natural origin seems necessary to understand our world. My goal here is to put on display many of those natural human mechanisms, which could be operative. Looking at these may provide a form of plausibility argument for the non-supernatural origins of religious systems. For the interested reader Daniel Dennett and Loyal Rue have both recently published excellent books offering evolutionary explanations for religion with their own best guesses at the particular scenario that got the wheel of supernatural belief turning. My own intuition is that dissociative or mystical experience played and plays a very important role in the initiation of most if not all religions.

Do We Have a Biological Tendency to Religious Belief?

Thou hast made us for Thyself and our hearts are restless till they rest in Thee.

—Saint Augustine, *Confessions* (1.1.1)

Many Christians seem very confident that you can't become a good, well-rounded, moral, and admirable human being without a belief in God, particularly the Christian God. Some offer this view at every opportunity and even claim that a "god belief" of *any* kind is better than atheism. With considerable effort and almost no supporting evidence, they have given atheism such a bad name that it is considered a public liability. In effect, those who hold a religious position, especially of leadership, congratulate each other that they are better than the skeptics, agnostics, and atheists—almost as propaganda to discourage any who might want to seriously examine the logical positions of the nonbelievers. In fact, one might say that atheists have the public image that religious fundamentalists deserve. Perhaps this demonization of atheists has worked so well because, indeed, we have a natural proclivity toward belief in powerful, personal, supernatural forces—with kind intentions toward us and our world.

Several facts suggest that the ability to believe in a good and caring "higher power" may be an innate property of human minds— one just waiting to be developed as we are acculturated. This system would be, somewhat like linguistic ability, relatively plastic when we are very young and growing more fixed as we mature. Such a tendency would explain the ubiquity of religion and the fact that only a very small minority of adults actually make major changes in their religious belief systems. My own experience is that when an adult becomes disillusioned with his religious tradition, he seldom develops an enduring attachment to a markedly different tradition. He may stay culturally near his old tradition, move to another similar tradition, or temporarily try something more avant-garde. For example Joseph Campbell, the famous scholar of myth, moved from Catholicism to Eastern religions—and back to Catholicism.[165] Les Payne, the Pulitzer Prize–winning journalist, returned to the Baptist Church after forty years of exploring secular and other spiritual world views.[166] The Mennonite and Hutterite customs of having young men go out and experience the larger world continues because these young men usually do not feel at home in that larger world, so eventually a large fraction voluntarily return to the community.

One would expect that this property of minds would start out as an eager belief in a caring and well-intentioned, higher power that was poorly defined in the child's mind. It is probably focused on the parent, at least initially. Over time the child is introduced to the idea of a godlike caring figure (Jesus, a saint, an ancestor, a bodhisattva). This new power figure offers another level of support and control—even if possibly imaginary. Such a figure may allow new confidence and optimism in facing the world. In fact the adaptive power that might explain the evolutionary success of this mental tendency would be its ability to support the natural human optimism or hope that allows us to go forward in the face of a hard life—even personal or community disaster—expecting things will get better if we keep trying and maintain our trust in our divine confidant.

The evolutionary success of this natural belief system would say nothing about its epistemic truth—actual facticity—but a great deal about its practical utility in a world such as that inhabited by our ancient biologic ancestors. It does not help us at all in deciding whether some god made us this way or the system evolved. Probably throughout the past some people, often privately, have found reason and the facts of the world in conflict with the communities' religious belief. Of tribal societies Huston Smith[167] says "the village atheist still turns up." In the modern era with more education, more time for reflection, and a greater understanding of the facts of the world, it is hardly surprising that there is some increase in the minority who question religion. However, the strength of the inbuilt urge and the enduring human need for refuge tends to overwhelm reason and science for most of us.

This same need or desire for a powerful caring figure may underlie the success of messianic politicians who promise utopia on earth for their followers. Hitler, Mussolini, Castro, Mao, and others came to power with violence—and continued that violence against any opposition. They, however, promised a form of earthly paradise for the common man, and eventually, if only temporarily, enjoyed durable and wide acceptance from the general public within their political entities. Even in our democracy there seems to be a tendency in times of stress to want an able, confident leader and to give him almost unrestrained power—as though he were a god. Julius Caesar's popularity in Rome and the growing expectations and power of the American presidency may be examples of this tendency to look for a savior; and finding one willing, to exalt that leader in unrealistic ways—to make this person superhuman.

Common Individual Experiences of the World

I hope for heaven, since the stars endure
And bring such tidings as our fathers had.

—George Santayana, *Sonnet 29*

There are a number of personal tendencies or common experiences of individuals that may contribute to the development or acceptance of religious ideas, or at least be sources of support for the religious impulse. In this section, I will attempt to review three such areas.

The Biologic and Psychologic Drives for Life and Immortality

One factor that may affect the widespread acceptance of religious ideas is the observation that, though most of us know we are mortals, we innately feel that we should be able to go on living indefinitely. This may partly come from our innate drive to avoid death—one shared with all living things. Most non-moribund humans do not think that there is ever a now when it is appropriate to die, as evidenced by the famous response to the question "Who would want to live to be ninety-five?" the answer being "Most ninety-four-year-olds." We are almost unable to think of the world without ourselves in it. Freud incorporated the idea of a life instinct into his psychoanalytic theory using the ancient Greek term *Eros*. Eros was a god of creativity, love, and sexuality—all involved in the life force.

We have never experienced non-existence, can't until we die, and are not even sure there is experience there. Therefore imagining it is very hard. Instead our evolutionary heritage seems to be that we come to the world with some sort of belief in a psychological continuity at death. Children three to five years old offer such a continuity analysis even more often than older children. These same young children seem to understand the end of biologic life and the lack of need for food and water after death. Those who study this say that young children readily hold these two somewhat conflicting concepts.[168] Thus our beliefs in some form of mental continuity after death probably don't originate with specific religions, though they are usually supported there.

We know that there is no immortality here, in our human world, so the only possible immortality is in some other place or time. It is true that much effort has been spent in many cultures creating elaborate burial monuments and providing expensive burial goods—apparently presuming that the dead continue their existence, in some place, where such things have meaning.[169] What little I know of ancient religion suggests that, in these cultures, the continuation was thought to be under the earth or in the heavens. Hope is often more powerful than reason, and this plus our innate mental tendencies may make us especially vulnerable to supernatural religious belief. Most religious traditions teach that we weren't made for this world, that our existence here is just a sort of "getting ready" for that other place. Thus religion encourages our innate beliefs and gets reciprocal support from doing this.

The Tendency to Anthropomorphize and Rationalize

We humans readily assign human personalities, names, and purposes to the rest of the animate world and even the plant and inanimate world. We find this a widespread and entertaining habit today. Our ancestors who knew almost nothing about nervous systems and neurophysiology probably took this much more seriously. From such practices, it seems rather likely that a form of animism might easily evolve with rivers, mountains, and animals given powers and purposes and accepting supplications and sacrifices for favors. This is promoted by a part of the human mind that functions as an "agency detection device" that at a subconscious level is always scanning for evidence of agency in the world around us. For our own safety, this system is very sensitive and leads to a lot of false alarms that are usually innocuous—as it seeks to protect us from dangerous agents. This may be the system that makes us so comfortable with anthropomorphizing.[170]

The rational human animal will always be attempting to improve its understanding and make its system more believable. One direction this takes is the desire to see some unity behind everything. We thus find that at least some apparently polytheistic systems came to think of one high god behind all. The Hindus have many gods such as Vishnu and Shiva, but behind all is Brahman, the ultimate single principle that animates everything in the apparent world. The Yoruba of West Africa have a very distant high god and supreme force, Olorun, to whom they must answer after death.[171] Meanwhile, they may sacrifice or appeal to lesser entities such as their ancestors. Another example from the ancient Greek world can be found in Plutarch's life of Pelopidas, where some of his military officers in rejecting a suggestion of the need to sacrifice a virgin say "that typhons and giants did not preside over the world, but the general father of gods and men."[172]

Awe and Natural Piety

Most humans are at least at some time in their lives deeply impressed by the beauty, vastness, and complexity of the universe, and our small piece of it. From this may come a certain natural humility and a respect for the quiet power of a nature that seems to contain something divine. This was especially expressed in American Transcendentalism, as typified by its most noted exponents, Emerson and Thoreau. It is probably easier to think that someone must have made all this as part of a design than to believe that it all evolved, over a long time, from the operation of a few basic laws controlling the interaction of energy, matter, and space. It thus seems reasonable to many people that some designer, some awesome mind or consciousness, lies behind everything. The "Intelligent Design" movement of our day can be considered one expression of this.

This sort of evidence is not specific in what type of god it supports. It could support a Deist type god who set it all running and has no more concern with the show that he has started. Of course, those who believe in a kind, all-powerful, and all-knowing god find this evidence is compatible with their position, though perhaps weak support. This belief in the universe as good, beautiful, and divine does not address or explain the natural and man-made catastrophes that plague human life. It has no answer to the injustices that have haunted the more sensitive observers of the human scene for thousands of years. Now probably just as thousands of years ago, it has a wonderful spell-binding power on a moonlight night or at sunrise or at sunset.

Cognitive Factors Shaping and Supporting Religion

As someone might say, brains are strange and wonderful things, making minds with remarkable complexities. There was a time in the past when most educated Western people thought that there was a soul—provided supernaturally—and this was what identified you, held your thoughts, and traveled on after you died. The Enlightenment followed by the rise of modern science has made this seem an unlikely belief. My own lifetime has seen great advances in the understanding of the structure and function of the brain and the mind, and I believe that in another fifty to one hundred years, we will see almost unbelievable changes in our understanding of who and what we are—and how our brains make us. Most likely our understanding of religion will be forever altered by these new insights. There are, however, some things that we know about minds that partially explain how they deal with religious ideas.

The Ubiquity of Theory

Any sufficiently advanced technology is indistinguishable from magic.
                                                                    —Arthur C. Clark

Child psychologists have observed that children are "naïve theorists" in the sense that already, when they are very small, at least by age four or five, they are forming theories about how their world works.[173] Even in their pretend play, they use intuitive theories about psychology, physics, biology, etc. They also have complex expectations about the roles and responsibilities of adults in their world. These ideas allow them to integrate information about the world and remember and apply it. The theories are refined as their experience grows. As adults, we have extensive internalized models of the expected behavior of other people, animals, liquids, gases, and solid objects. Our most demanding intellectual challenge is our attempt to understand other humans. Without these theories about what things do, what they are good for, and how they relate to each other and us, our sensory data would be just a buzzing, booming, incomprehensible confusion.

Even the least educated people I have known have often had complicated stories about how institutions and other people should or will behave. It seems to me that this natural human tendency to develop theories might readily lead to our postulating supernatural forces to explain things that just don't seem explainable by other means—as we try to refine our models of reality to give them greater explanatory and predictive power. The hope would be to develop more useful models, and magic is one form of explanation. Unfortunately, even if the models didn't work well, they might persist—if there were no good competing ideas. Modern science has offered new explanations for some of these things, but it is still far from a complete understanding of the universe, so the old supernatural models, perhaps with some refinements, continue to have real power for many observers.

The Place and Power of Dissociative Experiences

Dissociative experiences (visions, dreams, trances, glossolalia) may be one of the most important sources of religious validation—and sometimes even creativity. This was especially true in the past and is still true for some groups and cultures. For instance, a visit to a Pentecostal church service almost any week will find people who privilege such experiences as manifestations of the divine. Less demonstrative believers in more mainstream churches will also often assure you that their religious beliefs are validated by some personal experience of God. See our prior discussion of these phenomena in the section "The Criteria of Belief" in chapter 10: Religion and Science and Reason. Such experiences are both ancient and widespread in the religious world.

The shaman of many primitive groups provided them a connection to the supernatural world. This has been well documented among native peoples of North America but seems to be a role recognized in most cultures over thousands of years. This supernatural connection is facilitated through rituals including music, dance, sometimes plant extracts (for instance cactus and mushroom), fermentation products from grains such as barley, gases (ethylene etc) such as found at the Delphic oracle and the shrine of Apollo at Klaros, solitary meditation, fasting, sleep deprivation, repeating a prayer or phrase hundreds of times, etc. Some people seem to enter dissociative states much more readily and have been thought by their contemporaries to have a stronger connection to the supernatural. Such people make better shamans or in contemporary culture better mystics.[174] This seems to be a point of continuity between ancient and current primitive religions and between these and the more sophisticated of current religions—all appreciate and possibly need some connection to the supernatural and mystical experiences regardless of how they are induced appear to provide this important connection.

In many settings, those who have or have had such experiences, and those around them, have associated these experiences with the supernatural. This has something to do with the expectations of the individual and of the community and with how the experiences are framed. Typically, an experience is interpreted as religious if there is such an expectation or if it occurs in or is framed by a setting with visual and auditory stimuli that are accepted as religious by those involved. Such experiences are filtered through individual and community filters and only occasionally contain completely new and unexpected ideas. Often they serve to validate and expand on ideas already in the community. They may also function as a powerful validation for one's own belief in God. It is presumed to be evidence or a sign that God has chosen you, loves you, and is pleased with your worship and beliefs. For many people, it is the supreme form of validation for their religious views. The skeptic usually finds these experiences subjective, private, and unconvincing—possibly even wish fulfillment.

Dreams are another category of dissociative experience, widely viewed as confirming the supernatural. Dreams provide a sense of existing outside of one's body, thus for some observers, supporting the idea of an immortal soul—and by a ready extension life after death. From antiquity to the present day, dreams have been taken as giving warnings and information about the future—as a way for the supernatural to communicate with us. The Bible provides examples, such as the dreams of Joseph and Daniel. Widely varying illustrations can be found in poetry and literature where dreams appear as warnings or information about the future. Authors ranging from Plutarch to Milton have included these. My own personal experience suggests that this is in fact a common folk belief in the United States today. Even present day folk music includes predictive dreams in some of its tragic ballads.

Several lines of evidence suggest that dissociative experiences are properties of minds and do not depended on a supernatural intervention. Karen Armstrong reported that mystics in the Christian, Jewish, and Islamic traditions used similar practices to induce their experiences.[175] Among the large number of ways of inducing dissociative experiences are physical and sensory deprivation or overload, and various chemicals. Texts in the Avesta thought to be on the order of 3000 years old report experiences of the supernatural obtained by using a plant based preparation named "Soma."[176] Psychoactive substances, such as the cactus derivative peyote, are used by native peoples in North America for religious ceremonies suggesting these states of mind are related to human not supernatural activity. Another example comes from recent work with the mushroom extract psilocybin[177] which has been shown to induce mental events having properties very similar or identical to those of mystical experiences induced in other ways. Thirty-six spiritually active volunteers participated in this study receiving the active agent in a blinded fashion before one of two or three meditation sessions. Even fourteen months after the experimental session, the majority of subjects (67 percent) reported that the psilocybin "enhanced" meditation was one of the five most spiritually significant experiences of their lives. The experimenters also reported that the majority met criteria for a "complete" mystical experience when using the psilocybin. Placebo was less successful in inducing these effects.

Some students of psychoactive substances believe that these have made real contributions to the development of religions both primitive and sophisticated. For instance, it is possible to construct an apparently plausible interpretation of the Genesis story of the Tree of Good and Evil and the loss of the Garden of Eden based on a knowledge of psychogenic mushrooms and their place in some ancient cultures.[178] More recently, a well-argued paper has proposed that plant hallucinogens, especially those from ergot may have contributed to the visionary experiences recorded in the New Testament.[179] It thus seems that an evolving neuroscience may explain dissociative experiences on the basis of the properties of minds and their reactions to their chemical and experiential exposures—rather than depending on the supernatural.

One likely example of the role of dissociative experiences may be that of validating the major figures involved in founding or reforming a religious tradition. We will address Jesus and Mohammed in more detail at the end of this chapter. Other major foundational religious figures who report probable mystical experiences include the founders of Buddhism, Methodism, the Quakers, the Church of Latter Day Saints, and the Seventh-day Adventists—a very incomplete list. In each case, the founder provided an evolving interpretation of these experiences and then the followers took over—constructing a rationalizing and explanatory theology. On this, over decades and centuries, a great and always evolving religious edifice is built, one that depends on the founders experience but usually not on continuing mysticism.

The Power of Imagination

The human imagination is very powerful, and when unleashed by those with time and need, it can construct complete alternate realities, with fine detailing. This power develops early, as small children often create imaginary playmates for themselves and sometimes ask other people, including grownups, to meet their imaginary friends. As we mature, many of us continue to visit fantasy worlds for relief of stress or frustration or to replace a real life that is unsatisfactory. Some are remarkably good at this, and such people may go on to create the vast literature of the imagination. The protagonists in such literature may seem so real to such a large group of people that they come to symbolize a group or an era. For instance, think of Tom Joad, Robinson Crusoe, Don Quixote and

Sancho Panza, Hamlet, Macbeth, or Leopold Bloom—or from film James Bond or Luke Skywalker.

Thus the human imagination seems quite adequate to create the most complicated stories about the supernatural or divine realm. Most people have no trouble accepting this imagination as the source when it comes to the many stories of the Gods that were told two to five thousand years ago and are still told in some primitive societies. The major religions of the modern era are, of course, excepted from this interpretation by their own groups of adherents, but not because the human imagination is inadequate for the job of creating these more sophisticated religious forms.

Neuroscience and Religion

The study of the mind and its underlying physiology and anatomy is an exciting part of current science. We have known a lot about how individual neurons work for decades, but we are just starting to understand something about how the brain creates the mind. Consciousness sits on top of a boiling mass of unconscious processing. The single most important activity of a mind is processing information about other humans—ranging from their locations, through their suspected or feared intentions, to their reported or expected opinions about us.

A recent book by Todd Tremlin[180] provides a thoughtful discussion of how this is being applied to religion. I will attempt the briefest of summaries of a few interesting points from this book. Minds are continually scanning their environment for other intentional agents, both human and nonhuman, and for protective or survival reasons, and tend to be overly sensitive to possible evidence. This makes a leap to anthropomorphic explanations come quite readily—as we seek to interpret our world and eagerly avoid missing any intelligent agents there.

Much of our social processing is done at the subconscious level, leading to intuitive decisions that come to consciousness preformed with an emotional overlay. We only have certain ontological categories. One of these categories is the person category, and when we conceive of a god, we use that category with all its associated relational baggage. God concepts with limited or minimal counterintuitive properties, for example humanlike but with great power and immortality, are very attractive to most human minds and tend to produce powerful and memorable images. Regardless of the sophisticated theology of the religious professional, most believers worldwide associate their religion with such powerful supernatural beings. This is part of the explanation of why folk religion is often quite different from that of the theologian. Probably this rapidly advancing field will greatly increase our understanding of the religious impulse, but it is unclear how, if at all, it will impact day-to-day religious practice.

The Effects of Our Manner of Rearing

Another factor impacting the shape and acceptance of religion, and possibly its origins, can be seen when we examine the usual forms of acculturation of children. Children are reared by parents, who are as "gods" to them, providing all their needs including security, food, shelter, and interpretation of the world. As the children mature, they eventually find out that the parents are limited and vulnerable humans like the children. The attractiveness of replacing the parent with a good, kind, and caring, powerful personal God is reasonably obvious. In fact the child's acculturation may explain the "God centered hole" in humans that some religious authorities use as an argument for the existence of God. The following quotation is from the student first describing this possible relationship.

The God-Creator is openly called Father. Psychoanalysis concluded that he really is the father, clothed in the grandeur in which he first appeared to the small child. The religious man's picture of the creation of the universe is the same as his picture of his own creation.... He therefore looks back on the memory-image of the overrated father of his childhood, exalts it into a Deity, and brings it into the present and into reality. The emotional strength of this memory-image and the lasting nature of his need for protection are the two supports of his belief in God.

— Sigmund Freud, *New Introductory Lectures in Psychoanalysis* [181]

This need for a powerful and prescient ally persists throughout the rest of our lives and certainly may have something essential to do with the success of the religious traditions. The human life cycle is thus arranged in a way that seems to support the religious impulse. We would also note that the Abrahamic traditions have portrayed their gods as divine parents, with all the demands for obedience and the concerns for the welfare of the worshiper that would be expected of a good parent. This is found repeatedly in the Bible, for instance in the Lord's Prayer, and in countless pieces of religious music.

Most parenting is done by both a mother and a father, and we would note that many religions have some divine representation of a mothering god. Catholicism has Mary, the mother of God and many female saints; Hinduism includes powerful goddesses; and Buddhism in some strands offers female bodhisattvas. Perhaps unfortunately, the Protestant, Islamic, and Jewish faiths have very limited female representation in their pantheon or sub pantheon—at least as far as I can determine

The Plasticity of the Record Both Oral and Written

The fluidity of verbal history or story is another important consideration in understanding religious traditions. Everyone who has played the game of "telephone" knows how a verbal version of a story may be modified during multiple retellings. In my own experience, I have found colleagues who reported stories of some of my abilities that exceeded any reality. People seem to enjoy embellishing stories most likely because it makes the stories more interesting and compelling to the listener—and more fun to tell.

At least two respected biographies of Henry V of England (victor in the Battle of Tours) published on the order of one hundred years after his death were filled almost completely with fallacious material. These were based on previously printed material—some of it dating back to within fifty years of the King's life.[182] It repeated stories about him that circulated among the admiring populace—stories that couldn't have happened. The mythic status of the stories only became known because he was the crown prince and there were extensive family records. Lord Raglan thinks that there are rough rules about how myths and miracles may be associated with historical characters. First, he thinks that enough time must pass, typically fifty years or so, for the details of the career to have been forgotten but the highlights of fame or infamy remembered. Second, the person must have been notable in some ways that become pegs upon which the legends can be hung. Third, miracles must be believed in by those who will repeat the myth.

Other examples include stories such as the *Iliad* and the *Odyssey*, which though wonderful stories filled with comments on human nature, are also stylized. The numbers of people are inflated far beyond our best guesses about the original figures, and the gods are almost continually interfering in the human drama. These heroes probably lived four to five hundred years before their story was recorded, allowing for much evolution of the stories during verbal transmission. The exploits of Gilgamesh and his friend Enkidu, in the Epic of Gilgamesh,[183] are also clearly tales that relate in some way to a historical character, Gilgamesh, found on the list of the kings of Urek but now covered with myth and miracle—the reality long buried in the sands of time.

As long as the only record of a religious tradition and its founders remains verbal, it will be evolving. Once put into writing and copied a few times, it must move toward a fixed, unchanging story. This became especially true with the development of the printing press and its output of thousands of copies. Until the printing press, there was still some flux since each handmade copy was unique with its own errors and possible modifications to fulfill the copyist's agenda. This was unavoidable—as it took about a year of a scribe's time to hand copy a large document such as the Bible. Thus there were never many copies of any document. After the printing press, the only evolution became one of interpretation and of the attempt to reconstruct some long-lost original text from archeological and literary sources. Language itself evolves over time so that in a century, or a few centuries, what was once clear may become obscure as word meanings, grammar, and usage may change.[184] Attempting to read and understand an unannotated copy of Shakespeare will quickly demonstrate this. Some of his words are little used now and some have changed their common meanings.

A further complication for those basing their religious beliefs on ancient written texts is that few, if any, of those using these texts are native speakers of the languages in which they were originally written. Most readers have to depend on translations, single or serially, into other languages with all the known difficulties of carrying subtle concepts and nuances between languages. In the case of the Qur'an, there are no official translations, so converts are supposed to learn Arabic. It is unclear that the amateur devotee—learning Arabic just to read the Qur'an—will make a better private translation than would be made by some expert. And this amateur will likely never be fluent in Arabic, so in effect will be translating. What is clear is that the religious leaders by avoiding an approved translation do not have to officially face up to ambiguities and problems in interpretation that would be brought out in an attempt at translation.

The Many and Possible Gods

We men have made our gods in our own image.

—Hesiod, *Works and Days*

(Pierre) Janet says that there is no real religion where there are no Gods.

—Henri Ellenberger, *The Discovery of the Unconscious*

It is possible to conceive of a religion without a God in charge. Buddhism has demonstrated this feat—being alive and well, and having a worldwide following. The Buddha himself remains, however, a godlike figure and some strands of Buddhism have provided bodhisattvas—a kind of saint with godlike powers—who may be appealed to for help on the road to enlightenment. Most of the religions of today and of historical time have, however, had a god, or a pantheon of gods, as a central or primary feature. One great question then is "what kind of a God do you worship?" The Abrahamic traditions have claimed a god with unlimited or infinite power, knowledge, and goodwill toward his human worshipers. This same god is portrayed in the Biblical Old Testament as a very angry god willing to kill people over victimless rule breaking and willing to destroy all the men, women, children, and animals in a city that worships a rival deity. Other conceptions of god include a concerned god who made the world but can't interfere now because it would negate our "free will"—assuming we have that property. The "Intelligent Design" supporters would bring forward a creator god, but perhaps they can provide nothing more; that leaves them with a god similar to that of the Deists. In one of the exchanges in his *Dialogues Concerning Natural Religion*, David Hume[185] offers the entertaining suggestion that possibly the god who made this world was an ingénue at creation, botched the job, and has been sent on to other work by his superiors, leaving this world to run on by chances. There are also those, such as Spinoza, who believe that God and the universe are the same thing, a form of pantheism. A further refinement is panentheism, which holds that God includes the universe but is also something more than the universe. This does not exhaust the possibilities but at least illustrates the complexities of trying to talk about a god figure.

A god with omnipotence, omniscience, and omnibenevolence seems the most useful God to postulate, since he cares about everything and can do anything. This postulate runs head-on into what is sometimes known as the "theodicy problem." How can one claim that there is a good god with great power in the face of a world of much injustice and evil, both natural and originating in us humans? Most of us have found no simple, generally convincing answer to this concern. Some religions, not surprisingly, hold that the answer comes in another place and time when we are rewarded or punished for what we did here. A Hindu or Buddhist variation on this theme is to propose that what happens now is related to what we did in some past lifetime. In both cases, this god or religious system is able be absolved of any responsibility for providing apparent justice in this time and place. Finally, there are those who would say, "Just trust God, someday you'll understand," "God's ways are not man's ways," and "We finite humans should not be so presumptuous as to expect we could understand such problems."

A thriving branch of Western Philosophy has grown up attempting to address these difficulties, including attempts to prove god's existence by logical arguments. The first major effort in this area was provided by Thomas Aquinas, who offered five ways of proving God's existence, in his *Summa Theologica*. The Teaching Company offers a fascinating lecture series by James H. Hall titled *Philosophy of Religion*[186] that reviews the various philosophical arguments for and against the existence of God in a very evenhanded way. Dr. Hall's conclusion is that neither pro nor con arguments are compelling to an uncertain truth seeker. My conclusion is that the "proof of God" arguments are plausibility arguments, ones that wouldn't be considered seriously if someone didn't already believe, for other reasons, in the existence of a God. One form is the argument, based on our human experience in the world, that everything must have some first cause or initiator. This world must have had such a "prime mover" and that prime mover should be known as God.

A further question is to ask just how the presumed god would relate to the individual human, especially the worshiper. Is he responsive to individual requests acting in the context of the day-today life and needs of the petitioner? Can he be argued with and gotten to change his mind? Is he the "forces of history" that were envisioned by Karl Marx? Is he found in the triumph of the dominant political entity of each era, as envisioned by Hegel? Is he found in the natural world, both good and bad, or is he the good part of the natural world and some evil force accounts for the bad—God versus the devil in Christianity or the dualism of good and evil gods of Zoroaster? Or is he the force that created a world with a gradual and erratic evolution towards a better moral order as proposed by Robert Wright?[187] Or perhaps is he some perfect being, somewhere contemplating perfection and uninvolved in the imperfect world in which we live?

Possible Historical Examples

Jesus, the founding figure for Christianity, claimed to speak directly with God—called his Father. At times he spent whole nights in meditation, a practice that can be effective in inducing dissociative experiences such as trances. None of the Gospels were written by Jesus or his own followers, but at closest were written by the followers of the followers. This puts them at least thirty to fifty years and at least two human memories away from the described events, allowing for substantial evolution of the material while it was in oral or unrecorded form. Bart Ehrman, among many others, has reviewed the history of the documents that now make up the New Testament and the human factors at work in their creation.[188] In the beginning there were many strands of Christianity and a proliferation of sacred documents supporting these strands. It took on the order of two hundred years to select the current documents, and the official canon of the New Testament wasn't finalized till about 400 CE. In the era before the printing press, the individual copyist was in charge of the text. There were few copies of many texts, and changes by the copyist either by error or by intention, honest or otherwise, might sometimes have a durable effect as they were propagated by future copyists. Failure to be copied, at least in Europe, usually meant that a text disappeared in a few generations. The world of Christian documents thus came to be dominated by texts screened for their being authorized versions of the past, approved by clerical leaders, and therefore eligible for the expense and effort of copying. These texts and their official interpretations were used to suppress new or schismatic versions of the faith such as that of the Montanists and the Marcionites. The Christian church found that dissociative experiences could undermine clerical authority and be disruptive and difficult to control, and such experiences were largely suppressed or otherwise kept under church discipline after the first century.

Mohammed claimed visitations from an angel, who brought him God's word. These episodes tended to happen in places and times of deep solitary meditation, a practice known to be capable of inducing dissociative experiences. The Qur'an was not written down by Mohammed, who was illiterate, but was collected from written fragments created by his hearers and especially from living memories some years after the prophet's death. It is supposedly a record of what the angel told him when he was in trance—the words being sent by Allah. Reportedly, the current document was created by Zaid ibn Thabit and associates, under orders of the caliph Othman (died in 656), and all other codices were ordered to be destroyed. The reality was that all other codices were not immediately destroyed, and the writing system was still evolving so that final textual stability for the Qur'an was probably not achieved for another two to three hundred years.[189] The original text was one to several human memories from the supposed divine original, and the final text has some uncertainty in its relation to the original text. (See also prior comments on this in the chapter: Religion and Change.)

We thus see that the plasticity of oral tradition and of human memory may be deeply involved in both traditions. Both have probably some of their roots in mystical or dissociative experiences of the founders and possibly later of some of the followers, such as the "gift of tongues" in Acts. A further human factor, one that can only be hinted at, but must be a real concern, is that the actual recorders of these stories were deeply committed to the worldly success and acceptance of the traditions they were describing—so would tend, possibly subconsciously, to put them in the most favorable light possible—leaving out unpleasant material or alternative interpretations.

Final Comments

The above discussion offers many non-supernatural mechanisms for the development and spread of religious ideas. These are, of course, plausibility arguments, and how it actually happened is uncertain. Most likely multiple mechanisms were and are involved.

My personal interpretation is that religion probably arises in mystical or dissociative experiences and from their interpretation by the agent and his community. The other mechanisms we've discussed above provide the plasticity and the support that is necessary to create the complex documents and institutions of a major religion.

The ubiquity of religious belief suggests that it offered a survival advantage but tells us little about how it may have started. Perhaps over millions of years of evolutionary change, our ancestors had a gradual enrichment in some features of minds that are particularly adapted to supernatural belief. This would suggest a range of attractiveness for religious belief but not a preprogrammed necessity. Evidence and rational decision making would still be an option for those attracted to that process, though this may come less naturally and require more educational effort. Pascal Boyer has provide a well-informed commentary following this line of thought.[190]

The illusion for each religion is that it came into being through an act of the divine will changing the world. The reality would seem to be that multiple human forces, both individual and communal, have worked over time to create these complex and nuanced traditions with their many strands, their functional overlap, their dependence on prior traditions, and their heroically defended differences. The multiplicity of strands for all major religions is one significant argument for their origin within the always evolving human world.

12. The Universals and the Particulars of Religion

To find place and power in the human world a religion must have mechanisms of fulfilling many or most of the roles we discussed in the chapters on usefulness and power. Furthermore, to justify its independent existence, a religion must have unique beliefs not shared by its competitors. I will try to outline how some of this appears to work—from my own limited reading and observations.

Possible Universals

Immortality, Happiness, Justice, and Other Worlds

Some things seem to be present in all or almost all current religious traditions and perhaps must be there for a religion to fill its many roles. One is a belief in some form of human immortality. All the major religions teach that this world as presently constituted is not our intended place—not where we really belong. We are to seek a better existence in a better place. This may include a continued personal existence or a possibility of union with a god or eternal good spirit (nirvana). Whether or not we find happiness in our current lives on earth, we are encouraged to maintain a hope for a future with some form of eternal happiness in a spiritual or physical existence here or somewhere else.

Another widely present feature is a belief in eventual justice. This justice may come at some final judgment day, or it may come in this world—over a series of lives through the principle of Karma as believed in the "wheel-of-life" religions. Both these routes to justice support the hope for a happier future life as mentioned above, especially for the person who is having a hard life now. They also offer some satisfaction to the sensitive person who sees a world full of anger, cruelty, and injustice. The proposal of a better future life and of eventual righting of wrongs is so intuitively good, right, and just that most of us find it irresistible. It fulfills our dreams and hopes for how the universe should work.

Ethics and Social Support

Religion must also have some good and admirable personal ethic. This ethic must be available to guide the convert in his life. It must also be available for the supporters of the religion to point to when they are asserting the value of their religion for the world. This ethic is especially applied to fellow believers and to the poor and weak. The extension of the ethic to those who do not support the religion and especially those who have power and oppose the "truth" is often problematic (see the section on ethics). In fact this dichotomy may be necessary for the religion to function in some of its roles such as uniting and protecting the community—recreating the archaic tribe.

We humans seem to prefer a simple world of truth versus error, black versus white. Religious claims of unique truth can be used to justify such a categorization. We often balk at the intellectual demands of a world of uncertainty and complicated understandings of contingent truth—a pluralistic world. Such a view makes for less confident decisions. If you can really tell the good people from the bad people, you can have a basis for action—even for destroying evil. Religions, to be politically and socially useful, often find it best to offer a dichotomized world of good and not good with every relevant thing categorized. Coping with the downside of this black-and-white vision remains a serious problem. Such confident categorization limits the possibility for compromise, negotiation, and pluralism.

Thus those rejecting the religion's great truths are viewed as flawed in some important way. Those who share the belief system are portrayed as better people and more ethical than others. They are encouraged to love and care for each other, to do business with each other, to marry each other, and to seek to proselytize others to join the group and be "saved." This description seems to apply to most religious groups. Thus a religion's success may be partly from creating an identifiable "tribe" within a large community, a place where a person may find a comfortable and rewarding social home, a "divinely" blessed but earthly attempt at a realizable utopia.

The Gods

Here I venture a few comments from a theological novice. One may interestingly but maybe somewhat arbitrarily divide the realm of gods or supernatural beings into two broad classes. First, we may think of the anthropomorphic gods or supernatural figures that have some humanlike characteristics. These are the gods who can feel our pain, hear our entreaties, respond to our needs, and guide us on the way to some form of salvation. They seem to be intuitively believable and attractive to many, even most, human minds (see "Neuroscience and Religion" in chapter 11). Supernatural beings of this type may be found somewhere in most religious traditions.

In Christianity, various strands have concepts of Jesus, Mary, saints, and angels who fill this role. The children's song "Jesus Loves Me" was one example that I grew up using. Similarly, some strands of Buddhism have the Buddha and a variable pantheon of bodhisattvas who may help the devotee on his path to enlightenment. Hinduism has one great God—and many expressions of that god, such as Krishna, Indra, and Shiva, that the believer may beseech for help. Islam has angels, both good and bad, and from its Sufi wing a tradition of saints that are revered and often worshiped by believers seeking their assistance. Powerful caring beings are so attractive to the human mind that most long-running religions include strands or branches with such figures.

Alternatively, all religious traditions include some more sophisticated god concepts. Such gods are regarded as not like humans, in fact "other" and even indescribable for the human. They are everywhere and sometimes no particular place. They may respond to entreaties or may let the world go on according to natural law. They usually have complete power, knowledge, and good will. For the Buddhist, the laws of Karma guaranteeing eventual justice and offering union with the divine are the equivalent of a god. For the Hindu, Brahmin is that ultimate power behind everything, and we are all expressions of that power—part of this almost inconceivable deity. Christians, Muslims, and Jews are often said to be worshipping the same great god, though there is certainly some variation of concepts depending on the theological substrand to which they adhere.

Mysticism and Origins

Mysticism or dissociative experience in its several forms seems important in the founding of many current major religions—at least Christian, Islamic, Jewish, and Buddhist traditions. See our prior discussion in the chapter Possible Sources and Shaping Factors for Religion. In my limited personal observations of smaller religious groups, such as Seventh-day Adventists and Mormons, and some of their schismatic subgroups—such as the Branch Davidians and the Fundamentalist Church of Jesus Christ of Latter-day Saints—they have put forward the claims that their leaders had divine inspiration, as shown for instance in mystical experiences bringing prophetic messages. Certainly, religions may be conflicted and split over interpretations of ancient documents, rituals, and beliefs, but those offering the new interpretations seem to be more compelling when they can cite experiences that they interpret as of divine origin.

It is my impression, or even theory, that new religions—which commonly arise from schism of a prior group—usually depend on mysticism as a connection to the supernatural and gradually evolve their own orthodoxy. This new orthodoxy must somehow control, suppress, or marginalize further expressions of mysticism. For the first few centuries, Christianity dealt with many heresies that seemed based in mysticism, including Montanism and forms of Gnosticism. Mysticism seems to be a widespread human activity that is hard to completely suppress, so, even in well established religions, it continues at the margins or in controlled situations such as monastic orders, the Sufis in Islam, and in Pentecostal meetings. Those empowered by a mystical experience seem to have more confidence than those empowered by rational study, as they know the truth by an "experience of the divine."

Mysticism is a widespread but minority human activity. These are real human experiences that are to some degree reproducible. They are widely associated in human minds with the supernatural. The shaman provided this important connection for many if not all primitive religions. Thus mysticism or some equivalent appears to be an important and almost ubiquitous player in the world of religion perhaps because it provides a perceived connection to the supernatural and this is a widely accepted justification for religious claims.

Sacrifice and Memorial Architecture

It seems that most if not all religions ask the believer for some form of sacrifice. Personal possessions or wealth and animal or human life are the usual examples of the sacrifices demanded by religion. Some form of sacrifice seems universal to both historic and prehistoric religion. The Romans and Greeks gave up human sacrifice over two millennia ago, but other groups such as the Norse continued through most of the first millennium of the Christian Era, and it was still practiced in the Americas till the Europeans destroyed the native cultures.[191] Christianity, Buddhism, and Islam have not promoted killing life as a sacrifice to the supernatural. They do, however, encourage their believers to dedicate their lives to the religion. This is most obvious in the monastic traditions of Christianity and Buddhism.

One result of the believer's donation of his goods to his religion is the accumulation of wealth by the organization. This has allowed essentially all large and enduring religions to build memorial architecture consisting variously of altars, pyramids, shrines, temples, mosques, synagogues, churches, and cathedrals. Sometimes these may be interchanged from one religion to another just by changing decorations. Mosques and cathedrals have been exchanged following a change in political control, as have temples and mosques. Such structures are found all over the world and go back for thousands of years. Recently, the oldest large stone temple was thought to be one dating from about 3200 BCE on Malta dedicated to the worship of the Mother Goddess.[192]

Religion, Sexuality, and Family Life

Many strands of religion teach that the highest forms of religious devotion require giving up sexual relationships and family life. The iconic figure at the center of Christianity never married or was responsible for a family, and the Apostle Paul advocated the unmarried state as being better than marriage. The revered Hindu holy men have usually given up family life as have Buddhist and Christian monks and nuns. The Islamic world doesn't support a monastic tradition, but some of its strands suppress sexual expression with a very heavy hand putting women as much as possible out of public life, covered with excess clothing and without power. The Jewish tradition seems more accepting of the role of sex and family, but at the extremes, even it, during the first century CE at Qumran, supported a monastic community that seemed to be all male. Thus it appears that most religious traditions consider sexuality and family life to be in conflict with the highest and most dedicated religiosity—and in some way give special honor to those who give up sex and family to devote themselves to a pursuit of the divine. *No one seems to notice that such people, with a less than a full experience of being human, might not represent the highest emotional and intellectual development of the human mind.*

One Proposed Model for the Structure of a Religion

Anyone with more than a very parochial experience of the religious world has probably had the feeling that the various religions have significant similarities—both in beliefs and in strategies for controlling and aiding their supporters. Despite their obvious and often emphasized differences, religions mostly do the same work in the human world—implying that some common description might apply. In a recent book[193] Loyal Rue has proposed a theory or model for the structures that make up a religion. His model seems to have explanatory power for a wide variety of religions, and he presents a discussion of the application of his ideas to the Jewish, Christian, Muslim, Hindu, and Buddhist traditions. I will briefly outline his proposal, but you will have to read his book to appreciate the sophisticated description of the emotions and of the mind and how these are affected by religions.

Religions must have, at their core, a narrative myth that relates what is and what ought to be, the facts of the universe, and the responsibilities or ethical duties of the believer. This myth must be treated as absolute truth about the universe and about people's needs. The myth must be plastic enough to allow some reinterpretation—when the believing group is under stress from new forces in the culture or new interpretations of reality. The orthodoxy of the myth must be maintained without letting its interpreters, the priests or clerics, get so much power that they try to exercise totalitarian control over society, applying their interpretation of the myth to every detail of human life.

Dr. Rue describes a group of ancillary strategies that support the core narrative tradition or myth and are an essential part of a functioning religion. These include intellectual, experiential, ritual, aesthetic, and institutional dimensions that "collectively shape the religious life." The intellectual strand seeks the best and most coherent interpretation of the central myth. The experiential strand seeks to promote an experience of the ultimate power described in the myth. The rituals seek to make the myth real by dramatic practice. The aesthetic program seeks to make the myth real by objectifying its stories and characters—for instance in artistic representations. The institutional program is responsible for maintaining an authorized version of the myth and its interpretation and making sure the other elements support this official version of reality.

Different traditions use the different strategies to varying degrees. These ancillary strategies may be thought of as making the myth more real and keeping it in working memory so that it will affect the believer's daily decisions, ethical and otherwise. They also serve to educate the emotions and to change the believer's personal goal hierarchies to correspond better with the religious worldview. These things go together to support a "socio-symbolic system of interdependent elements." Dr. Rue believes such systems to be natural entities that have emerged through the normal selective processes that have brought diverse and complex life and social evolution to our world. Their goals are the creation of "personal wholeness and social coherence."

An interesting study in the adjustment of religions to change—the plasticity of the myth—and in their reluctance to make such adjustment can be seen in the dealings of Christianity with science over the last few centuries from Galileo to the current controversies about the origins of life. The controversy with Galileo is well resolved, and the heirs of those who persecuted him have made a very late official apology. The origins controversy is, however, in full swing. Some Christian groups have found evolutionary processes compatible with their interpretations of scripture, and others have totally rejected scientific work in this area—insisting on the priority of Biblical myth over scientific reconstruction of the past, even though the latter is validated by multiple lines of evidence coming from many branches of science including at least physics, chemistry, geology, anthropology, paleontology, and molecular biology.

The Uniques

It is necessary for religions to have their own unique interpretations of the world and the universe. The hold on the followers and the power of the leaders depends on the belief that this particular religion is the only one that really understands the human situation. Religions tend to have at least two groups of unique features. One set of uniques is related to their supernatural beliefs, and another is related to their cultural origins and exposures. Cultures seem to leave marks on religions probably most powerfully the culture in which it originates and to varying degrees the cultures in places where it is transmitted. All religions founded in historical time were founded by people who already had a set of religious beliefs and a culture—

which included those beliefs. The religion had to consciously, or unconsciously, create a new structure that would be acceptable to people already acculturated to the old traditions. For instance, Mohammed kept Mecca and the Ka'ba important in his new religion but changed the attached meanings. He also seems to have been relatively egalitarian as related to woman's rights, but the societies that took up his religion were very patriarchal, and today most Muslim societies demand this as part of their religion.

The most important differentiating features of religions are probably provided in their beliefs about metaphysical or supernatural questions, since these are untestable. Thus unique and sometimes even bizarre beliefs may be promoted with no chance that they can ever be proven wrong. These beliefs are used to separate religious communities from one another. If the difference from some other community is small, then the leaders focus on whatever differences there are and emphasis their claimed importance. Usually the *believers must hold all alternate religious interpretations of the universe as wrong, as fatally flawed*. These believers are also usually encouraged to feel a personal responsibility to convert others to their unique truths. This encourages them to have confidence in their particular belief system and encourages them not to really seriously consider alternate systems. Else they may lose their "faith." The public commitment of teaching others is almost certainly more important in strengthening the "faith" of the believer than it is in getting new converts for the group—but the goals are intertwined.

Conflict between Religions

It is almost axiomatic that there will always be conflict in the religious world. The very existence of each religion depends on maintaining its distinctive supernatural claims. The jobs of the leaders, and to a lesser degree the hopes of the followers, would disappear if the uniqueness claims were vacated. There can be no appeal to observations of the universe to resolve differing claims, and no one can trust any expert but his own. Differing claims cannot be mediated as there is usually absolute inflexibility on these matters—such is a point of religious education and of heroic resistance even to martyrdom. The saints held up as exemplars are often made this way. In the Jewish tradition in the time of the Maccabees, those who were killed for refusing to eat pork were held up as martyred heroes—

according to Paul Johnson[194] the first martyrs for religious belief. The Protestant Reformation created similar heroes.

Carl Popper[195] believed that only flexibility in claims or demands could allow two parties to reach a compromise. Claims of love toward the other party are in fact irrelevant in settling disputes where the disputants hold rigid positions. He called such irrational belief systems based on ideology or religion "oracular irrationalism" and observed that differences between such belief systems could seldom be settled peacefully. The conflicts of the religious world do not have to be violent, but if a religion has or seeks political power, violence is only a short step ahead. Examples include the European wars of religion, set off by the Protestant Reformation, the present Muslim Jihad or terrorism, our own abortion clinic violence and any number of other world "hot spots" where religion is used to justify violence.

Within Religion Conflict: The Moderate versus the Fundamentalist

Within each religious tradition there is the possibility of conflict between people who are concerned with maintaining the original purity of the "faith" as it was at the founding and the moderates or progressives who would modify and change the tradition to adjust to a changing world. Typically the moderates are inclusive and see a world of shades of gray. They value the tradition, see it as their tradition, and emphasize its best features. They also see a complicated, pluralistic human civilization, with many other religious traditions that may each have value. They may even accept some compromises to have a "live and let live" world.

In contrast, the fundamentalists serve a demanding, and often angry god. This god has given them the "truth" through the founder's work. They have a dream of the past that is a continual rebuke to their experience of the present. They are driven to purify the religion and take it back to the beliefs of the founders. They have complete confidence that they know the "truth" and must act to support it and assure its victory. They can't compromise since they know the mind of God, and it would be a curious thing for God to be mistaken even in small matters—but especially in enormities. The moderate has a difficult time resisting the fundamentalist as the moderate claims to believe that same tradition—which the fundamentalist takes to its logical extreme by saying that it is "truth" and it must conqueror over all other ideas, since "it comes to us from God."

The moderate would like a peaceful accommodation, while the fundamentalist looks at the founding documents and sees that violence is there. He knows he is right and he must act, so he is willing to resort to anything, including violence, in doing God's work. A small number of violent people can control a much larger number who disagree with them but are unwilling to take the disagreement to a violent conclusion. This violence is in all the monotheistic traditions but maybe most on display in Islamic history—as its founder engaged in what would now be called terrorism in his war on Mecca and after his death, the first four caliphs, his replacements, were all assassinated over religious differences.[196] The "Assassins or Ismailis-Nizari" operated in the Islamic world for almost two centuries from 1090 to 1275, killing those who were not keeping the faith pure enough, hoping thereby to spread a "pure" version of Islam.[197] This tradition of violence, arising in particular interpretations of Islamic documents and history, continues to the present, as the actions of Osama Bin Laden and Al Qaeda are not just directed against the West but also against Muslims who have not kept the faith carefully enough—or not kept the right version.[198] Diderot wrote that "there is only one step from fanaticism to barbarism"[199] and the world has certainly seen that move.

Summary

All major religions and most minor ones believe in some form of human immortality, in eventual justice, in some admirable ethical code with supernatural exceptions, in the uniqueness of their knowledge of a divine mandate, and in mysticism as a source of divine truth, at least at some point in time. They all practice memorial architecture, demand various personal sacrifices from their followers, give special status to those who abstain from sex and family life as more devoted, and have at least some strands with powerful anthropomorphic figures able to aid the devotee on the path to "salvation."

A wide range of unique supernatural beliefs and rituals can be used to organize religious people into social groups and provide them with many of the advantages or useful features that the religious traditions offer. Each group has to have its own set of supernatural beliefs and must usually claim that theirs is the only true belief system. In practice this often means that they must demonize and denigrate those outside their tradition or at least those who clearly reject their tradition. This then may on some occasions, become the driving spring for violent action by a group of believers who think of themselves as good and of those who don't share their beliefs as sub-human.

The illusion is that religion is here to give us peace and togetherness. The reality is that it does this but usually in practice does it on a limited, piecemeal basis, with the ever-present risk of intense violence, or at least intolerance between conflicting visions. When each tradition claims that there is only one "truth" and that "truth" is in their possession, the ultimate loss can sometimes be the chance of peacefully sharing a common human heritage.

13. Atheism and Religion

There is no God, and the human being is His prophet.

Belief in a ruling, judgmental God, that is the last great illusion of humanity, and what then, when that is gone? Then people will be wiser; but richer, happier? I can't see it.

—From *Niels Lyhne* by Jens Peter Jacobsen

Agnosticism is a term widely used to signify uncertainty about the existence of God. It is unclear if it is actually in practice significantly different from atheism, and we will not separately address it in this text. I will assume it is a less "in your face" sort of atheism.

Atheism, Acculturation, and Individualism

For many thousands of years, most people in the major civilizations of the world have been acculturated to one or another religious tradition as part of their early training. Within Christian, Muslim, Jewish, Hindu, and Buddhist societies most people do not switch traditions but spend their lives within the tradition to which they were acculturated. Human religious loyalty suggests that there is something about implanting these beliefs and symbols at an early age that makes them become central in the self that we are creating. We obviously have deep discomfort with suggestions of changing them.

In the Western world that I have experienced, most atheists were and are so as individuals who have evaluated evidence and made rational, considered, and often reluctant choices. This doesn't apply to the officially atheistic Marxist world—see a following discussion. Some Greek philosophers such as Heraclitus and Epicurus seemed to have reached essentially atheistic positions after careful consideration of the options. People are not usually atheists because they know this as truth "in their hearts." They were not usually acculturated to atheism but reached this position after years of discussion, review of evidence, and internal dialogue. My own limited experience suggests that because of the kind of individualistic, internally directed people who tend to become atheists, one does not find them readily aggregating into groups that look like religious groups.

For some people, atheism may be best seen as a rejection of such religious systems as they have met in their experience of life. Life is short and busy, and few of us have time to examine many religious systems in detail. People may find a place in our religiously based culture and accept the beliefs of those around them but be unpersuaded themselves. For such people, atheism is a private matter, and you would not know of it without asking or carrying on a more than superficial conversation with them. They do not change the world or create a substitute for religion. Some may even cherish the hope that somewhere there is a "true" religion that they might find believable.

Exceptions to this description apply to those aggressively acculturated to atheism in the Marxist communist world in the twentieth century and to a small group of Western atheists such as Madelyn O'Hair (deceased) who spend their time in agitation against religion. Muslim terrorism has perhaps increased some of the antireligious activity of intellectually prominent atheists with books by Sam Harris, Daniel Dennett, Richard Dawkins, Christopher Hitchens, and others, appearing in the years since the World Trade Center catastrophe, arguing the atheist case—but so far I see no equivalent of a religion rising amongst such people.

Short Review of Some Arguments Supporting Atheism

If they (the Gods) have the will to remove evil and cannot, then they are not omnipotent. If they can but will not, then they are not benevolent. If they are neither able nor willing, they are neither omnipotent nor benevolent. Lastly, if they are both able and willing to annihilate evil, why does it exist?

—Epicurus, *Aphorisms*

Greek rationalism is probably the first time that there was any systematic attempt to reject the Gods. Heraclitus was one of the pre-Socratic philosophers whose own writings are largely lost except for quotations that others thought memorable and some fragments. He felt that religion was a noble disease. Epicurus was eighteen years old when Alexander the Great died, so he spent his life in the Hellenistic world created by that figure. Epicurus did not deny the existence of the gods, he simply said that they had nothing to do with men or this world and that there was no supernatural available to us.

Despite our almost universal acculturation to religious belief, most populations contain significant minorities (occasionally majorities) who have given up such belief. I will make an attempt to present some of the points that would need to be addressed to understand the arguments about atheism versus theism for many people. This is an incomplete but illustrative set of concerns.

1) *Theodicy or the justice of God.* This is a recurring problem for all religions. Justice and injustice are widely available in the world, and it would seem reasonable to expect a religious system to provide an explanation for their distribution. In the Abrahamic traditions, it is generally handled by saying that justice will be taken care of in the future in a place such as heaven or hell. In the wheel-of-life religions this is usually explained by invoking Karma, in essence saying that if you are having an unpleasant life this time, it is because of something bad you did in a previous lifetime, now haunting you. Another way to handle this problem is to say we aren't capable of understanding God's justice now, but he will help us understand in a future existence. For many people exposed to these traditions, none of these solutions are satisfactory. I personally find it hard to understand how some future reward will make up for the excruciating pain and death of a child or of an apparently kind and peaceful adult.

2) *The question of the supernatural.* The central narrative myth of every great religious tradition contains a supernatural claim. Folk versions of the religion often contain many more such claims. These claims seem always to be unavailable for public evaluation. The rules of evidence applied to scientific concerns and practical life are not generally accepted as applying to these claims. The supports of the supernatural claims come from the inaccessible past or the equally inaccessible subjective. Many skeptical minds reject these claims because of their inability to evaluate them objectively and publicly and their failure to be confirmed by the daily experience of most humans.

3) *Exclusivity in ethics.* Most religions have an admirable and universal ethical mandate written into their foundations. In

actual practice, this is often interpreted as applying only to the community of believers—or exceptions are made on God's word (as provided by the leaders of the religion). Thus religious wars can be justified and have been repeatedly in the histories available for us all to review. This is exactly what you would expect if religions were human institutions serving human purposes. In one sense, they reproduce the ancient tribal structure and its fight for survival. If some divine will created and guided the religion, one would think this could be managed more skillfully and less violently.

4) *Use as a tool for domination.* The first enduring and officially atheistic governments in human history were the Marxists countries of the twentieth century. Karl Marx believed that religion's chief use was to control the underclass by promising them a good life next time around if they bore their burdens well in this current dark world—that religion in effect justified oppression. This was Marx's understanding of the historical record, and at one point millions of people shared his view—and millions still do. Other authors such as Jared Diamond and Upton Sinclair have largely supported this view of religion. Seeing a religion functioning in this fashion will drive some thoughtful people to atheism at least about that religion, though they might still be attracted to some alternate religious practice.

5) *Direct disagreement with scientific studies.* Various religious teachings such as the immortal soul, the resuscitation of dead bodies and a theistic creation of all life only a few thousand years ago have become less tenable as science has evolved and developed its understanding of life and of the past. Some religions have adjusted and gone on, while others remain conflicted and are losing some of their educated adherents. Specific claims about documents and artifacts have been debunked by dating technologies and by critical analysis of texts. Such studies genuinely undermine the faith of some individuals, but others simply ignore the studies (try an Internet search on the Shroud of Turin to see the "true believers" and the skeptics giving their arguments).

6) *The multiplicity of competing religions.* The large number of competing religious traditions all basing their claims on

similar evidence—usually particular interpretations of ancient documents of uncertain origin or else private experience or both—leaves many people suspicious that all religions are about equally to be trusted or doubted. For the more skeptical, doubt is the usual response, but there are some who accept all religions as roads to God or truth.

People do not usually leave a religion because they want to be evil and the religion is restraining them. They leave for many reasons that may include rejection of the supernatural truth claims, disillusionment with the practical ethics, objections to the exclusivity claims, and a personally expanding scientific understanding of the world. Some people will just tell you they don't believe anymore, it no longer makes sense to them. Those who reject scientific materialism and claim there is another way of knowing have yet to offer a method for separating illusion, delusion, and truth about that reality which we often call "the universe."

Atheism and the Marxist World

For the period of about seventy years from approximately 1919 to 1990 the largest official block of atheists were found in the Soviet Union and its satellites. This was undoubtedly the largest group of atheists in the history of the world. Communist Party members were atheists, and the schools taught atheism. Religion, within the larger society was, despite claims of religious freedom, repressed as far as was convenient. The collapse of the Soviet Empire led to a remarkable emergence of religious sentiment as multiple religious organizations from the West found fertile soil for their proselytizing. Acculturation to the Communist worldview had apparently been much less successful than the usual religious acculturation. In fact, long before the collapse, the great Russian writer Solzhenitsyn[200] wrote of a hope that the Russian Orthodox religion would again become an important part of Russian life.

Several things may have contributed to the Communist failure to establish an enduring atheism. For one the party may never have created a vision like the religious vision that extended to all men and filled all or most of the useful roles outlined in our earlier section. This is a difficult task and, with a God substitute as nebulous as the "forces of history," would have required a considerable imagination. With the Communist Party being largely an elite organization there may never have been a buy-in by the common man. Thus acculturation of the young would often not have occurred at a family level but only in school or child care programs. The intimate association of this atheistic belief system with a tyrannical and oppressive political system may also have undermined the credibility of the atheistic beliefs.

Thus when the Soviet Empire collapsed, a great bastion of official atheism was also gone. For many involved, this belief was imposed by political violence, and they were happy to be rid of it. This failure, after having almost three generations to acculturate and thereby create an enduring substitute for organized religion, may be a comment on what we humans need for emotional support. The intellectual merits of the Bolshevik system were, however, seriously questioned from the start.[201] Those in charge may have failed to understand religion, to replace it creatively, and to maintain the ethical standards we humans need and expect. It seems that they thought human nature infinitely plastic—a blank slate—and especially they didn't appreciate our intrinsic or intuitive morality. At any rate, the system created was a failure at making a desirable human home. Most of us are glad it is largely gone. My Christian friends who lived for years under Romanian Marxism have only bad things to say about that experience.

Paul Gabel has documented much of this history in his recent book *And God Created Lenin: Marxism vs. Religion in Russia, 1917–1929.*[202] He notes that a narrow interpretation of religion as primarily a tool for domination by the ruling class made Marx, Engels, and Lenin unable to appreciate religion's adaptive power—the multiple human drives and needs that it serves. In a recent article,[203] he gives an account of the Soviet attempts to suppress religion during the rest of their time in power and then reports that five years after the fall of Bolshevik Communism, the Russian Orthodox Church claimed 72 percent of the population and less than 19 percent reported a lack of religious affiliation. Gabel feels that the religious impulse is so innate to human nature that the Bolshevik attempt to suppress religion was a "hopeless quest."

Philosophy, Religion, and Atheism

For most students, philosophy is the rational search for truth about the human condition. It addresses many of the same concerns as religion including morality and how a human life can best be lived. For most practitioners, it makes these evaluations without appeals to the supernatural but on the basis of the kinds of beings we are and the kind of world in which we live. Religion also claims a search for truth but allows a contribution from avenues that many philosophers would not accept as rational analysis. The religious traditions are, however, eager to be rational themselves—within the limits of their central myth. They have often employed philosophers to explain and rationalize their religious belief systems and give them a relationship to the rest of human ideas. St. Augustine, Thomas Aquinas, and many others have done this for the Christian tradition. This is an ongoing project, and some universities have active professorial chairs dedicated to the philosophy of religion.

Possibly more notable to the public may have been philosophers of the last few centuries, such as David Hume and Bertrand Russell, who have rejected religion and the supernatural—and done so eloquently. Friedrich Nietzsche also spent a lot of time proclaiming "the death of God" and what this might mean for our civilization—and his concerns still echo in our discourse. The post-modernists, as a group, seem to reject the absolute certainties of religious belief. Even some ancient philosophers, such as Heraclitus, found religion unbelievable. Thus one long-running strand within philosophy rejects the supernatural, and the study of this strand of philosophy offers an alternative to religious belief for the restless and inquiring mind.[204] Such study may become the occasion if not the cause for the development of personal atheism. Philosophy, however, offers no systematic social support system such as that of religion and so is not in any practical sense a functioning alternative to religion in the day-to-day business of the world.

Is Atheism an Alternative to Religion?

As already alluded to in the first section of this chapter, I see atheism as a rejection of belief in the supernatural but not as a replacement for religion. In practice atheism has no program of its own but is simply the negation of the theistic worldview. It therefore does not easily and automatically step into society and fill the many private and public roles of a religion. In fact, it may be fair to say that the time and energy devoted to personal and social support by any atheistic group has been trivially small compared to that invested by the typical religion. It is, however, possible to use the atheistic worldview to consciously create substitutes or alternatives for religion in its many roles in the human sphere. One must note, however, that atheism is primarily supported by its intellectual appeal while religion appears to be primarily supported by its emotional appeal.

The Council for Secular Humanism (www.secularhumanism.com), which publishes the journal *Free Inquiry,* provides one example of a contemporary effort to make atheism more attractive by making real efforts to address the psychological and ethical needs of humans who reject religious solutions. To me it appears that this approach has merit and possibilities, but I think it will always have a hard time competing with belief systems that are embedded by acculturation starting in early childhood and represented weekly at your neighborhood church along with a strong, caring social support system. It also would seem to lack the wonderful emotional appeal of a religion that promises a kind, caring, all-powerful, and all-knowing god who answers the prayers of small children and adults alike. It seems that for the majority of humans, emotional appeals trump intellectual arguments.

Is Atheism Dying?

In 2004 Alister McGrath published *The Twilight of Atheism: The Rise and Fall of Disbelief in the Modern World*[205] in which he gives his view of the recent past and expected future. By atheism he means confident rejection of belief in God. He would not include agnostics or those uncertain about the god question. Since many nonbelievers consider themselves fallible, he would make them agnostics, thus in effect classifying people often thought of as atheists, such as Shelley and Darwin, as more likely agnostics, with a soft spot in their heart for some sort of good god.

One of his observations is that atheism has lost ground because it failed to create better people than those created by the religious traditions. He also bases his predictions about atheism's future on the collapse of the international Marxist version of Communism with its dedicated rejection of supernatural religion and gods. He thinks this political change has made atheism less attractive and has reminded us that religion is not the only source of man's suffering.

At least supporting McGrath's belief in atheism's decline, Peter Berger has edited a book titled *The Desecularization of the World: Resurgent Religion and World Politics.*[206] He and his contributors see religion as a resurgent force in widely disparate parts of the world. In contrast, Tom Flynn recently published an article reviewing evidence that secularism and atheism are doing as well as ever.[207] Perhaps we are ordained to a future of competing secularism and theism with neither ever completely in control but the balance tipping toward theism as the majority will usually share that view. My hope is only that a pluralism of voices can be always welcomed.

Atheism and Atrocity

In his essay *The Pursuit of the Ideal*[208] Isaiah Berlin quoted Alexander Herzen, the nineteenth-century Russian radical, as saying "that a new form of human sacrifice had arisen in his time—of living human beings on the altars of abstractions." His comment was driven by the European revolutions of 1848, but it might also be reasonable to say that much killing in the past had been done over differences in religious belief—for instance the Inquisition—a form of abstraction. The government managed destruction of human life in the twentieth century far exceeded any previous period in human history. In this century again, the pursuit of an abstraction was the justification for much of the human sacrifice.

The Bolsheviks and their International Communist Party probably destroyed prematurely over 100 million human lives in their futile attempts to create utopian Communist states. Some would say that atheism killed these people. I would maintain that it was not atheism that killed them but instead a "faith-based ideology" that had its own prophet, canon of scripture, and eschatology or hopes for the future. Atheism was just an incidental part of this system. Only a faith-based system can have the necessary absolute confidence in its ideology that will allow it to destroy millions of those who disagree. Thus instead of atheism itself causing the deaths, it was a confident belief—a faith in the usual religious sense—in a Marxist interpretation of history, society, and the future.

The Marxian version of Communism was not scientific any more than are our openly religious ideologies. In fact, Marx rejected rational analysis and planning for the future saying this was "bourgeois logic."[209] Marx may have started with an attempt at using scientific materialism, but he went far beyond anything scientific to create a vision of a future utopia built on a misunderstanding of human nature as being a blank slate with unlimited potential for manipulation—he also misunderstood some other things such as economics. His followers could not question his understanding, because this was a faith-based movement—in daily practice like a religion—not a scientific enterprise. Its leaders spent their time debating interpretations, not studying how the world worked.

The atrocities of Mussolini and Hitler, who also killed their millions, cannot even loosely be blamed on atheism, as their governments maintained good relations with the official Christian churches. Instead, their evil actions were based on their "absolute faith" in belief systems or ideologies that included plans for utopian futures. To again quote Shadia Drury: "The worst atrocities have their source in the zealous pursuit of a sublime ideal."[210]

Summary

Atheism's future is not possible to predict. Clearly, there is no current atheistic belief system or organization that has been able to fully fill the role of religion in any human society. Disbelief is probably most attractive in times of religious excess. E. O. Wilson in his book *On Human Nature* gives a very pessimistic evaluation of scientific attempts to discredit religion. He concludes that these logical attacks have almost no effect on the religion or the believer. "Their crisply logical salvos, endorsed by whole arrogances of Nobel Laureates, pass like steel-jacketed bullets through fog."[211]

Despite the improbability of atheism replacing religion in society in any formal sense, atheism will probably remain a very viable intellectual position. Substantial numbers of educated and thoughtful people will end up in this position either openly or covertly. In much of Western Europe, a majority of the population does not claim a religion or a belief in a god, and there is little reason to expect this to change in the foreseeable future. Thus atheism is about as likely to die as is religion.

14. Conclusions and Futures

We shall not cease from exploration
And the end of all our exploring
Will be to arrive where we started
And know the place for the first time

—T. S. Eliot, *Little Gidding*

Religions do not disappear when they are discredited; it is requisite that they should be replaced..

—George Santayana, *The Life of Reason*

The Evolution of Religion

All the major current religions should probably be thought of as the results of a long cultural evolution—at least thousands of years. Hinduism was built on an earlier tradition whose hazy remains we find in the Vedic hymns. It has now been evolving for on the order of three thousand years. Buddhism was built on Hindu roots about twenty-five hundred years ago and continues to split and evolve. The Jewish God should probably be traced back to the ancient Canaanite pantheon.[212] Jewish religion achieved a rough consistency with its current beliefs about twenty-five hundred years ago but continues to have splits and reinterpretations. Christianity was built on Jewish roots but with significant contributions from the Greek philosophy that permeated the culture in which it grew. Originally, there were many strands of Christianity (Docetists, Montanists, Marcionites, Ebionites, Gnostics, and others), but this was narrowed after the church obtained political power in the fourth century CE. A thousand years later, the Protestant Reformation brought another explosion of Christian sects and viewpoints.

Islam, the youngest of the major religions, started about six hundred years after Christ. The founder incorporated pieces of Jewish and Christian history in his holy book. He largely got rid of the animism that preceded his religion—but he never got rid of the suppression of women and the violent insistence on controlling belief.

He had only been dead a short time when his followers went to war against apostate desert tribes. As would be expected, his religion has broken into several strands. The tendency to violence has been much on display in recent years, but there is also a peaceful pluralistic interpretation that is less well-known. For instance, an Internet search on the name Fethullah Gulen will turn up an extensive literature supporting this interpretation. Robert Wright has given us a sympathetic interpretation of the Qur'an as related to the evolution of Mohammed's own life and stuggles.[212]

Christianity has had a competitive evolution over the last five hundred years. Political domination has become less possible, and many strands of Christian religion have had to compete with one another on the basis of what they offered in this world and the next. Perhaps this has lead to more sophisticated concepts of god and eternity and more pluralistic and humane treatment of the human condition on this earth. One student of religion, Rodney Stark, believes that Christianity has developed the best concepts of God.[213] He refers to it as "discovering God" and thinks it is a real process of discovery. Despite these observations, Christianity still includes branches of violent fundamentalists who would use physical power to control the human world and of Pentecostal groups who celebrate a primitive Christianity in some ways similar to first-century Christian mysticism.

Adam Smith in his famous treatise, *The Wealth of Nations*,[214] first wrote about a limited versus an open religious marketplace. He felt that state control and backing created an unresponsive and passive religion while an open, competitive market created vibrant religions responsive to the needs of their members. Rodney Stark has applied Smith's ideas to ancient Rome, which may have been the first such religious marketplace.[215] He also notes that Europeans today are relatively much less involved with religion, probably because they have spent their lives with conservative state-sponsored religious establishments—in contrast to North America with its open and enthusiastic religious marketplace.

Regardless of the sophistication of a religious tradition, the common believer looks to have a useful religion—for social and personal support, for emotional and even sometimes physical help. The intellectual believer would like a religion that does these things but also has minimal conflict with science and reason and allows for some pluralism of interpretation. Within groups of humans there is variation in what we find plausible and in how much of our lives we wish to make religious. To some degree, the Roman Catholic world has dealt with this by having many religious orders that do have some variation in theology and emphasis. The Protestant world has dealt with it by having many denominations. In an increasingly interconnected civilization, all religions are evolving and having to cope in some way with the same concerns. Those unable to evolve are likely to eventually be replaced.

The Good of Religion

One might ask if religion has been good for the human race. I believe that, overall, in its thousands of years of existence, it has been a positive force. It has usually supported education, decreased barbarism, supported morality, increased the chance that people would be treated as individuals, not objects, and organized communities to support good—and sometimes heroic goals. Certainly Thomas Cahill portrays Ireland as a much nicer place in which to live a human life for several hundred years after St Patrick brought Catholicism there.[216]

Perhaps the greatest downside has been religion's support of hierarchy. The aristocracy in many cultures has found religion useful in justifying the oppression of the common man for the benefit of the elite. Even this is a two-edged sword, as religion's support of a just and good ruler may improve the chance that the society will prosper and be a happy place. Nevertheless, some observers, maybe most notably Karl Marx, have found this abusive and unacceptable—especially as Marx saw it in nineteenth-century Europe.

Some believers have accused me of writing about nothing but the downside of religion. This has in no way been my intention, as I set out to document how religion, as a human construct, actually worked—to achieve its great successes in our world. Its plasticity and use for both good and evil is, I believe, somewhat of a surprise to many believers, as they have limited their religious evaluations to positive interpretations. The traditions present themselves as though they were products of the supernatural sent to benefit our world. Looking at the plethora of traditions, the many human needs served by religion, and the weakness of evidence for the supernatural, makes belief in a human origin most plausible for some of us.

In an attempt to judge the benefits of religion, we might ask what a society without religion would look like. None has ever existed, so we can only imagine. The Marxists tried to have a society without god—though they offered a limited religious substitute—the "party." It didn't work well enough to make the rest of us jealous. Perhaps society as we know it isn't even possible without religion, or something very similar, filling its place in the culture. Clearly cultural evolution seems to have favored religion. Maybe other ways could be found for meeting the many human needs that a religion covers, but in practice it appears that one of the common religions is probably the most parsimonious way of satisfying these needs.

The most powerful aspects of a religious tradition are probably related to its god beliefs. They are so powerful because they are desirable and essentially intuitive. We find it seems natural to believe that there are omnipotent and kindly figures controlling the world and wishing us well. In practice, almost every religion includes such figures, even Buddhism that started out without a god. This may be both a result of and reinforcement for human optimism.

The Possibility of a Universal Ethics

Karen Armstrong has recently written a wonderful commentary on the religious past and her hopes for its future. Her book *The Great Transformation*[217] is a history of religious ideas focused on the Axial Age, which she dates from approximately 800 to 200 BCE. Here she finds the roots of all the major religious traditions dominating the world today. Her art (and possibly the world's salvation) is to find, within every tradition, thinkers who transcended the violent and the egoistic. These thinkers believed that the highest spiritual development comes through learning to respect others and ultimately all living things. Reaching Enlightenment, the perception of God, The Way, nirvana, etc., is thought to come from a sophisticated and broad application of something like the Golden Rule. Theological doctrines become unimportant. The human world has obviously struggled for over two thousand years with these ideas, and the ideas still have very limited currency. They have persisted as the esoteric, attractive to intellectuals and mystics and experientialists, but nearer the fringes than the center. The Indian ascetic and politician Gandhi is probably the only major figure in my lifetime to attempt to follow these ideas and to have some real political impact. Unfortunately, this is not the useful everyday religion that wins elections, builds cathedrals, fights wars, and comforts soldiers in fox holes.

We can however still have hopes. There is a fundamental similarity of this view of religion and the view of human responsibility provided by Emmanuel Kant's categorical imperative—that we would desire to have the principles of our behavior generalized to all people, or that we not treat other humans as objects. The Scottish Enlightenment (David Hume, Adam Smith, and others) understood ethical human behavior as originating from our empathetic identification with others. This seems to also be dependent on a deeply similar interpretation of human nature and need. There might be room here for more development of a common human ethics that transcended sectarian religion. Unfortunately, sectarian religions would lose some of their power if they gave up this area of control, so progress may be difficult, slow, or impossible. A vision of increased human peace and prosperity could be a driving force, but what power group would find an incentive for promoting this?

It is a bit of a dream, but perhaps a modern democratic society could agree on the development of a universal system of moral or ethical education for its youth and a set of universal ethical principles to which all citizens would subscribe. Religious groups that refused to support this would not face violent suppression but would have to face having this information regularly on public display so that all in the culture would be aware of their rejection of the ethical standards. These would be standards higher than the legal code, not prosecuted in a court of law but expected of the most exemplary of citizens. Having ideals may be beneficial even if you can't always reach them, just as our dreams may motivate us.

Accommodation with Science

Religion and science may be viewed as fundamentally different human activities. The main goals of a religious group are emotional support of the individual and the community and appeasement of the supernatural, while the goals of a scientific society are to critically examine and understand the natural world in its biological, chemical, and physical principles—exploiting these where possible to increase human thriving. When religion makes supernatural claims, science can only say it doesn't go there and has no tools to evaluate such claims. Reason can comment on the epistemology of such beliefs but never disprove them. When religion's claims relate to nature, history, geology, paleontology, etc., then science can offer a reasoned commentary.

One way that religion might control its conflicts with science would be to keep its commentary on the evaluable natural world tentative and able to be revised. In the long run, religion must live with science if it wants to thrive. Science will not go away and has been too successful to be easily discounted. It can't be suppressed in a given culture without putting that culture at risk of losing out to cultures that encourage science and technology. Some religions may have to make major changes—such as new approaches to the mind-body problem, to the origin of life, and to the history of the earth. For instance, the development of neuroscience is making it much harder to believe that there is some immaterial soul, which carries our mind or is our mind going from this existence to some future existence, here or elsewhere.

Carl Sagan reportedly said, "A religion that stressed the magnificence of the universe as revealed by modern science might be able to draw forth reserves of reverence and awe hardly tapped by traditional faiths. Sooner or later, such a religion will emerge."[218] The history of human civilization is filled with religions that have been replaced. Most of them were preliterate, so our knowledge of them relies on the discoveries of archeology. We do know that "new" religions tend to include pieces of older ones—as mentioned in our section on the evolution of religion. The prediction of a genuinely successful new religion is most problematic, but it is noteworthy that our world regularly sees attempts to found new religions. These are usually small and local, but maybe someday one will emerge that is science-friendly and has other features allowing the possibility of a broad attraction. A widespread following is at least a possibility. Universality is not to be expected—we humans are too diverse. Most likely a universal religion would last for a golden moment and then be fractured by the faithful into smaller subsets.

Tolerance and Pluralism

The increasing availability of rapid communications and high-speed travel has been gradually shrinking our world, especially for the last century. Most recently, we are becoming a global television community as TV audiences worldwide may watch an Olympics, a papal funeral, a war, or some other monumental event. The audience may include billions of people. One effect of this on the religious world is to put particular religions on worldwide display, for better or worse. The violence of the Islamic world has been particularly on display in the last fifteen to twenty years. Christian violence has been demonstrated in the Balkan wars of the 1990s, in murders related to abortion clinics in the United States, and possibly in the American attempt to change the government and maybe the culture of Iraq, sadly playing into the hands of a violent Islam. The Jews have provided their own public violence both against the Arabs, and in murdering their own prime minister over a religious disagreement. This violence is a strong negative for the religious traditions, but the media do not always expose it for the terrible insanity that it represents. The media people may perhaps find it difficult to provide a critical commentary because they share or sympathize with some of the religious sentiments driving the violence.

Another way the shrinking world affects religions is by offering the opportunity for global competition for power. Violence may be delivered over great distances if the followers of one sect have enough anger toward another. Hopefully, this fact plus the public exposure of religiously based violence will eventually lead to a rejection of violence as an acceptable part of any religious tradition. This is certainly a vain hope for the near future, as many so called "fundamentalists" of the Christian, Islamic, and Jewish traditions accept violence as a needed path in fulfilling their goals. Violence between Hindus and Muslims, and between Hindus and Sikhs, has also been a huge problem in India to varying degrees for centuries. Divorcing religion from violence may be extremely difficult but might help religion's long-term survival as a desirable human institution.

A further religious concern is that the suicidal beliefs of some fringe religious groups could conceivably put the whole planet at risk sometime in the future. In fact, many strands of Christianity, and strands of some of other religions, contain within them the apocalyptic idea of a returning savior god, coming at the end of time to save the faithful. Some Christians think that obedience and faith, even expressed violently, will bring his return, just as the first-century Jews fighting the Romans at the fall of Jerusalem and Masada thought that they would be saved by a powerful messiah. The end result is the opposite of what is hoped—cataclysmic loss for those expecting salvation.

Every religious tradition has many strands. Suppression of the violence and emphasis on the humane aspects of each religion would change the religion and our world. Who has the power, or the will, to do this? Resorting to violence allows a small group to control a much larger group. Fundamentalist leaders of all traditions, who appeal to violence, seem all too frequently to find an eager following—successfully reaching the young and inexperienced by glorifying the violence. One opinion would be that to change these violent traditions would take powerful leadership emboldened by some human catastrophe and willing to use both public opinion and violence, or its threat, as necessary to alter the traditions. We can hope for nonviolent social evolution, but it is unclear if those truly driven to violence by religious beliefs will be so easily restrained.

At this point, I would note that it is a human tendency to dichotomize the world into one's own group—who are the good people—and the others—who are usually not trustworthy, and possibly malicious or evil. Primitive people do this routinely[219] and so do more sophisticated racial groups—for instance at times in history European, Arian, Chinese, and Japanese cultural groups or subgroups have claimed superiority over the rest of the world. Religion seems one of the most powerful ways of motivating and justifying such a splitting of the world into us and them. The underlying propensity seems likely to be put there by evolution and useful in protecting the group and improving the chance of survival for the individual, especially in the days of our hunter-gatherer existence.

Since religious education is largely a non-rational education, given especially to young children, it seems unlikely that religions will ever be selected by some objective criteria. We might, however, ask for more effective teaching of tolerance. A hopeful note for me was an article by Carrie Kilman titled "One Nation Many Gods" published in the fall of 2007.[220] She described the only required U.S. high school course on world religions—which had been in place in Modesto, California for seven years. In 2006, interviewers explored the effects of this class and reported it made the students more tolerant and understanding of other religions than their own. None of those interviewed had, however, any interest in switching traditions. This would seem a nonthreatening improvement.

The Future—Seen Darkly

Over several generations, I would expect that the conflicts of religion and science would decrease as most institutional religions evolve and extricate themselves from this useless contest. On the other hand, the world may never be completely safe from messianic cults that rise in response to the message of some mystic. These groups are often semi-secret, typically include some apocalyptic expectations, and seem to appeal especially strongly to those who have a deep belief in the supernatural. They do not appear to be confined to any particular religious culture. One example from this genre was the 1995 release of lethal saran gas on the Tokyo subway by members of the Aum Shinrikyo movement or cult.[221] Other recent examples of tight bonding, unusual religious beliefs, apocalyptic expectations, and suicidal solutions come from the Heaven's Gate cult mentioned in the second chapter and from the mass suicide in 1978 of the People's Temple cult in Jonestown (Guyana)—lead by Reverend Jim Jones.[222]

I do not believe the world would be better off if one religion—even a "good" one—were dominant everywhere. Pluralism is safer for us and for our religions. Rodney Stark, Alfred Whitehead, and others believe that Christianity has the greatest truth and that the development of science was dependent on that truth. It may be that Christianity's acceptance of the world as real and important and its attempt to develop a rational theology created an environment conducive to the development of science—at least more conducive than other places in the world. Perhaps of equal or greater importance the Protestant Reformation removed the single controlling mother of society, and freed a dynamism of thought and a competitive spirit that led Europe to conquer and colonize the world, and that same spirit lead to the attempt to conquer nature—that we call science. Shadia Drury supports my contention writing, "It is because we have dethroned Christianity that our societies are more free and prosperous than the Islamic societies."[223] Christianity may be an excellent religion, but no religion deserves unchallenged control of a civilization.

Recalling Carl Sagan's comments mentioned earlier, I would note that E.O. Wilson has suggested[224] that humans come equipped with an emotionally powerful "mythopoeic drive." He thinks we should concede that scientific materialism is a mythology but a noble one. Its central core is the "evolutionary epic." Many of its very plausible assertions can never be proven with absolute finality. Wilson thinks that scientific materialism may someday come to understand the complexity and power of our inherited tendencies to religious belief. It is his hope that by doing this and by showing in so many other areas the power of knowledge over ignorance, scientific materialism may eventually become the dominant mythology for human culture. Even he is, however, unable to see belief in God completely disappearing, though at one point he refers to our religions as "a jerrybuilt foundation of partly obsolete Ice-Age adaptations."

I agree that religion similar to what we have is likely to maintain a place in human culture. For thousands of years we have used religions in our attempts to find community, stability, justice, hope, and even immortality in a world where these are all in very limited supply. Religion has also been the road to power, wealth, and fame for a smaller number of people. There are good reasons to think that religions will remain with us. Their wide power may decrease in the future, but there will almost certainly be individuals and groups who choose to build their lives around religious practice. Cordwainer Smith, who wrote science fiction set five to ten thousand years in the future, included in his future, mostly secular society, adherents to a small mystical religious sect. I would tend to agree with him. Not every man can face a cold and rational universe. Beliefs such as our religions provide are so attractive to many that they can be expected to endure in some form through the foreseeable future.

Summary

Religions evolve because the human world evolves and their conditions of success change. They are associated with many good things in our societies—but there are also negatives such as the support of oppressive power. The possibility of a universal ethics is very attractive to some of us. It would, however, require religions to give up the position that God or the supernatural, through them, is the definer of our ethical responsibilities—sadly, this may not be an option in the near future. Science has immensely altered the conditions of our lives in the last three hundred years—with increasing rapidity. To have long-term success, religions must find ways to avoid conflict with science. Such conflict decreases the credibility of religion for at least the educated part of the population.

Most religions are inherently intolerant of those not sharing their belief system. With varying degrees of intensity, they subscribe to the doctrine of one truth. We can hope that exposing school-age children to the basics of a wide variety of religious beliefs might allow them to be more tolerant and able to support a religiously pluralistic society— the possibility of more than one truth. The future is hard to predict in a world dominated by rapidly changing technology and its many empowering products. Our current religions have lasted for thousands of years and are seemingly more sophisticated than the religions that they replaced. Religion seems likely in some form to persist far into the future.

I have two particular fears. One of these is the possibility of small fundamentalist groups with apocalyptic beliefs—which may justify any insanity in pursuit of some "holy goal"—acquiring access to military hardware allowing them to kill millions of people. The other fear is the use of religious belief in times of societal stress to justify the selection of minority groups as scapegoats for oppression or extermination. Ruthless and pragmatic politicians may use and have used such schemes to deflect criticism and to increase their political power.

15. Personal Postscript

There is no wealth but life.

John Ruskin, *Unto This Last*

The essence of being human is that one does not seek perfection, that one is sometimes willing to commit sins for the sake of loyalty, that one does not push asceticism to the point where it makes friendly intercourse impossible, and that one is prepared in the end to be defeated and broken up by life, which is the inevitable price of fastening one's love upon other human individuals.

—George Orwell, *Reflections on Gandhi*

An alternative title I considered for this text was: *Memoir from a Life Lived Near Religion*. A lot of such time as I could spare has been spent in trying to understand the human condition and its opportunities and limitations—to make sense of my own life in the human context. In this section, I may allow myself to be even more opinionated than previously.

The Necessity of Ideology

Ideology is necessary because we all must have goals and values to function in the world, and we will always feel that we must have an explanation or justification for these goals and values. Our explanation is our ideology in some narrative or other form. Here we relate our personal goals and values to some larger story about the world or universe. A religion is the most common way this is done. Throughout human history, this has probably been the most simple and straightforward way of creating a story with widespread participation and understanding.

We humans learn values and goals early in life. We live with other people and from them we probably learn most of these things. If we are acculturated to a religious tradition, it will provide part of this education–formally if possible. However, it seems likely that the experiences of living in a family, on a playground, and in a schoolroom are more powerful and immediate for the young and wonderfully impressionable mind. We are especially open to such learning when we are quite young, perhaps less than ten years old. Religion has filled this role so successfully that the vast majority of us die within or near the religious ideology into which we were born and/or acculturated. In fact, I refer to myself as a cultural Seventh-day Adventist, since my manner of living has changed little, even as my metaphysical understandings have undergone major alteration.

Though much of common religious belief seems seriously compromised by any rational analysis of the human experience in the world, this fact is almost irrelevant to the credulous believer who cites his knowledge by "faith." This "faith" seems to mean an inner equanimity with the belief set in question, probably because of deep psychological structures created during his acculturation. A method of acculturation without belief in the supernatural but with a deep respect for all life might take some people out of the religious cycle, while maintaining their chance of being "good people" with happy fulfilling lives here on earth. Would this be better for our world? We may never know, but it seems to work for some people.

Varieties of Need for Religious Belief

In primitive societies, the cultural anthropologists have suggested that magic and religious ritual were used to deal with important events whose outcomes were unpredictable—with things like ocean voyaging, planting time, marriage, and death.[225] Malinowski suggested that these rituals were a way of supporting the natural optimism of the human. In the modern urban world, these rituals persist, especially for marriage, for death, and sometimes for illness. For many people, the rituals still help maintain an optimism that keeps hope and planning for the future alive.

There is, however, great variation from one person to another in the need for and appreciation of religious belief. Some have no problem with believing we are alone in the universe, and they seem to be no less ethical or good in their behavior than those who claim strong religious conviction. This is my own experience, and John Stuart Mill claimed a similar experience. Other men can only find meaning in their lives when they throw those lives into some larger cause. Some men's greatest satisfactions are found in emotional experiences, while others find their most compelling rewards in rationally addressing intellectual challenges. Our propensities for these different activities are probably not simply matters of choice but are most likely significantly determined by both genetics and early conditioning.

We thus should not expect that there will ever be some universal ideology or religious program that satisfies the emotional needs of all. The most desirable human society in terms of freedom, happiness, creativity, and productivity may well be a society that contains and protects a wide variety of religious beliefs, without letting any particular orthodoxy become dominant or controlling. Its only desired orthodoxy would be respect for others and their beliefs—a sort of shared civil religion as some have suggest we have had in the United States. The failure to achieve this may very well destroy the society. The one unacceptable belief is the belief in intolerance; the belief that any member can and may force others to conform to his particular ideology because it "is right." The attempt to force uniformity of belief is a crushing burden for any society and may make it an unhappy and dangerous place to live. .

Emotion and Reason

Most people do not hold their religion as the result of a rational conscious analysis of the world. It is usually the result of an acculturation, of the instruction of respected authority figures, and sometimes the result of emotional experiences. One's social world is usually deeply intertwined with one's religion. The result is that our religious loyalties are enmeshed with powerful emotions. For most people they are not dispassionate judgments that can be readily weighed and changed on the basis of negotiation.

Some religious people maintain that faith and reason are alternate ways of obtaining knowledge. My judgment is that faith is not a trustworthy source of knowledge, though it is clearly used to support religious belief in many traditions. The very fact that it supports a wide variety of conflicting religious beliefs makes it seem unreliable to this observer. Beliefs about the supernatural are, however, usually backed by faith claims, since they are not generally grounded in reason or science. Such beliefs, however, fit very well into the majority of human minds and evoke powerful positive emotions.

Our theologians are ask to provide a rational scaffold on which to hang our religious beliefs, and they do their best to oblige, but their effort seldom convinces those who don't already believe the tradition in question. Their work attempts a formal rationalization of the tradition, but my limited experience suggests that it is often almost irrelevant for the average lay person—though it provides an official explanation for the shape of the religion. It thus appears that much of religion's power lies in its involving deep emotional structures in the brain. Positions not arrived at by reason are not easily defended by reason—they are defended by appeals to strong emotions.

The Price of Refuge

"Every form of refuge has its price" is a line from a song the Eagles made popular decades ago. Religion, the great human refuge, is no exception. It has significant material, emotional, and opportunity costs, and I can offer only a limited accounting of these. Most people would say it is worth the costs—maybe judging this because of eternal implications—but I doubt that many people have seriously and objectively attempted any systematic accounting.

Within the Christian tradition typically, the material expenses of religion may include the cost of its lands and buildings, the cost of educating and employing its clergy and its missionaries, and the cost of administering its properties and workers. All this wealth is generally obtained from the lay members of the organization via regular appeals for funds for "the Lord's work." Laymen who can afford it are expected to give generously and many do respond—to some combination of love, guilt, and hope for heaven. To quote Opus (comics) we have a "loving and perfect creator who asks only to be worshipped, praised, and paid plenty."

To the individual the emotional consequences of religion often include a narrowing of one's community in order to separate one's self from the evil "world." The believer may find it difficult to look on the world and appreciate her role as another human in a long tradition. She may not be able to read Homer, Plutarch, and Shakespeare and appreciate what she shares with the heroes and villains of these human stories. This narrowing of community may lead to cruelty toward other people—even family members that do not share the desired belief system. Another emotional cost of religion is guilt over victimless rule breaking—"picking up sticks" on the Sabbath or reading a banned book—and over not being "good enough." Christianity even offers "original sin" guaranteeing that you are intrinsically evil, with the "true" religion being your only hope.

One of the opportunity costs of religion is often nihilism about this world. This comes easily if you believe that the only important life is that later, possibly immortal life, for which this life is but preparation. You do not fight for your best interests in this life if you think that your job is to be humble and accept the poor place in the world that God has arranged for you. Nietzsche criticized Christianity for this. In *Beyond Good and Evil* he wrote: "The Christian Faith from the beginning, is sacrifice: the sacrifice of all freedom, all pride, all self-confidence of spirit; it is at the same time subjection, a self-derision, and self-mutilation."[226] Many Christians actually rise above this, but such attitudes make religion useful as a tool for domination of the majority, by those with economic, political, or ecclesiastical power. A similar devaluation of the present occurs for those strands of religion that propose an imminent end of the world. Saving for the future, education for the future, and ecological concerns may become almost irrelevant as the adherents urgently seek salvation.

Most of the religious traditions of the world privilege the male over the female. Some humans, more often men than women, completely devote themselves to these traditions, abandoning domestic love and duty, procreation, and sex. They completely devote a human life to what seems to be a sacred fantasy, leaving the real, mundane, and possibly better world to the rest of us. In this regard it may be noted that there are good reasons to think that human sexuality is not just about procreation but is also important in pair bonding and the creation of a home for children.[227] To give this up may be to give up something for which we are especially fitted. One also suspects that a celibate ascetic life is at risk of being impoverished in terms of the moral and practical dilemmas and the emotional rewards that are common in family life.

Certainty

She believed in nothing; only her skepticism kept her from being an atheist.

—Jean Paul Sartre, *The Words*

Ideological beliefs that are held with confidence or certainty contain within that confidence a demand to control others, so as to make them do what is in their own best long-term interest. Such hubristic claims have been, and are, the seeds of religious war, of the Inquisition, of the Holocaust, of Stalin's and Mao's purges, and of today's suicide bombers. Certainty about belief systems harbors the danger of terrible error and fuels the willingness for violence. Probably the only safe certainty we can maintain is a certainty that our best understandings are conditional and always seeking improvement. Even this "certainty" might best be considered a conditional human judgment for a world such as we have. We can be sure that years, decades, and centuries will refine and change our understandings.

All ideologies that, confident of their truth, seek to demonize those who reject that ideology will then tend to withdraw their ethical concerns from the nonbelievers. These nonbelievers may then be portrayed as less than fully human, and the "true believers" will be allowed or even encouraged to treat them in ways that would be considered evil if directed toward those within the believing community. Certainty is the necessary ingredient to make this happen.

The Religious Case against Belief[228] is a recent attempt at a new approach to the question of certainty. In this book, James Carse, a very well-informed student of the religious world, redefines religion as a long-running—at least many centuries, preferably millennia—discussion of the great human questions such as the meaning of life and the meaning of death. He thinks these questions have no answers, only an annotated presentation of the possibilities by a long series of discussants. He thus argues that religious history itself militates against our certainties. One could hope that good people would pay some attention to his clear pragmatic argument for a relaxation of the world's religious certainties—though perhaps that is hoping for too much.

One cannot lightly take away certainty, especially from the Abrahamic traditions, for they depend on it in daily cultural practice. To a significant degree, they would be emasculated by giving it up. How could a religious leader demand that you devote your life and your wealth to his organization if he could not offer you the certainty that he understands God's will for you and for the universe? One might wish that such leaders could at least give up believing that their God only accepts one route to his kingdom—and they hold the keys.

Certainty is one great enemy of the open and pluralistic society that many visionaries would hold out as America's goal.

The Supernatural

The existence of the supernatural has been a postulate of many, if not all, successful religious systems, and many religio-philosophical systems such as Stoicism and Platonism. There is no known test of the existence question for the supernatural, no proof or disproof that can satisfy those who seek an objective answer. Those who claim they can answer in the affirmative usually give private experience or ancient texts as justification. Public answers or proofs are not offered. In the ancient world, prophecy and healing were also considered evidence of the divine or supernatural. These have not passed well into the modern world, as people have become more able to objectively evaluate such claims.

Many observers, looking closely and carefully at a complex world, see no evidence of a kind and caring providence. They see good and evil delivered to humans regardless of their personal qualities. Like David Hume, I have become skeptical about the existence of a kind and caring divine power. If there is some divine power, it seems unconcerned with the course of human affairs or with the realization of outcomes that we call good or evil. This, of course, does not prove that no divine power or god exists. It just says that such a power seems uninvolved in the world as we experience it. The Intelligent Design (ID) debate is irrelevant to this concern, as it only seems to addresses an origins question. Some would try to retrieve a kind caring God through these arguments but I can't see how.

Origins

All confident statements about ultimate origins seem to be statements of "faith." Religions often teach that they have true and certain knowledge about such things, while science offers conjectures based on reasoning, models, and extensions of known scientific principles. Religions think that their understandings are for all time, but at least scientists—if thoughtful—know that, over decades and centuries, their models, ideas, and conclusions will evolve, possibly in very unexpected ways.

The ID movement offers a reasoned commentary on the probability of life arising spontaneously versus coming from some "creator." One difficulty is that their analysis is usually biased toward very unlikely evolutionary scenarios. These are then "straw men," that can readily be shown to be extremely improbable.[229] There are often alternative scenarios that skilled commentators have offered, and that seem reasonable to many of us, but are summarily rejected by the ID representatives. For instance, the chance that an enzyme composed of 120 amino acids would form from a pool of over 20 amino acids in the proper sequence on a random basis is ridiculously small. If, however, one recognizes that enzymatic activity is mainly dependent on much smaller active binding sites (one or two such sites), the chance of spontaneous formation becomes much higher, though still small.

Having rejected evolutionary schemes, the ID proponents are then left with the equally difficult task of supplying and explaining a creator god who would make a world like this with its good and its evil, its life form relationships, and its appearance of great antiquity—in a universe of even greater antiquity. Having made a universe characterized by relentless change, is this god himself eternal and unchanging, or does he also evolve in some way? Generally, instead of taking on these issues, they retreat to a religious commentary that "God" did it. The ID proponents seem to be a combination of religious people seeking to protect religion from possible inroads of science, and anti-science people who feel that science, at least in its attempts to study origins, has gone beyond its limits.

There will be no compelling answer to this debate for all involved, at least in our lifetimes. It is, however, notable that an evolutionary paradigm has become pervasive in explaining the world of biology, and its extensive interdependences, especially at the molecular level. Many religious people find the scientific explanations compelling and participate in both traditions. For instance, see Francis Collins's book *The Language of God*.[230] For many of us, the scientific work remains exciting and satisfying regardless of who or what started the show.

Religion as a Political and Practical Tool

Out of timber so crooked as that from which man is made nothing entirely straight can be built.

    —Immanuel Kant (See preface to Isaiah Berlin's *The Crooked Timber of Humanity* for alternate translations)

Some of our politicians eagerly hold up their religious claims to justify their political goals. This is frightening and dangerous, because politicized religion is dangerous religion. Those with a political agenda ignore the dark face of religion, pretending it is only fair and good. They either lie or have no sense of or knowledge of history. Though the religious have marginalized atheism in the political discussion, they have probably marginalized the less dangerous player. The real danger to a human society is a confident "faith-based" belief in intolerance—namely that a particular group has absolute truth and should forcibly spread that truth to the larger world around them. Such a group has no possibility for compromise or negotiation. From such beliefs come the Gulag, the Inquisition, the Crusades, and modern religious terrorism.

Religions claim to be completely devoted to doing good things in our world. Their documents and organizational structures seem to be supportive of this claim. The one thing that they obscure is that they are really human organizations, run by humans, for humans. These remarkable structures can be thought of as complex ideological tools that are very powerful; therefore capable of great good and great harm, depending on the ends to which they are applied, and the skill of those who would use them. Many people find in them solace for this life and some hope for the future. Others find the emotional support that sends them on a life of service to the sick, orphaned, or homeless. For instance, most American cities have missions for the destitute that are based on a religious salvation and healing model with food for both the body and the soul.

Other men use religion for personal aggrandizement and material enrichment—see many of the television ministries. Some men have used religion to justify violence, both Christian and Muslim, while others such as Gandhi and Martin Luther King, used religion to justify nonviolent action to lift up the weak and downtrodden. The Holocaust in Europe found the pope signing a concordat with Hitler, and most of the official religious organizations of Germany supporting the Nazis. On the other side, many Christians used their faith to justify protecting and aiding Jews to escape Nazi power. It thus seems that something human outside of or beyond religion—most likely a complex of motives—contributes to or controls how a particular religion is applied to a particular human situation. Usually religion, in some form, is exploited on both sides of any serious, durable conflict—for instance the American Civil War.

Thoughts for Life Regardless of Religion

The end is nothing
The way is all

—Unknown

Where I live in a constant endeavor to fence against ill health and the other evils of life by mirth, being firmly persuaded that every time a man smiles, but much more so when he laughs that it adds something to this fragment of life.

—Lawrence Sterne, *Tristram Shandy*

The world we live in, the universe beyond the world, and the complexities of life are glorious and astonishing whether the result of natural or supernatural forces. I am, at this stage of my life, satisfied with natural explanations based on our limited but expanding understandings of physical law. Nevertheless, I stand in awe of that which we may call the "creation." I have no quarrels with those who would invoke a distant creator god to explain these things. To those who would invoke a caring personal deity, I would say I believe I understand why, though I can't share the belief. There is a kind of spirituality available to even "nonbelievers," and I would claim that spirituality.

Over many years, I have collect in my thoughts a few concepts or ideas to use in living and in thinking about my own life and its complications. This is a very incomplete unsystematic collection of comments that I present only with the hope someone else may find some of them interesting or helpful.

Happiness is now. Simple things may bring pleasure, depending on our attitude—and such things can be found at any time if we stop and think, and if we educate ourselves for this. Our attitudes and expectations have a marked effect on what we find in our world. Alternatively, one can say, "We only live now and after that we are dead."

Respect all life. All life represents a struggle, perhaps not always so poignantly felt as for the human, but still a struggle deserving respect. Karen Armstrong found this an important strand in all the great religions and I was pleased with her analysis, though I think formal religion isn't the only way there—in fact it often doesn't get there.

The best source of happiness is to make another being happy. The famous atheist Robert Ingersoll said, "If you want to be happy, make someone else happy." It is remarkable how true and easily verified is this assertion.

The universe, both local and extended, is full of much beauty. Sometimes there is a lot of ugliness, but if you look for it, there is also great beauty.

Most people are doing the best they can with the hand they have been dealt. If you think they are wrong, try to get inside their world, to understand their decisions. I was once given an American Indian saying: "Before you judge a man, walk three days in his moccasins." Often, though not always, you will get a new appreciation of the "why" in someone else's life.

The most wonderful and rewarding thing in life is to create. I believe that the most important thing we ever create is ourselves. One of Bob Dylan's songs has the lines "That he not busy being born, Is busy dying."[231] This is the work of a lifetime—of being born and reborn, creating and recreating ourselves as long we have such power. This of course only makes sense if you think that humans have some freedom of action. Like Jean-Paul Sartre, I would say *freedom is what you do with what has been done to you.*[232]

Life may have no meaning beyond what we give to it. To live it well is to give it meaning. To rise above some infirmity, to reach some major goal or achievement, to make the world a better place for your fellow humans—all seem to give meaning to a life. Few of us can truly change the world, but most of us can find achievable victories that we think are worth the struggle and may be major defining points for our brief lives.

Having humor about our life and it's never ending struggles helps us to relax and enjoy this life, and yet to have perspective and humility about our own and humanity's place and accomplishments in the great pageant of the Universe.

Many of the god models of the ancient religious texts seem to be built on the idea of the ultimate oriental potentate. I would like to suggest that if there is some good god, he must be better and more charitable than the best human being you ever knew. He wouldn't torture anyone, and he wouldn't kill people over theological details or believing wrong things. If such a god existed, we could all admire him—but the supporting data seems strangely unavailable.

16. Brief Document History and Acknowledgments

For over twenty years, I have been a regular participant in a Saturday morning discussion group sponsored by a local Seventh-day Adventist church and supervised by Loma Linda University professors of religion James Walters and Dalton Baldwin (retired). Certain topics seemed to come up repeatedly in our discussions, so in the summer of 2005, I decided to write a commentary on some of these that I might pass out to friends for their feedback. My efforts to organize my thoughts about religion as a human project lead to what seemed better personal understanding and an expanding commentary over the next couple years. After two years work, I shared my commentary with friends, including the members of the discussion group. The leaders of the group decided to make my project the focus of our meetings, devoting about three months to giving me critical feedback and alternate views that aided me in revising and improving my manuscript. Since that time, I have continued to study, and intermittent revisions to the manuscript have seemed appropriate through October 2010.

My strongest motivation to complete this project was my perception that few of us understood why religion was so important in our ever-evolving world. In midlife I had come to doubt its truth claims but had not been able to appreciate why it was so ubiquitous and powerful. As I got older and I watched people use their religion and observed the accolades they gave to it, and understood that these were sincere and intelligent human beings, I came to better appreciate the place and power of supernatural belief in human society. Writing this manuscript eventually became a way to improve my own understanding and an attempt to share that improving grasp with others who might have similar interests.

There are many people to whom I owe thanks for anything that may be right about my work—the faults are mine alone. Two friends who encouraged me to continue this work from the start were running partners Doug Will and Elber Camacho, with Doug having endured several versions of the manuscript. Max Phillips made an appreciated but unrequested early edit of my work that helped to clarify it as did a later edit by my son Colin Wilbur. The presenters for the discussion group reviews were Dennis Hokama, Ervin Taylor, Max Phillips, Lee Greer, James Walters, Richard Rice, Michelle and Dave Scharfenberg, Jan Long, Mailen Kootsey, Birthe Thomsen, John Testerman, T. Joe Willey, and Petre Cimpoeru. They all provided erudite commentary that challenged me to improve my efforts. Others who have given me feedback and support include (in no particular order): Ken Walters, Robert Rentschler, Todd Kessler, Lisa Mackey, Robert Whitsett, Barbara Orr, Richard Jellerson, Washek Pfeffer, Glenn Foster, Ivan Blazen, David Larson, Ronald Anderson, John Buccholz, Todd Burley, Donna Reeves, Keith Colburn, George Grames, Doug and Janet Hackleman, William Jarvis, Elmer Kelln, Carl and Joyce Jordon, Cherry Orne, Marvin and Kimberly Payne, Bill Shull, Lucerne Snipes, John Thiel, and Bob Wonderly. There were almost certainly some other people who attended our discussions or privately reviewed my work and whose names I can't cite.

Bibliography and Notes

1. Johnson, Luke Timothy. *Early Christianity: The Experience of the Divine,* The Teaching Company, Chantilly, VA, 2002 (a 24 lecture course available at www.TEACH12.com).

2. Seldes, George (compiled by). *The Great Thoughts,* Ballantine Books, New York, 1985. (This reference has been used for many quotes from authors whose originals I don't have available).

3. Yeats, William Butler. Quoted in: Brooks, Cleanth. *The Hidden God: Studies in Hemingway, Faulkner, Yeats, Eliot and Warren,* Yale University Press, New Haven, CT, 1963.

4. James, William. *The Varieties of Religious Experience: A Study in Human Nature* (Centenary Edition). New York: Routledge, 2002 (first published 1902).

5. Murray, Charles. *Human Accomplishment: The Pursuit of Excellence in the Arts and Sciences, 800 BC to 1950,* HarperCollins, New York, 2003.

6. Anonymous. *Multidimensional Measurement of Religiousness/ Spirituality for Use in Health Research: A Report of the Fetzer Institute/National Institute on Aging Working Group,* 1999 (reissued 2003), available at www.Fetzer.org.

7. Reese, William. *Dictionary of Philosophy and Religion: Eastern and Western Thought,* Humanity Books, Amherst, NY, 1996.

8. Ecklund, E. H., et al. "The Religious and Spiritual Beliefs and Practices of Academic Pediatric Oncologists in the United States," *Journal of Pediatric Hematology and Oncology* 29(11):736–42, 2007 (Nov).

9. Jones, Charles B. *Introduction to the Study of Religion,* The Teaching Company, Chantilly, VA, 2007 (a 24 lecture course available at www.TEACH12.com).

10. Comte-Sponville, Andre (translator Nancy Huston). *The Little Book of Atheist Spirituality,* Penguin Books, New York, 2008.

11. Hume, David. *Principle Writing on Religion* including *Dialogues Concerning Natural Religion* and *The Natural History of Religion*, (edited by J. C. A. Gaskin), Oxford University Press, Oxford, UK, 1993 (originally published 1779 and 1757).

12. Blackburn, Simon. *Truth: A Guide* (Chapter 1), Oxford University Press, Oxford, UK, 2005.

13. Ehrlich, Eugene, and Marshall De Bruhl, (compiled by). *The International Thesaurus of Quotations,* HarperCollins, New York, 1996.

14. Jenkins, Philip. *The Next Christendom: The Coming of Global Christianity*, Oxford University Press, Oxford, UK, 2002

15. Hand, Learned. *The Spirit of Liberty: Papers and Addresses of Learned Hand,* quotes found at the Web site www.commonlaw.com/Hand.html (accessed 17/Nov/2008).

16. Durkheim, Emile. *The Elementary Forms of the Religious Life*, (1912, English translation by Joseph Swain: 1915), The Free Press, 1965, new English translation Karen Fields, 1995.

17. Ibid.

18. Stark, Rodney. *Discovering God: The Origins of the Great Religions and the Evolution of Belief*, HarperCollins, New York, 2007.

19. Dostoevsky, Fyodor. *The Brothers Karamazov: A Novel in Four Parts with Epilogue* (translated by Richard Pevear and Larissa Volokhonsky), Farrar, Straus and Giroux, New York, 2002 (original published in 1880) (the quotes I use all come from chapter 5, "The Grand Inquisitor").

20. See the entry for "Heaven's Gate (religious group)" at www.wikipedia.org for a very adequate discussion (accessed September 12, 2008).

21. Durkheim, *Elementary Forms*.

22. Holland, Glenn S. *Religion in the Ancient Mediterranean World*, The Teaching Company, Chantilly, VA, 2005 (a 48 lecture course available at www.TEACH12.com).

23. Hale, John R. *Exploring the Roots of Religion,* The Teaching Company, Chantilly, VA, 2009 (a 36 lecture course on the archeology of religion available at www.TEACH12.com).

24. Solomon, Robert C. *No Excuses: Existentialism and the Meaning of Life*, The Teaching Company, Chantilly, VA, 2000 (a 24 lecture course available at www.TEACH12.com).

25. Kimball, Charles. *Comparative Religion*, The Teaching Company, Chantilly, VA, 2008 (a 24 lecture course available at www.TEACH12.com).

26. See multiple papers in *Whatever Happened to the Soul: Scientific and Theological Portraits of Human Nature*, Brown, Warren S., Nancey Murphy, and H. Newton Malony, eds, Fortress Press, Minneapolis, MN, 1998.

27. Pinker, Steven. *The Blank Slate: The Modern Denial of Human Nature*, Penguin Books, New York, 2002.

28. I do not have the Upanishads available as texts, but many Web sites have long quotations and www.Hinduism.co.za/upanisha.htm had the quotation presented here.

29. Wilson, Epiphanius ed. *The Wisdom of Confucius*, (translated by William Jennings 1900), Wings Books, New York, 1982.

30. Camus, Albert. *The Plague*, (original 1947, translated Stuart Gilbert 1948), Vintage Books, New York, 1991.

31. Camus, Albert. *The Myth of Sisyphus and Other Essays*, Vintage Books, New York, 1991.

32. Frankl, Viktor E. *Man's Search for Meaning*, (original 1946, first English edition 1959), Washington Square Press, New York, 1985 (see especially page 170).

33. Diamond, Jared. *Guns, Germs, and Steel: The Fates of Human Societies*, W. W. Norton & Company, New York, 1997 and 1999.

34. Ellenberger, Henri F. *The Discovery of the Unconscious: The History and Evolution of Dynamic Psychiatry*, BasicBooks, New York , 1970.

35. Hoffer, Eric. *The True Believer: Thoughts on the Nature of Mass Movements*, Harper & Row Publishers, Inc., 1951.

36. Diamond, Jared. *Collapse: How Societies Choose to Fail or Succeed*, Viking, New York, 2005.

37. Johnson, Luke Timothy. *Mystical Tradition: Judaism, Christianity, and Islam,* The Teaching Company, Chantilly, VA,

2007 (a 36 lecture course available at www.TEACH12.com); Johnson, *Early Christianity*.

38. Trimble, Michael R. *The Soul in the Brain: The Cerebral Basis of Language, Art and Belief*, The Johns Hopkins University Press, Baltimore, MD, 2007.

39. Seldes, *Great Thoughts*.

40. James, *Varieties of Religious Experience*.

41. Joyce, James. *A Portrait of the Artist as a Young Man*, Penguin Books, New York, 1976 (originally published 1916).

42. Rue, Loyal. *Religion Is Not about God: How Spiritual Traditions Nurture our Biological Nature and What to Expect When They Fail*, Rutgers University Press, Piscataway, NJ, 2005.

43. Martin, David W. *Psychology of Human Behavior*, The Teaching Company, Chantilly, VA, 2006 (a 36 lecture course available at www.TEACH12.com).

44. Stark, *Discovering God*.

45. Finkelstein, Israel and Silberman, Neil. *The Bible Unearthed: Archaeology's New Vision of Ancient Israel and the Origin of Its Sacred Texts*, Touchstone, New York, 2002.

46. McWhorter, John. *The Story of Human Language*, The Teaching Company, Chantilly, VA, 2004 (a 36 lecture course available at www.TEACH12.com).

47. Ehrman, Bart D. *Misquoting Jesus: The Story Behind Who Changed the Bible and Why*, HarperCollins, New York, 2005.

48. Warraq, Ibn. *The Origins of the Koran: Classic Essays on Islam's Holy Book*, Prometheus Books, Amherst, New York, 1998 and *Why I am not a Muslim*, Prometheus Books, Amherst, New York, 2003; Reese, *Dictionary of Philosophy and Religion*.

49. Finkelstein and Silberman, *Bible Unearthed*.

50. Ehrman, *Misquoting Jesus*.

51. Reese, *Dictionary of Philosophy and Religion*.

52. Warraq, *Origins of the Koran*.

53. See Wikipedia article on the Hadith at http://en.wikipedia.org/wiki/Hadith.

54. Wright, Robert. *The Evolution of God*, Little Brown and Company, New York, 2009.

55. Rue, *Religion Is Not about God.*

56. See Wikipedia article on Luther and anti-Semitism. His major work was *On the Jews and Their Lies* published in 1543 (http://en.wikipedia.org/wiki/Martin_Luther_and_the_Jews).

57. Benjamin, Daniel, and Steven Simon. *The Age of Sacred Terror: Radical Islam's War against America,* Random House, New York, 2002.

58. Kimball, Charles. *When Religion Becomes Evil*, HarperCollins, New York, 2002.

59. Dalton, Dennis. *Power Over People: Classical and Modern Political Theory*, The Teaching Company, Chantilly, VA, 1991 (a 16 lecture course available at www.TEACH12.com).

60. Liulevicius, Vejas Gabriel. *Utopia and Terror in the 20th Century*, The Teaching Company, Chantilly, VA, 2003 (a 24 lecture course available at www.TEACH12.com).

61. Tzu, Lao (translation by Victor Mair). *Tao Te Ching: The Classic Book of Integrity and the Way*, Bantam Books, New York, 1990.

62. *The Bhagavad Gita*, translated by Juan Mascaro, Penguin Books, 1962.

63. Nelson-Pallmeyer, Jack. *Is Religion Killing Us? Violence in the Bible and the Quran*, Trinity Press International, Harrisburg, PA, 2003.

64. Sinclair, Upton. *The Profits of Religion*, Prometheus Books, Amherst, New York, 2000 (first published 1918).

65. Seldes, *Great Thoughts.*

66. Williams, Douglas E. *Truth, Hope and Power: The Thought of Carl Popper* (quotes on page 142), University of Toronto Press, Toronto, 1989.

67. Drury, Shadia B. *Terror and Civilization: Christianity, Politics, and the Western Psyche*, Palgrave MacMillan, New York, 2004.

68. Juergensmeyer, Mark. *Terror in the Mind of God: The Global Rise of Religious Violence*, 3rd ed., University of California Press, Berkeley, 2003.

69. Randi, James. *The Faith Healers*, Prometheus Books, Buffalo, NY, 1987.

70. Hackleman, Douglas. *Who Watches? Who Cares? Misadventures in Stewardship*, Members for Church Accountability, Morrison, CO, 2008.

71. Hoffman, Joseph R. "The Morality of Historical Skepticism: Enlightenment and Biblical Criticism," *CSER Review* 2(1):3–7, 2007.

72. Mill, John Stuart. *On Liberty*, Prometheus Books, Buffalo, NY, 1986 (first published 1859).

73. Stark, Rodney, *Discovering God*

74. Muesse, Mark W. *Religions of the Axial Age: An Approach to the World's Religions*, The Teaching Company, Chantilly, VA, 2007 (a 24 lecture course available at www.TEACH12.com).

75. Krakauer, Jon. *Under the Banner of Heaven: A Story of Violent Faith*, Doubleday, New York, 2003.

76. Seldes, *Great Thoughts*.

77. Swift, Rod. *The Results of the Christians vs. Atheists in Prison Investigation* at http://holysmoke.org/icr-pri.htm (accessed 21/Nov /2008).

78. Hauser, Marc, and Peter Singer. "Morality without Religion," *Free Inquiry* Dec 2005–Jan 2006 issue, 18–19 (also found at www.secularhumanism.org).

79. Stenger, Victor J. *Do Our Values Come from God? The Evidence Says No*, available at www.colorado.edu/philosophy/vstenger/ Godless/Vales.htm. The Web site also reports the same material is in his book: *God: The Failed Hypothesis: How Science shows that God does not Exist*, Prometheus Books, Amherst, NY, 2007.

80. Wilson, Edward O. *On Human Nature* (with a new preface), Harvard University Press, Cambridge, MA, 2004 (first published 1978).

81. Wikipedia contributors. *Euthyphro Dilemma,* Wikipedia, the free encyclopedia accessed on line at http://en.wikipedia.org/wiki/ Euthyphro_dilemma (accessed 21/Nov/2008).

82. Koterski, Father Joseph. *Natural Law and Human Nature*, The Teaching Company, Chantilly, VA, 2002 (a 24 lecture course available at www.TEACH12.com).

83. Kane, Robert H. *The Quest for Meaning: Value, Ethics, and the Modern Experience*, The Teaching Company, Chantilly, VA, 1999 (a 24 lecture course available at www.TEACH12.com).

84. Tremlin, Todd. *Minds and Gods: The Cognitive Foundations of Religion*, Oxford University Press, New York, 2006.

85. Pinker, *Blank Slate*.

86. Wikipedia contributors. *Frans de Waal* online at http://en.wikipedia.org/wiki/Frans_de_Waal (accessed Sept 7, 2009).

87. de Waal, Frans. *Primates and Philosophers: How Morality Evolved*, Princeton University Press, Princeton, NJ, 2006.

88. Preston SD, de Waal F. "Empathy: Its Ultimate and Proximate Bases," *Behavioral and Brain Sciences* 25(1), 1–20, 2002 (February) (accessed on line through a Wikipedia link at www.bbsonline.org on Sept. 7, 2009).

89. Rue, *Religion Is Not about God*.

90. Tremlin, *Minds and Gods*.

91. Frohnmayer, Dave. *Situational Ethics, Social Deception, and Lessons of Machiavelli* a speech posted at http://president.uoregon.edu/ (accessed 22/Nov/2008).

92. Wikipedia contributors. See *Sharia* in www.wikipedia.org for an extended discussion of this complex topic (accessed 12/July/2009).

93. Whitecross, Richard. "Separation of Religion and Law? Buddhism, Secularism and the Constitution of Bhutan," *Buffalo Law Review* 55:707–711, 2007 (access on line July 12, 2009).

94. Wikipedia contributors. See *Hindu law* in www.wikipedia.org for an extended discussion of this topic (accessed 12/July/2009).

95. Sowell, Thomas. *Race and Culture: A World View,* Basic Books, New York, 1997.

96. Sisci, Francesco. "China's Catholic Moment" in *First Things*, June–July, 27, 2009 (#194).

97. Jenkins, *Next Christendom.*

98. Holland, *Religion in the Ancient Mediterranean World.*

99. Larson, E. J. and L. Witham. "Leading Scientists Still Reject God," *Nature* 394(6691):313, 1998 (see table and references).

100. Blanton, Dana. *10/28/05 FOX Poll: More Believe in Heaven than Hell* posting on www.FOXNews.com reporting the results of a Fox News survey conducted October 25–26, 2005 reporting the opinions of 900 registered American voters (accessed 22/Nov/2008).

101. Anonymous. *Religious Views and Beliefs Vary Greatly by Country, According to the Latest Financial Times/Harris Poll* found at www.harrisinteractive.com by selecting Financial Times/Harris Poll. Poll conducted online between November 30 and December 15, 2006 with about 2000 participants per country for each of six countries (accessed 22/Nov/08).

102. Newcott, Bill. "Life After Death," *AARP The Magazine*, September & October 2007, 69 (available at www.aarpmagazine.org/people/life_after_death.html).

103. von Mises, Ludwig. *Socialism: An Economic and Sociological Analysis*, Liberty Classics, Indianapolis, Indiana, 1981 (Translation by J. Kahane, 1936, originally published 1922).

104. Wikipedia contributors, *American Civil Religion*, Wikipedia, The Free Encyclopedia, http://en.wikipedia.org/wiki/American_ civil_religion (accessed November 7, 2010).

105. Smith, Adam. *An Inquiry into the Nature and Causes of the Wealth of Nations*, (edited by Edwin Cannan), The Modern Library, New York, 1994 (originally published 1776).

106. Stark, *Discovering God.*

107. Zuckerman, Phil. "The Virtues of Godlessness: The Least Religious Nations Are Also the Most Healthy and Successful," *The Chronicle Review* B4–B5, Jan 30, 2009 (section B of the *Chronicle of Higher Education* LV (#21)) (see also his book: *Society without God*).

108. Letters to the Editor. "The Complicated Relationship between Religiosity and Social Well-Being," *The Chronicle Review*, B22–B23, Feb 20, 2009.

109. Wikipedia contributors. *History of European Research Universities*, found at www.wikipedia.org (accessed July 2, 2009).

110. Wikipedia contributors. *Hospital* at www.wikipedia.org (accessed August 28, 2009).

111. Nagamia, Husain F. *Medicine in Islam* at www.iiim.org (accessed August 28, 2009).

112. Wikipedia contributors. *Christian Reconstructionism*, at http://en.wikipedia.org/wiki/Christian_Reconstructionism (accessed August 19, 2008).

113. Sugrue, Michael. *Thucydides and the Dawn of History*, Lecture 5 in the second section of the first edition of *Great Authors of the Western Literary Tradition*, The Teaching Company, Chantilly, VA, 1996 (an 80 lecture course possibly available at www.TEACH12.com).

114. Dostoevsky, *Brothers Karamazov*.

115. Johnson, Paul. *A History of Christianity*, Touchstone, New York, 1995 (c. 1976).

116. Action, Lord (Dalberg-Acton, John E. E.). *Essays in the History of Liberty* (Selected Writings of Lord Acton), Liberty Fund Inc., 1985.

117. Will, George. "Cato: Upholding the Idea of Liberty," *Cato's Letter* 4(3):1–6, 2006 (Summer 2006).

118. Fremantle, Anne. *Introduction to Fyodor Dostoevsky: The Grand Inquisitor*, Frederick Ungar, New York, 1956 (accessed August 20, 2008 at www.dartmouth.edu/~karamazo/fremantle.html).

119. Grasso, Joseph. "Buddhism: Blood and Enlightenment," *Free Enquiry* 28(2), 51–52, 2008).

120. Finkelstein and Silberman, *Bible Unearthed*.

121. Holland, *Religion in the Ancient Mediterranean World*.

122. Liulevicius, *Utopia and Terror in the 20th Century*.

123. Johnson, Paul. *A History of the Jews*, Harper & Row, New York, 1987.

124. Rashid, Ahmed. *Taliban: Militant Islam, Oil and Fundamentalism in Central Asia*, Yale University Press, New Haven, 2001.

125. Soros, George. *The Age of Fallibility: Consequences of the War on Terror*, PublicAffairs, New York, 2006.

126. Orwell, George. *Politics and the English Language* included in *A Collection of Essays*, Harcourt Inc., Orlando, FL, 1946.

127. Williams, D. R., and M. J. Sternthal. "Spirituality, Religion and Health: Evidence and Research Directions." *Medical Journal of Australia* 186 (10 Suppl): S47–S50, 2007.

128. Anonymous. *Americans Who Are Religious and Older People Are Happier* found at www.harrisinteractive.com (accessed August 14, 2008). This was an online poll conducted March 11–18, 2008 and reported as Harris Poll #46, April 22, 2008.

129. Pargament, K. I. *"Is Religion Nothing But ...? Explaining Religion versus Explaining Religion Away,"* *Psychological Inquiry* 13(3): 239–44, 2002.

130. Powell, L.H., et al. "Religion and Spirituality: Linkages to Physical Health." *American Psychology* 2003 Jan; 58(1):36–52.

131. Williams and Stearnthal, "Spirituality, Religion, and Health...".

132. Simpson, W. F. "Comparative Longevity in a College Cohort of Christian Scientists."*JAMA.* 1989 Sep 22-29; 262(12):1657–8.

133. Anonymous. *Religion's Role in Treating Addiction* at www.religionlink.org/tip_060508.php (accessed August 25, 2008 at the home page by selecting "drugs" under "Social Issues").

134. Geppert, C. et al. "Development of a Bibliography on Religion, Spirituality and Addictions." *Drug and Alcohol Review.* 2007 Jul; 26(4):389–95.

135. Holland, *Religion in the Ancient Mediterranean World.*

136. Johnson, *Early Christianity.*

137. Mackie, J. L. *The Miracle of Theism: Arguments For and Against the Existence of God,* Oxford University Press, Oxford, 1982 (see chapter *Miracles and Testimony* for a discussion of Hume's position).

138. Jantos, M., and H. Kiat. "Prayer as Medicine: How Much Have We Learned?" *Medical Journal of Australia* 186 (10 Suppl): S51–S53, 2007.

139. Galton, Francis. "Statistical Enquiries into the Efficacy of Prayer," *Fortnightly Review* #68, New Series, 125–35, August 1, 1872.

140. Tessman, Irwin, and Jack Tessman. *"Efficacy of Prayer"* in *Science and Religion: Are They Compatible?* Paul Kurtz, ed., 257, Prometheus Books, 2003.

141. Roberts L., I. Ahmed, and S. Hall. "Intercessory Prayer for the Alleviation of Ill Health." *Cochrane Database of Systematic Reviews* 2007, Issue 1.

142. Cha, K. Y., and D. P. Wirth. "Does Prayer Influence the Success of In Vitro Fertilization-embryo Transfer? Report of a Masked, Randomized Trial," *Journal of Reproductive Medicine.* 2001 Sep; 46(9):781–7.

143. Masters, K. S., and G. I. Spielmans. "Prayer and Health: Review, Meta-analysis, and Research Agenda." *Journal of Behavioral Medicine.* 30(4): 329–38, 2007 (Aug).

144. Roberts, L., I. Ahmed, S. Hall, and A. Davidson. "Intercessory Prayer for the Alleviation of Ill Health." *Cochrane Database of Systematic Reviews* 2009, Issue 2 (April 15), CD000368.

145. Johnson, *History of Christianity.*

146. Hecht, Jennifer M. *Doubt: A History: The Great Doubters and Their Legacy of Innovation from Socrates and Jesus to Thomas Jefferson and Emily Dickinson,* HarperCollins, New York, 2003.

147. Harris, Sam. *The End of Faith: Religion, Terror, and the Future of Reason,* W. W. Norton & Company, New York, 2004.

148. Brown, James Robert. *Who Rules in Science: An Opinionated Guide to the Wars,* Harvard University Press, Cambridge, MA, 2001.

149. Camus, Albert. *The First Man,* Vintage Books, New York, 1996 (translated by David Hapgood).

150. Taves, Ann. *Fits, Visions and Trances: Experiencing Religion and Explaining Experience from Wesley to James,* Princeton University Press, Princeton, NJ, 1999.

151. Ellenberger, *Discovery of the Unconscious.*

152. James, *Varieties of Religious Experience.*

153. Principe, Lawrence M. *Science and Religion*, The Teaching Company, Chantilly, VA, 2006 (a 12 lecture course available at www.TEACH12.com).

154. Bucholz, Robert. *Foundations of Western Civilization II: A History of the Modern Western World*, The Teaching Company, Chantilly, VA, 2006 (a 48 lecture course available at www.TEACH12.com).

155. Dennett, Daniel. *Breaking the Spell: Religion as a Natural Phenomenon*, Viking Penguin, New York, 2006.

156. Pinker, Steven. *The Stuff of Thought: Language as a Window into Human Nature,* Viking Penguin, New York, 2007, 403.

157. Gould, Stephen Jay. *Rocks of Ages: Science and Religion in the Fullness of Life*, Ballantine Books, New York, 1999.

158. Blackburn, *Truth*.

159. Miller, Kenneth R. *Only a Theory: Evolution and the Battle for America's Soul*, Viking (Penguin Group), New York, 2008.

160. Principe, *Science and Religion*.

161. Wilson, *On Human Nature*.

162. Hale, *Exploring the Roots of Religion*.

163. Burenhult, Goran. *The Megalithic Builders of Western Europe*, in Burenhult, Goran, ed., *People of the Past: The Epic Story of Human Origins and Development*, 291–312. Fog City Press, San Francisco, 2003.

164. Dennett, *Breaking the Spell*.

165. Holst, Wayne A. "Thou Art That: Transforming Religious Metaphor. Spirituality – Book review," *National Catholic Reporter*, Dec 7, 2001.

166. Payne, Les. "My Dance with Faith." *AARP Magazine* March & April 2008, 62–65.

167. Smith, Huston. *Why Religion Matters: The Fate of the Human Spirit in an Age of Disbelief*, HarperSanFrancisco (HarperCollins Publishers, New York), 2001.

168. Bering, Jesse. "The End? Why So Many of Us Think Our Minds Continue on After We Die." *Scientific American Mind* 19 (5):34–41, 2008 (October–November).

169. Hale, *Exploring the Roots of Religion.*

170. Tremlin, *Minds and Gods.*

171. Higgins, Kathleen. *World Philosophy*, The Teaching Company, Chantilly, VA, 2001 (a 24 lecture course available at www.TEACH12.com).

172. Plutarch. *The Lives of the Noble Grecians and Romans*, Modern Library, New York, (Plutarch lived about 46–120 CE, and this work was translated by John Dryden, revised by Arthur Hugh Clough 1864).

173. Watson, Malcolm W. *Theories of Human Development*, The Teaching Company, Chantilly, VA, 2002(a 24 lecture course available at www.TEACH12.com).

174. Hale, *Exploring the Roots of Religion.*

175. Armstrong, Karen. *A History of God: The 4000-year Quest of Judaism, Christianity and Islam*, Ballantine Books, New York, 1993.

176. Muesse, *Religions of the Axial Age*

177. Griffiths R, W. Richards, M. Johnson, U. McCann, and R. Jesse. *"Mystical-type Experiences Occasioned by Psilocybin Mediate the Attribution of Personal Meaning and Spiritual Significance 14 Months Later,"* Journal of Psychopharmacology 2008 Aug;22(6):621–32. Epub 2008 Jul 1.

178. Wasson, R. G, S. Kramrisch, J. Ott, and C. A. P. Ruck. "Persephone's Quest: Entheogens and the Origins of Religion," *Yale University Press*, New Haven, CT, 1986.

179. Matossian, Mary K. "Visions and the Origins of Christianity," *Free Inquiry* 29(4), 46–51, 2009 (Sept–Oct).

180. Tremlin, *Minds and Gods*

181. Seldes, *Great Thoughts*

182. Raglan, Lord. *The Hero: A Study in Tradition, Myth, and Drama, Part II*, published in *In Quest of the Hero*, Princeton University Press, Princeton, NJ, 1990.

183. Maier, John (ed.). *Gilgamesh: A Reader*, Bolchazy-Carducci Publishers, Inc., Wauconda, IL, 1997.

184. McWhorter, *Story of Human Language.*

185. Hume, *Principle Writings on Religion.*

186. Hall, James H. *Philosophy of Religion*, The Teaching Company, Chantilly, VA, 2003 (a 36 lecture course available at www.TEACH12.com).

187. Wright, *The Evolution of God*

188. Ehrman, Bart. *Lost Christianities: Christian Scriptures and the Battles over Authentication*, The Teaching Company, Chantilly, VA, 2002 (a 24 lecture course available at www.TEACH12.com).

189. Warraq, *Origins of the Koran.*

190. Boyer, Pascal. "Religion: Bound to Believe," *Nature* 455: 1038–9, 2008 (23 October 2008).

191. Hale, *Exploring the Roots of Religion.*

192. Ibid.

193. Rue, *Religion Is Not about God.*

194. Johnson, *History of the Jews.*

195. Williams, *Truth, Hope, and Power.*

196. Armstrong, Karen. *Islam: A Short History*, Modern Library Edition, Random House, Inc., New York, 2000.

197. Stern, Jessica. *Terror in the Name of God: Why Religious Militants Kill*, HarperCollins, New York, 2003.

198. Benjamin and Simon, *Age of Sacred Terror.*

199. Seldes, *Great Thoughts.*

200. Solzhenitsyn, Alexander et al. *From Under the Rubble*, Regnery Gateway, Washington, D.C., 1981 (translation 1975 by A. M. Brock and others, original copyright 1974).

201. von Mises, *Socialism.*

202. Gabel, Paul. *And God Created Lenin: Marxism vs. Religion in Russia, 1917–1929*, Prometheus Books, Amherst, NY, 2005.

203. Gabel, Paul. *An Elemental Impulse: Religion Is So Powerful that Even Soviet Antireligious Policy Failed*, Skeptic May 30, 2007 (accessed Sept 12, 2008 at http://www.skeptic.com/eskeptic/07-05-30.html).

204. Hecht, *Doubt.*

205. McGrath, Alister. *The Twilight of Atheism: The Rise and Fall of Disbelief in the Modern World*, Doubleday, New York, 2004.

206. Berger, Peter (ed.). *The Desecularization of the World: Resurgent Religion and World Politics*, Wm. B. Eerdmans, Grand Rapids, MI, 1999.

207. Flynn, Tom. *"Secularization Resurrected," Free Inquiry* 27(5):15–16, 2007 (August/September).

208. Berlin, Isaiah. *The Crooked Timber of Humanity: Chapters in the History of Ideas*, Princeton University Press, Princeton, NJ, 1990 (Edited by Henry Hardy).

209. von Mises, *Socialism.*

210. Drury, *Terror and Civilization.*

211. Wilson, *On Human Nature.*

212. Wright, *The Evolution of God*

213. Stark, *Discovering God.*

214. Smith, *An Inquiry into the Wealth….*

215. Stark, *Discovering God.*

216. Cahill, Thomas. *How the Irish Saved Civilization: The Untold Story of Ireland's Heroic Role from the Fall of Rome to the Rise of Medieval Europe*, Doubleday, New York, 1995.

217. Armstrong, Karen. *The Great Transformation: The Beginnings of our Religious Traditions*, Alfred A. Knopf, New York, 2006.

218. Sagan, Carl. This quote is found at www.positiveatheism.org/hist/quotes/qframe.htm where it is stated that it was "quoted from the United Universists front page" (accessed September 12, 2008).

219. Fischer, Edward. *Peoples and Cultures of the World*, The Teaching Company, Chantilly, VA, 2004 (a 24 lecture course available at www.TEACH12.com).

220. Kilman, Carrie. *One Nation, Many Gods*, Teaching Tolerance, Fall 2007 (#32), pages 38-46 (can be accessed at www.tolerance.org/teach/magazine/features.jsp?is=41&ar=851).

221. Juergensmeyer, *Terror in the Mind of God.*

222. See the entry for "Jonestown" at www.wikipedia.org for a good discussion (access September 12, 2008).

223. Drury, *Terror and Civilization.*

224. Wilson, *On Human Nature.*

225. Fischer, *Peoples and Cultures of the World.*

226. Seldes, *Great Thoughts.*

227. Wilson, *On Human Nature.*

228. Carse, James. *The Religious Case Against Belief,* The Penguin Press, New York, 2008.

229. Miller, *Only a Theory.*

230. Collins, Francis S. "The Language of God: A Scientist Presents Evidence for Belief," *Free Press,* New York, 2006.

231. Dylan, Bob. Lyrics from the song "Its Alright, Ma (I'm Only Bleeding)," copyright 1965, found at www.bobdylan.com/#/songs/its-alright-ma-im-only-bleeding (accessed Dec 12, 2008).

232. Sartre, Jean Paul. This quote is found on many Web sites, and I first heard it twenty years ago, but no one I found has posted a source—for instance http://atheisme.free.fr/Quotes/Sartre.htm (accessed December 12, 2008).

LaVergne, TN USA
26 December 2010

210079LV00001B/2/P